UNSOLVED MYSTERIES OF THE MIND

Unsolved Mysteries of the Mind
Tutorial Essays in Cognition

Edited by

Vicki Bruce
University of Stirling, UK

Erlbaum (UK) Taylor & Francis

Erlbaum (UK) Taylor & Francis
27 Church Road
Hove
East Sussex, BN3 2FA
UK

British Library Cataloguing in Publication Data

A catalogue record for this book is available from the British Library

ISBN 0-86377-392-3 (Hbk)
ISBN 0-86377-393-1 (Pbk)

Printed and bound by Redwood Books, Trowbridge, Wiltshire

Contents

List of contributors

Vicki Bruce, Dept. of Psychology, University of Stirling, Stirling FK9 4LA, Scotland

Michael J. Morgan, Institute of Ophthalmology & Dept. of Anatomy and Developmental Biology, University College London, Bath Street, London EC1V 9EL, UK

Stephen Monsell, Dept. of Experimental Psychology, University of Cambridge, Downing Street, Cambridge CB2 3EB, UK

Andrew W. Young, MRC Applied Psychology Unit, 15 Chaucer Road, Cambridge CB2 2EF, UK

Ned Block, Dept. of Linguistics and Philosophy, Massachusetts Institute of Technology, Cambridge, Massachusetts 02139, USA

Philip T. Smith, Dept. of Psychology, University of Reading, 3 Earley Gate, Whiteknights, Reading RG6 6AL, UK

Susan M. Kemp-Wheeler, Dept. of Psychology, University of Reading, 3 Earley Gate, Whiteknights, Reading RG6 6AL, UK

Stephen E. G. Lea, Dept. of Psychology, University of Exeter, Washington Singer Laboratories, Perry Road, Exeter EX4 4QG, UK

Marthe Kiley-Worthington, Dept. of Psychology, University of Exeter, Washington Singer Laboratories, Perry Road, Exeter, EX4 4QG, UK

Preface

Why is there such powerful popular appeal in the career descriptions of "Rocket Scientist" or "Brain Surgeon"? I think it is because such phrases conjure up an image of technical wizardry combined with the potential exploration of the unknown. During the 1960s the race to land people on the moon captured the imagination of the American public. The 1990s are "The Decade of the Brain" in the USA, an indication of the excitement currently generated by the field of neurosciences and cognitive sciences.

Knowledge about cognition has been accumulated at an extraordinary rate, considering that the field—at least as studied by experimental psychologists—is so new. One result of this rapid accumulation of knowledge is, understandably, a tendency to concentrate in our teachings on summarising bodies of research concisely and effectively. What we tend not to do is to focus on the things that we don't know or understand. We don't necessarily take time to examine some of the broader issues behind the research we describe, or talk about the niggly little phenomena that no-one has yet quite accounted for (certain visual "illusions", or effects such as Stroop), or expand on some of the philosophical issues that underpin our science (what does it mean to have a mind—or to be conscious, at all?). This book presents a series of tutorial essays aimed at exploring some of the unknowns in the study of cognition, to introduce some history and perhaps some complexity and controversy, to complement the many excellent texts that provide a more comprehensive and even-handed coverage.

The book arose from a discussion at an Experimental Psychology Society dinner. Alcohol was consumed, and some of my friends rashly agreed to participate in my project to Mystify the study of cognition. The resulting text does not pretend to offer coverage of the full range of topics in cognition, but offers a sample of chapters that, we hope, will help stimulate tutorial discussion, debate, and further reading relevant to topics on visual perception (Chapter 2), visual cognition (Chapters 1 and 3), memory (Chapters 1 and 3), attention and skill (Chapter 4), neuropsychology (Chapters 4 and 5), cognition and emotion (Chapter 6), and thinking, or Artificial Intelligence (Chapter 7). Most importantly, I hope it will stimulate curiosity and enthusiasm among a new generation of students.

The final version of this text was helped along considerably by some very helpful reviews of the manuscript by Martin Conway and three anonymous reviewers. We think the book is much improved by our attempts to rectify shortcomings that they identified. Moreover, all contributors to the book, as well as reviewers of it, have helped shape the contents in general, and my own Chapter 1 in particular.

Each of the contributors, myself included, added in different ways to the delays in producing this book. We all thank Michael Forster, Rohays Perry, and their colleagues at Erlbaum (UK) for patient waiting, and for their excellent and speedy editorial and production process when the manuscript eventually arrived.

Vicki Bruce
March 1995

CHAPTER ONE

Introduction:
Soluble and insoluble
mysteries of the mind

Vicki Bruce University of Stirling

PREAMBLE

Students are attracted to psychology for a variety of reasons. Some are motivated by a desire to care for people who are emotionally distressed or disturbed, others want to understand childhood and parenting, others are fascinated by the differing abilities and personalities of people. All these issues throw up unsolved mysteries, but these are not the focus of this book. Instead, we are concerned with a rather different set of puzzles about the workings of the brain and mind. How can perception, memory, language, and reasoning—the elements of human intelligence—be explained? Would it be possible to build a machine to recreate such intelligence? Questions like these lie at the heart of contemporary cognitive psychology and cognitive science, and form the background to this book. When I was a student, cognitive psychologists were just beginning to work with other disciplines to develop new methods for understanding intelligent behaviour; in the past 25 years there has been dramatic progress in some areas of investigation. This progress has been aided by powerful new techniques which have allowed a convergence of evidence of different kinds. When laboratory experiments with adult volunteers, neuropsychological studies of brain-damaged patients, and computer modelling all provide mutual support, we can be much more confident in the theoretical progress achieved. Despite this progress, however, many puzzles remain. The aim of this book is to explore a selection of these "unsolved mysteries", with the hope of stimulating the next generation of scientists to take up some of the remaining challenges.

Psychology has existed as an experimental science, distinct from philosophy and biology, for only a little more than a century. Its history has been characterised by a series of fashions in terms of approaches to human nature, methods of investigation, and the problems that have been thought appropriate for psychologists to investigate. Initially, attempts were made to study mental processes by introspection, on the grounds that such events are directly observable only by those having them. Unfortunately, however, such methods often led to poor scientific replicability, as well as restricting enquiry to aspects of cognition of which we are aware. Introspective techniques such as protocol analysis are still used as one method of enquiry about aspects of thinking and reasoning (e.g. Rips, 1989), but have proved wholly inappropriate for the analysis of most other cognitive activities such as perceiving, remembering, or speaking. Partly because of the deficiencies of introspection as a scientific technique, during the 1930s and 40s, the dominant school of thought was that of behaviourism. Behaviourists only considered it legitimate to study, and enquire about, observable behaviour. During the behaviourist period, research into mental experiences such as imagery virtually dropped out of psychology, and Bartlett's (1932) seminal work on the organisation of human memory was largely neglected until a later generation rediscovered it. Indeed under the behaviourists it became somewhat sloppy to talk of the "Mind" at all—only the brain and the behaviour to which it gave rise could be the subject of scientific enquiry.

The cognitive revolution changed all this. It is difficult to date its emergence as a distinct paradigm. Some of the new technology developed rapidly during World War II provoked human factors research aimed at understanding aspects of decision and attention not readily captured by behaviourist analyses. Cognitive psychology then developed during the 1950s and 60s, with Broadbent's (1958) *Perception and communication* (the filter theory of attention) and Neisser's (1967) *Cognitive psychology* (the first text with this name) as important markers near the start of this era. Armed with new metaphors drawn first from communication technologies and then from computing, psychology was able to develop a paradigm within which the study of Mind could be conducted scientifically. Furthermore, even if the computational metaphor for human mind is not always universally accepted in a strong form (see Searle, 1980), advances in artificial intelligence have produced improved techniques for computer simulation of theories of cognition, forcing theorists to be explicit in order to produce simulations that can run. Recent advances in parallel distributed processing, or "connectionist" models have enabled cognitive scientists to draw closer parallels between computational processes and neurobiological ones.

Moreover, the revolution in information technology during the 1970s and 80s has produced a new set of challenges for cognitive psychology. The relationship between people and machines is now an intimate one—no part of our lives is untouched by computers, and we need to be able to design the interface between people and machines to maximise the potential of each. This requires an understanding of both sides of the interface. The interdisciplinary area of cognitive science reflects a growing linkage between the study of information processing in people and machines. The Macintosh personal computer is often given as an example of a user-friendly design which resulted from the application of psychology to computer technology.

Another interdisciplinary area that has emerged recently is that of cognitive neuroscience, where specialists from the disciplines of neurology, psychiatry, and psychology share an interest in understanding the neural underpinnings of cognition. An important contribution to this understanding is made by the methods of cognitive neuropsychology, where the deficits that arise as a result of brain damage can be used to explore and test models of normal cognitive function, and conversely, models of normal cognitive function can make precise the questions asked in the examination and diagnosis of a patient with cognitive impairments. Later in this chapter, and in those that follow, we will demonstrate how converging evidence from cognitive psychology and neuropsychology has been used to develop accounts of how mental processes are organised and sequenced. Most recently, new techniques of visualising the activation of different parts of the brain as normal adult volunteers participate in cognitive tasks are allowing cognitive neuroscientists to localise cognitive processes in the brain with much greater precision.

Despite the very rapid progress that has been made in the study of human cognition, there are many things we do not understand. This is sometimes because problems have been neglected, at other times because, although studied, they may not have been thought about, or investigated, in quite the right ways. Even in much-researched areas, where progress has been marked, some curious gaps remain in our knowledge. The aim of this book is to sample several different types of enduring puzzles about cognition, and to consider different perspectives which have in the past been brought to bear on each. We may attempt, in the course of these reviews, to redefine the problems in order to suggest more profitable future directions. The current generation of students should be better placed in terms of methodology, and wisdom of hindsight, to make progress on these issues.

QUESTIONS versus PROBLEMS

To begin, let us consider what it means to understand (or "solve") a problem (or "mystery"). Understanding why something happens in the way that it does involves a good deal more than simply answering an empirical question. There are a number of questions we can pose for which it is possible to provide answers on the basis of purely empirical research, but where the *reasons* why we get these answers remain mysterious. For example, we know quite a lot about the best way to learn information. Baddeley (1990) reviews evidence showing that learning is better when practice is distributed rather than concentrated within a single learning session, and that within a session there is more learning if presentations of each item are spaced rather than blocked together. The beneficial effects of distributed learning sessions and spacing of items have been demonstrated in numerous studies throughout this century, and have formed the basis of a new mnemonic strategy (Landauer & Bjork, 1978), but the reasons for the beneficial effects of distributing practice have not been satisfactorily explained. Indeed it may be the relative scarcity of adequate theories of such phenomena of human learning that has led to their neglect over the intervening years.

Similarly, psychology has been blessed over the years with a number of "laws", relating perception or performance to aspects of the environment. For example, Hick's Law states that the reaction time to make a particular choice increases as a linear function of the information value of the stimulus—the more informative the stimulus, in terms of the uncertainty reduced by its occurrence, the slower the response. Fitts' law states that the time to execute a movement is a logarithmic function of the distance of the movement divided by half the width of the target to which the movement is required; and Weber's Law states that the magnitude of a just-noticeable difference in some physical dimension of a stimulus is a constant proportion of the baseline value of the dimension. All these laws have proved to have considerable generality across a range of situations, but none of them is readily explained (although see, for example, Laming 1988 discussing Weber's Law and Meyer et al., 1988 for an explanation of Fitts' Law). A law in itself does not imply an understanding of the mechanisms giving rise to this systematicity.

Other phenomena seem to have the regularity and reliability in behaviour of laws, although without expression in quantitative terms.

For example, since Stroop (1935) showed that the meaning of colour words could interfere with the naming of the ink colours in which the words were written, the Stroop effect has been replicated, extended, and even applied to the analysis of clinical conditions such as anxiety and panic disorders (e.g. see Mathews, 1993), but the reasons why the effect occurs are still not clear (see MacLeod's 1991 review). Similarly, there is no dispute about the fact that the moon appears larger when on the horizon than when it is overhead, but a satisfactory account of the basis of this illusion remains elusive, despite numerous attempts (e.g. see Plug & Ross, 1994). Perhaps our problems here arise because we have been posing the questions in the wrong way. In two of the chapters of this volume, we examine the kinds of frameworks within which explanations of illusions (Morgan, Chapter 2) or phenomena of task control, such as the Stroop effect (Monsell, Chapter 4) have been considered.

One response to noting the rather extensive list of phenomena that await satisfactory explanation, is to bemoan the lack of progress that has been made by psychologists at understanding the basics of human perception and cognition. In 1973, in an influential critique of progress in the area of visual cognition, Allan Newell enumerated a list of phenomena (e.g. visual illusions such as the Müller-Lyer effect) and dichotomies (e.g. single versus dual memory stores) which appeared to characterise the interests of cognitive psychologists of that time. While commending the experimental ingenuity of his colleagues, he felt that such a piecemeal approach would ultimately fail to deliver a cumulative understanding of cognition—"You can't play 20 questions with Nature and win" (Newell, 1973). Newell exhorted his colleagues to develop *complete* processing models, in which control processes were specified. He urged the study and analysis of *complex tasks*, such as chess, rather than laboratory "phenomena" such as the Stroop effect. And he urged psychologists to think about developing *general* theories of cognition that would be applicable to many different tasks.

To what extent would Newell's complaints be valid today? Are we still studying a set of piecemeal phenomena and dichotomies? My own view is that in many areas there is now a much clearer direction to most research than there was in 1973. In a number of areas of human cognition, research has contributed to establishing a clear theoretical framework which unifies past findings, and sets an agenda for future study so that it is clearer what needs to be done to solve the orginal problem. Interestingly, progress in many areas has not required a *unified* theory of cognition of the kind envisaged by Newell, although progress on such unified theories has also been achieved (e.g. Anderson, 1993; Newell, 1991; see Monsell, this volume, for further discussion of

Newell's "SOAR" theory). Instead, progress has been achieved through *converging* evidence from different methodologies, and by an emphasis on understanding *real-world activities*, rather than laboratory phenomena, as the goal of the research. In this chapter, I will illustrate this with just two examples of areas where I feel that, in these terms, genuine progress has been made; the identification of faces, and short-term "working" memory. The examples I have chosen are ones where British research has been particularly influential, but are chosen not through chauvinism but through my own familiarity with the topics and their relevance to some of the material covered elsewhere in this volume. Other similar examples I might have chosen include early visual processing (but see Chapter 2), word recognition, and visual imagery (described at some length in chapter 3). Other readers could doubtless offer further examples.

As well as illustrating the historical developments that have led to the progress that I claim for these fields, these areas also serve to illustrate how progress in one domain often throws up, or highlights, new mysteries for the next generation of scientists to ponder.

FACE RECOGNITION

The reason why this topic proves appropriate here is that it is an example where initial ways of formulating the nature of the problem promoted rather a lot of empirical, but rather little theoretical, progress. At about the same time as the "verbal learning" tradition was losing its hold on the study of memory, psychologists began to marvel at demonstrations by Shepard (1967), Standing (1973), and others, that people were remarkably good at recognising once-viewed pictures—even when they were exposed to several hundreds or even thousands of them. For example, Standing, Conezio, and Haber (1970) found performance of 90% correct in a study where subjects initially viewed 2560 coloured pictures for 10 seconds each and later had to pick the previously studied items from pairs containing studied and unstudied items. This astonishing performance in picture memory tasks was (and is now) attributed to a variety of factors, including the heterogeneity of the items used. However, it was soon noted that people could be very accurate indeed at remembering large numbers of *homogeneous* items such as human faces (Goldstein & Chance, 1971). Now the accuracy of recognition memory for pictures of unfamiliar faces created an apparent paradox, because at about the same time the criminal justice system was beset by a number of cases where eye-witnesses had misidentified people suspected of particular crimes (Devlin, 1976). Thus a paradox arose—if face recognition is so good, why is witness identification so bad? Although the paradox promoted quite a lot of research into factors affecting memory for pictures of faces in the laboratory, this research did not lead to any clear understanding of face recognition in everyday life.

During the 1980s, psychologists argued that to understand face recognition required that we understand properly the different uses made of face information in everyday life, the relationships between these different uses, and the mechanisms involved in each. By understanding, for example, the processes that allow us to recognise that the person across the street is our neighbour, and to note that she looks tired and troubled, we may be in a better position to consider how this same face-processing system is deployed during an encounter with a stranger, and the factors that may promote, or inhibit, later memory for that face.

One of the first and most important outcomes of this shift in emphasis was to note the distinction between *picture* recognition and *face* recognition (Bruce, 1982; Bruce & Young, 1986; Hay & Young, 1982). Remembering that a particular picture of a face has been studied in a laboratory experiment can arise as a result of matches with a number of different kinds of information (Bruce, 1982). We can remember the details of the *photograph* (as a pattern of light and dark, with its flaws or blotches), the details of the *expression*, the *associations* that the image of the face invokes (looks like my Uncle Harry), details of the *viewpoint*, *lighting*, and so forth. When the same pictures are used as study and test items, as is true of many studies of recognition memory for faces, then any or all of these sources of information might allow subjects to recognise the faces. When slight changes are made to viewpoint and/or expression between study and test, face recognition performance drops dramatically (Bruce, 1982). To study the processes occurring in eye-witness identification would require at the very least an understanding of how we build up a represention robust enough to allow generalisation to an encounter with someone who may have a slightly different hairstyle or clothing, and be seen in a different light (Bruce, 1994).

Moreover, Hay and Young (1982) noted that person identification could fail in a number of different ways and for a number of different reasons. Even though memory for unfamiliar pictures was remarkably good, occasions of social embarrassment through failure to behave appropriately are reasonably frequent. All of us have encounters where we fail to recognise people that we know slightly, or from different contexts, or where we cannot think why a particular person seems familiar, or where we forget a person's name. A witness who fails to attribute correctly the source of perceived familiarity of a face in a line-up can wrongly identify a person on the basis of prior exposure to their photograph (in a mug-shot file, e.g. Brown, Deffenbacher, & Sturgill, 1977) or to familiarity from a quite different encounter. For such reasons it seemed that we needed properly to understand everyday person-identification processes, and the reasons for their failure, before applying such understanding to the eye-witnesses' situation.

In trying to understand the everyday uses made of facial information, it was necessary to develop tasks that tapped the kinds of decisions we usually make to faces. Rather than asking participants the question "did you see this face in the experimental list", we devised tasks where subjects were asked to decide whether or not faces were familiar, or belonged to particular occupational categories. We also took as important converging evidence the patterns of deficit observed in patients with impairments of face processing as a result of brain damage. Such patterns of deficit are particularly interesting where "double dissociations" are observed between functions preserved or affected in different cases (Ellis & Young, 1988; Shallice, 1988). In a classic double dissociation, one patient may be unable to perform Task A (say, identifying faces) but be normal on Task B (say, understanding emotional expressions), whereas another patient shows the opposite pattern, and is normal on Task A and impaired on Task B. Such a pattern cannot be explained by assuming that one task is just easier than the other, and is more usually taken to suggest that the two tasks involve different information-processing modules. An additional category of evidence used to inform theory was the mistakes and difficulties experienced by all of us in everyday life (e.g. Young, Hay, & Ellis, 1985).

Using converging information obtained from these different methods we were able to demonstrate that the different uses made of facial information, i.e. the analysis of facial expressions, lip movements, and face identification, appear to involve independent information-processing routes. Thus identification of faces may be achieved independently of the analysis of facial expressions, for example. Space does not permit a full account of the evidence here (see Bruce & Young, 1986; Young & Bruce, 1991 for a fuller discussion), but the convergence of evidence for the independence of expression analysis and identification is impressive, involving laboratory experiments with normal adults and children (e.g. Ellis et al., 1993; Young et al., 1986b); double dissociations in clinical patients (e.g. Bruyer et al., 1983 and Kurucz & Feldmar, 1979; Kurucz, Feldman, & Werner, 1979; also see Young et al., 1993); and neurophysiological evidence from single-cell recording in monkeys (Rolls, 1992), and from studies of cortical activation in humans (e.g. Sergent et al., 1994).

Although some aspects of face processing appear to proceed independently of each other, it can also be shown that within a particular processing route, certain other processes must happen in sequence. In order fully to identify a familiar face, e.g. to say "That is Diana Spencer, the estranged wife of the Prince of Wales", we must match the incoming pattern to a stored representation of the appearance of Princess Diana, then retrieve stored information about that familiar individual (e.g. "member of the Royal Family") and only finally retrieve a particular *name* for the individual who has been recognised. (Notice that this sequence violates the way that we would naturally use language to describe someone's identity, where, as in my example a few sentences ago, we typically report the name of the person first.) This three-stage sequence is supported by evidence of a number of kinds.

First, there is evidence from everyday errors and difficulties of person recognition. Young et al. (1985) asked volunteers to record in a diary all instances of difficulties or mistakes in person identification, and analysed the nature of the errors that were made. They found that the reported difficulties fell into consistent patterns. For example, people commonly reported the experience of seeing a person, thinking they had met before, but having no idea at all why they seemed familiar; and people commonly reported the experience of remembering everything about the person except their name. However no-one ever reported knowing a person's name but not knowing who that person was (e.g. "That's Diana Spencer—who is she?"). Investigations of the relative time it takes to access different kinds of information about people also supports the sequence of "match pattern–access identity–access name" outlined earlier. For example, Young et al. (1986a) showed that when subjects were asked to make yes-no decisions about the familiarity of faces, their occupations, or their names, familiarity decisions were always made most quickly and name decisions most slowly.

Neuropsychological evidence also favours the three-stage sequence of familiarity–identity–names. Prosopagnosic patients find all faces unfamiliar, an apparent failure of the first stage. Another kind of patient studied by De Haan, Young, and Newcombe (1991) found faces familiar, but did not know why, an apparent failure of the second stage, and a third category of patients such as EST studied by Flude, Ellis, and Kay (1989) appear to have specific problems at the naming stage.

These observations about the sequence of stages that seemed to underlie the complete identification of a face, and the independence of this route from others to do with expressions and lipreading, were captured in functional models of the processes involved in face identification such as that outlined by Bruce and Young (1986: see Fig. 1.1).

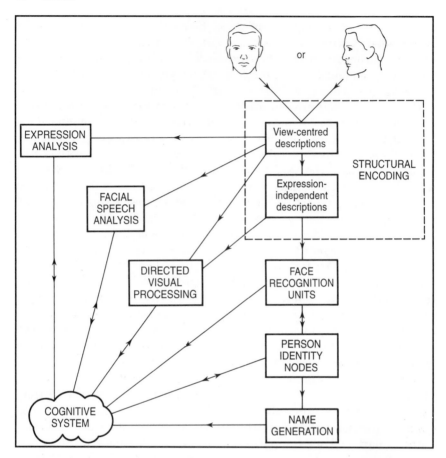

FIG. 1.1.   Bruce and Young's (1986) model of face recognition.

Space does not permit a detailed description of the different components shown in Fig. 1.1, and the reader is referred to Bruce and Young (1986) for these details. The important points to note here are the separation of routes for expression analysis and facial speech from the route drawn to the right, which mediates facial identification. Within the facial identification route, separate sequential stages are drawn for (a) the analysis of the structure of the face (structural encoding stage); (b) the access of stored representations of known faces (in face recognition units—see later); (c) the access of stored information about known people (at person identity nodes); and (d) the access of names.

Bruce and Young (1986) argued that the model shown in Fig. 1.1 should best be regarded as a framework, to summarise what was known, empirically, about the field, and to guide new research aimed at testing and refining the theory. This kind of model does not spell out the mechanisms of any of the "boxes" shown, but rather sets out in a simple diagrammatic form what is known and clarifies what needs to be explained. We can see this as an important *first stage* in understanding cognitive processes.

Since the development of this framework, progress has been made at exploring the nature and interaction of the different components of the identification route, using computer modelling techniques which have also proved useful in other domains (e.g. see Burton, Bruce, & Johnston, 1990; Burton et al., 1991). An implemented "IAC" model (for "interactive activation with competition", a particular variety of connectionist architecture) has allowed us to explain phenomena, such as covert recognition in prosopagnosia, where some patients show evidence of recognising faces subconsciously that they cannot recognise overtly, which seemed impossible within the "box-and-arrow" version of the model (Burton et al., 1991; see also Young & Block, Chapter 5, this volume). The model has also made new experimental predictions, not obvious in the "box-and-arrow" version, which are currently being tested and whose results may lead to further refinement of the theory. Research using the IAC framework can be seen as allowing us to explore in more detail how interactions between different sub-systems in the original framework can account in detail for empirical data.

Can we go further than this and spell out how each box does its job? Is it possible to build and access face-recognition units from real images of faces and show that patterns of confusion mirror those obtained by human subjects? There is now a large body of empirical evidence which supports the idea that faces are processed wholistically rather than as collections of discrete parts or local measurements (e.g. see Bartlett & Searcy, 1993; Rhodes et al., 1993; Tanaka & Farah, 1993), and that face representations preserve information about surface properties of pigmentation, texture, and shading (e.g. see Bruce & Humphreys, 1994; Bruce & Langton, 1994). Neural network techniques, operating directly on grey-level images of faces, or on images initially processed in ways consistent with early visual processing in the eye and brain, appear to hold considerable promise as psychologically plausible accounts of how structural codes are built and accessed. For example, O'Toole et al. (1994) have demonstrated that one such technique for coding face images does an excellent job of accounting for the variation in memorability of a set of face pictures.

These developments illustrate the *second stage* of understanding. Although we are not yet at the stage of having built a machine that recognises—and fails to recognise—faces in the way that people do, many of us are confident that this will be possible within a relatively short space of time, and that much of the progress now required is technical rather than conceptual. Where new conceptual advances may be required is in the broader area of visual image processing and connectionist modelling, rather than in the specific area of face recognition.

This raises a most important point, which is that the progress that has been achieved within the domain of face recognition has not been made in isolation from progress in other related fields of cognition. The theoretical framework for face recognition I have outlined here built opportunistically on advances in understanding the derivation of meaning from print. What was needed was to conceptualise the problem in these terms rather than as one of remembering pictures. By noting that face recognition was affected by context in a similar way to word recognition (e.g. Bruce & Valentine 1985, 1986) it became possible to borrow successful theoretical constructs from other domains and apply them to the task in question. Morton's (1969) model of word recognition, and the development of an interactive activation model (McClelland & Rumelhart, 1981) provided the core architectures with which to build accounts of person identification. Indeed in retrospect it seems most sensible that the central characteristics of such models *should* be pervasive: it would seem strange if a mechanism that is powerful enough to account for the interplay between sensory and cognitive levels in one domain was not exploited by the brain in several others. However, despite such similarities, different kinds of material also make specific representational and behavioural demands—which may be why different tasks such as object, face, and word recognition appear to rely on partially independent neurological structures.

What of the original problem of eye-witness testimony? Once we consider the representational demands of face recognition, we can see that an eye-witness has only a limited opportunity to view a face under the range of transformations that would normally build an enduring and robust representation. Recognition of previously unfamiliar faces is highly dependent on the reinstatement of precise viewing conditions (Bruce, 1982). When exposure has been made to several variations, there is still a limited ability to extrapolate beyond the range of exemplars seen (Bruce, 1994). However, a witness with a fragile representation of a face has considerable opportunity to be confused by superficial resemblance between the person apprehended and the actual culprit. A good example of this was the case of Mr Virag in the 1976 Devlin report, who was identified by several witnesses with great confidence as the person who had committed an armed robbery. The actual criminal had a face of a similar type to Mr Virag, but no-one who knew either man well could have mistaken the one for the other.

Moreover, it has been established in the witnessing literature (Brown et al., 1977) as well as in the everyday person identification (Young et al., 1985) that people are relatively poor at remembering the reason why a face seems familiar. Thus faces that have been encountered in photographs, or in innocent contexts, may be picked out of line-ups for entirely spurious reasons. One particularly vivid example is provided by Baddeley (1990) who describes how a psychologist who appeared on live television while a woman was being raped was later apprehended by police and identified by the woman as the rapist. The TV appearance of course provided the alibi that proved his innocence. The witnessing literature contains several further examples where false identification appears to have arisen for such reasons.

However, it would be wrong to suggest that no mysteries remain about face processing or person identification. For example, a number of us are perplexed about why proper names are so difficult to remember (e.g. see volume edited by Cohen & Burke, 1993). And we still don't know why people are so good at remembering lots of individual *pictures*!

WORKING MEMORY

A second illustrative area where I believe we now have an appropriate framework to guide research, and where research has been genuinely cumulative, is "working memory". This topic did not arise out of a single mystery or paradox, but rather out of a line of study—"short-term memory" which had become bogged down by sterile, and ultimately misguided, controversies about laboratory phenomena.

It has been known for a very long time that we have a strictly limited capacity to retain sequences of items in the short term—the "span" of short-term memory, compared with an apparently unlimited capacity in the long term. The existence of "primary" or short-term memory was acknowledged by William James and contrasted with the longer-term kind of memory that gives rise to a genuine recollection. However, although mental span was one of the items in early intelligence tests, it became disconnected from the study of *verbal learning* which became the focus of memory research during the behaviourist era in the United States. The verbal learning theorists explained all memory through the reinforcement of associations between stimuli and responses, and all forgetting in terms of interference between competing associations. In this context, the rediscovery by a number of psychologists, mainly in Britain (but, for example, see Miller, 1956), of a limited capacity short-term memory from which forgetting appeared to be due to *decay* rather than interference, was initially controversial. However, the controversies were not on the whole productive ones. During the 1960s an enormous amount of experimental effort went into trying to resolve the question of whether there really were two sorts of memory or only one, and whether forgetting was really all due to interference or could also occur through decay. (Incidentally, the question of why we forget things is still not one for which a ready answer can be found—see Baddeley, 1990.) What was missing from this territory was an attempt to link short-term memory (and long-term learning, for that matter) with real world activities. I believe this has been admirably rectified by the approach taken by Alan Baddeley and his colleagues over the past 20 years. This clarification of the mechanisms and purposes of short-term memory, however, has in turn served to highlight our ignorance about the control or executive processes, which remain deeply mysterious.

An excellent concise summary of the empirical and theoretical approach that I am sketching here is provided by Baddeley (1992), and a more extensive review by Baddeley (1986). The theory of working memory that Baddeley developed with Hitch (Baddeley & Hitch, 1974) built on the considerable body of empirical evidence about short-term memory accumulated during the 1950s and 60s, which described a limited-capacity, short-term store within which coding was phonologically based, in contrast to the apparently unlimited capacity long-term store within which coding seemed to be semantically based. Within the short-term store, a small number of items—such as the digits of a telephone number—could be retained as long as they were rehearsed, but rapidly forgotten in the absence of rehearsal. Because it appeared to be the case that the longer items were rehearsed, the more likely they were to be retained in the long term, it was rather natural to think of the short-term store as reflecting the information processing bottleneck in the verbal learning system. The short-term store appeared to be the limited capacity channel into which sensory material had to be selected and through which it had to be squeezed before arriving at the limitless repositories of long-term memory (Atkinson & Shiffrin, 1968; Broadbent, 1958). The common or "modal" model of memory, which emerged in the late 1960s saw a short-term store as maintaining, through rehearsal, information on its way to the long-term store. The short-term store in this model was also the proposed site of control processes and retrieval strategies, as well as acting as a more passive store.

The distinction between a short-term store (STS) and a long-term store (LTS) was supported by a double dissociation between different types of memory disorder. Whereas patients suffering from amnesia tended to have a normal short-term digit span but impaired long-term memory (Baddeley & Warrington, 1970), some other patients with language rather than memory disorders were observed to have impaired digit span but normal learning (Shallice & Warrington, 1970). Although supporting the distinction between two types of store, this double dissociation immediately suggested that the modal model of memory must be wrong. If STS was the crucial information-processing channel, how could someone with a severely damaged STS not be affected on a range of cognitive tasks? Patient KF, with a much-reduced digit span (Shallice & Warrington, 1970) had difficulties with language understanding, but was otherwise intellectually capable. It was the amnesic patient HM (Scoville & Milner, 1957), living permanently in the present, who was intellectually the more impaired.

The first steps towards re-thinking the nature of short-term memory were taken by Baddeley and Hitch (1974). First they established that the performance of a patient like KF could be mimicked in normal subjects, by showing that "filling up" the short-term store with digits had remarkably slight effects on other cognitive abilities in tasks of reasoning, long-term learning, and free recall. A three-digit load had no significant effect on performance, and a six-digit load impaired performance but did not abolish it. Clearly the attempt to model a patient with short-term impairment was successful. Like the patients, normal subjects with considerable imposed short-term memory limitations (through the use of concurrent loading) were able to function quite well at a range of other tasks which—on the basis of the modal model—should make demands on this same capacity.

Such observations led Baddeley and Hitch to conceive of short-term memory rather differently from the modal model. Baddeley and Hitch's (1974) working memory model proposed that short-term memory had a number of different components which could be deployed, or impaired, to some extent independently of each other. The model has developed in a number of ways over the years but retains the original three components of the articulatory or phonological loop (the latter term being the preferred name in more recent versions of the model), visuo-spatial sketch pad, and the central executive. The phonological loop and visuo-spatial sketch pad function as "slave" systems which can be used for particular storage tasks in order to reduce the load on the central executive. The fractionation of the short-term store into sub-systems specialised to deal with phonological and visuo-spatial material accounted neatly for the results of an experiment by Brooks (1968), described in more detail in Chapter 3. Briefly, Brooks found that a task that required short-term storage of a verbal sequence was performed better if responses were signalled by pointing, rather than speaking, and a task that required short-term storage of a visual image was performed better when responses were spoken rather than pointed.

In terms of Baddeley's framework, this result can be explained if the imagery task and pointing compete for some of the same (visuo-spatial sketch pad) resources, and the verbal memory task and speaking share some of the same (phonological loop) resources. Tasks are performed better when the response requirements make demands on a different system from that used for the short-term memory task itself.

Baddeley and his colleagues have made extensive use of the patterns of interference obtained between primary and secondary tasks in the further development of the model. For example, one characteristic of short-term memory performance is that people can retain longer sequences if spoken words are of shorter duration. The span for short words such as "mad, run, tip" is greater than for long words such as "information, territory, politics". The word-length effect is abolished if subjects are asked to engage in a task of articulatory suppression, where they are asked to say something such as "the,the,the" repeatedly during the presentation and recall of the list. This is explained if we assume that the word-length effect arises because longer words take up more space in the limited-capacity phonological loop, and that articulatory suppression competes for this space. I do not have space here to elaborate further on this large body of research, though some of it will be covered in Chapter 3. The reader is referred to Baddeley (1986, 1992) for full accounts.

The working memory model allows the patterns of deficit observed in patients with short-term memory impairments to be explained. On this model, patient KF had a defective phonological loop and hence was impaired at retaining sequences of verbal items, or at tasks such as the comprehension of complex sentences that required such retention. However, as the central executive and other components of the working memory system were spared, KF could function quite normally in most everyday tasks of learning, reasoning, and planning. Other patients with phonological loop deficits seem similarly unimpaired in most everyday activities, unless these involve phonological coding skills. Recent research by Martin (1993) has helped to clarify under what circumstances an impaired phonological loop may impede linguistic functioning, consistent with the idea that there may be other temporary stores associated with syntactic and semantic processing (e.g. see Monsell, 1984). Furthermore, Hanley, Young, and Pearson (1991) described a patient, ELD, who seemed to have a specific deficit in the visuo-spatial sketch pad, with impairments in tasks of short-term spatial memory, but with preserved short-term memory for sequences of letters even when presented visually. Interestingly, ELD is also impaired at learning new faces and objects, and this deficit in the encoding of new visuo-spatial material may form a parallel with a deficit in learning novel vocabulary items reported for a "phonological loop" patient, PV, by Baddeley, Papagno, and Vallar (1988).

The working memory model has proved useful in understanding the role of phonological memory in language development, and learning to read, and the role played by memory in chess-playing (Baddeley, 1992). It is now being applied to other tasks that seem to make short-term storage demands, such as mental arithmetic (e.g. Logie, Gilhooly, & Wynn, 1994). I will discuss the application of the working memory model to the domain of imagination in Chapter 3, and consider how hallucinations exhibited by psychiatric patients may be explicable in terms of this framework. These domains illustrate the key development in working memory research which is a shift in emphasis from the study of memory stores, to thinking about how the cognitive system is adapted to the demands made of it. The cognitive system evolved to allow people to communicate using language, or find their way around their environments. Such activities impose cognitive demands that require temporal and spatial storage systems respectively. The other major theoretical approach to memory which arose with the demise of the modal model, Craik and Lockhart's (1972) "levels of processing" framework, also attempted to redefine memory as a by-product of processing, and in this sense was similar in spirit to Baddeley's approach, although taking a very different theoretical stance (see Baddeley, 1978 for a critique).

The original working memory framework thus set an agenda for short-term memory research of understanding the kinds of temporary information stores required for everyday cognitive activities, and the re-thinking of the modal model was brought about through converging evidence from experiments with normal and brain-damaged adults. In the 20 years or so of the working memory model, there have been revisions and refinements to accommodate new experimental and neuropsychological findings, but the basic three-component model has survived remarkably intact. Interesting recent developments involve the use of connectionist modelling to implement parts of the model (Burgess & Hitch, 1992) and the use of brain imaging techniques to pinpoint distinct brain areas which are activated when tasks involving the phonological loop or visuo-spatial sketch pad are conducted (Baddeley, 1993). These recent developments are exciting and innovative, but would not have been possible without the earlier, less technically sophisticated, first stage of model development, on which the second stage of computer modelling and brain imaging techniques crucially depends.

However, although the phonological loop component of working memory has now provided a very thorough explanation of a range of effects found in memory for short sequences of words or digits, and, as I will show in Chapter 3, the visuo-spatial sketch pad component seems to bear an uncommon resemblance to the buffer store proposed as the medium for visual imagery, the study of working memory has highlighted our ignorance about the third component, the "central executive". In Atkinson and Shiffrin's (1968) modal model of short-term memory, a unitary short-term store was the seat of control and executive processes as well as storing and rehearsing list items. Although we have a much clearer idea of the storage functions in the tri-partite model, the control and executive processes remain both mysterious and elusive (e.g. see Allport, Styles, & Hsieh, 1994). Stephen Monsell considers the issue of control in Chapter 4.

These two examples, of face recognition and working memory, are ones where—whatever the merits or remaining deficiencies of the current theories—there was never any doubt that progress *could* be made. When we turn to other areas of cognition, some have suggested that we delve into murkier waters.

INSOLUBLE PROBLEMS

Some of the topics covered in the later chapters of this book appear to raise deeper issues than those that were encountered in the domain of person identification, or short-term memory, at least if we are to believe Fodor (1983). According to Fodor, we know little about "central" aspects of cognition such as the activities of thinking, reasoning, and belief, but rather a lot about peripheral input systems (modules) such as those to do with faces or language. Fodor suggests that input modules get on with their particular jobs of analysing specific types of input, uninfluenced by other types of input (they are "informationally encapsulated"), or by higher levels of belief or intention (they are "cognitively impenetrable"). However much we are told, or already know, about a particular visual illusion, for example, we still go on seeing it, suggesting that the lower levels of perception cannot be influenced by other modules, such as language, or by higher levels of cognition.

Central processes, however, are rather different. Fodor suggests his "First Law of the Nonexistence of Cognitive Science"; "the more global … a cognitive process is, the less anybody understands it" (1983, p.107). Unlike peripheral modules, central processes are not limited in their scope, but as a result, according to Fodor, there are all kinds of problems in trying to understand them. A key problem in trying to understand the central processes of cognition is that of characterising how to constrain the search through all the possibly relevant pieces of knowledge as a result of the access or activation of any other. He suggests that thought processes are diffuse and inscrutable within the current paradigms of psychology and neuropsychology which are so successful at tackling the "modular" input systems. Now several of the "mysteries" that we pursue in later chapters are mysteries to do with consciousness (Chapter 5: Young & Block), emotion (Chapter 6: Smith & Kemp-Wheeler); and thinking and belief (Chapter 7: Lea & Kiley-Worthington) which at least superficially appear to enter the central territory that Fodor claims is currently unknowable. If we take seriously Fodor's thesis, such processes will remain mysterious: "The ghost has been chased further back into the machine, but it has not been exorcised" (Fodor, 1983, p.127).

Happily, however, I think we can reject Fodor's suggestion that the processes of reasoning and belief do not lend themselves to the cognitive psychological paradigm. For example, Fodor (1983, p.119) suggests that it is not possible to have a neuropsychology of thought, because thought is not modular. However there have recently been some very successful demonstrations of how aspects of thinking and belief can profitably be studied in exactly this way.

The first example is that of the ability termed "Theory of Mind" (Premack & Woodruff, 1978; Wimmer & Perner, 1983; see also Lea & Kiley-Worthington, Chapter 7, this volume). Understanding another person's mental state—what they know or believe to be true—is an essential prerequisite for communication. It governs every aspect of conversation from the chosen topic to the use of pronouns. Normal children appear to acquire the ability to understand another person's beliefs at around the age of 4, as demonstrated by "False Belief" tasks. A typical task of this sort involves giving a child a private glimpse of an unexpected state of affairs—for example showing them that a Smarties (M&M's) tube contains a toy animal rather than sweets (candies)—and then asking them what a third party, not present at the private viewing, would think the tube contained. Before about 4 years old, a normal child cannot understand that the other person may hold a different (in fact, false) belief, and attributes to the other person their own privileged knowledge of the contents of the box. However, older children can correctly deduce that an uninformed observer most likely thinks that a Smarties (M&M's) tube contains sweets (candies). Research at the MRC Cognitive Development Unit in London has shown that it is a characteristic of autistic children that they generally fail such False Belief tasks, whereas Downs Syndrome children of mental age 4 and above generally succeed (Baron-Cohen, Leslie, & Frith, 1985). It seems that understanding other minds may depend on a specific ability or "module" whose function can be impaired by the neurological condition that provokes the autistic syndrome (Frith, 1989; see also Frith & Happe, 1994, who describe additional cognitive characteristics of autism to supplement the theory of mind account). Indeed Fodor himself views theory of mind competence as among the modular subsystems on which intelligence depends (Fodor, 1992), although he disagrees with some developmentalists about the specific reasons why 3-year-olds fail false belief tasks.

Moreover, other kinds of thought disorder also prove amenable to the cognitive neuropsychological paradigm. C. Frith (1992) and others have recently embarked on an extremely interesting attempt to account for the symptoms of schizophrenia in terms of the breakdown of central processes to do with supervision and willed action. Norman and Shallice's model of attentional control (see Chapter 4 of this volume) has proved a useful framework for understanding schizophrenic symptoms. I will discuss in more detail in Chapter 3, "Reality and Imagination", how the working memory model may additionally provide a framework for understanding certain kinds of hallucination as misattribution of self-generated phonological loop activity to external sources. Recently, there has been considerable interest in explaining how certain bizarre delusional states may arise as a result of damage to specific information-processing routes. For example both the Capgras syndrome, where patients think their friends and relatives have been replaced with doubles or impostors, and the Cotard syndrome, where patients believe that they are dead, may be understood in neuropsychological terms as resulting from damage to the neuro-anatomical pathway responsible for appropriate emotional reactions to familiar events (Young, 1994: see also Young & Block, Chapter 5, this volume). Such developments in abnormal cognitive development and cognitive neuropsychiatry appear to refute Fodor's suggestion that thought processes cannot be studied or understood with current cognitive techniques. Indeed this book contains several other examples of the apparent modularity of other "central" cognitive processes. For example, in Chapter 4 we encounter examples of the fractionation of executive processes.

However, Fodor has raised other difficulties for our understanding of the processes of "central" cognition, not least of which is the Frame problem. The Frame problem (see the collection edited by Pylyshyn, 1987) is a crucial issue for artificial intelligence: The problem is, how can we limit the amount of relevant information that can be brought to bear on the possible solution of a problem, without cutting off any possibility for novel or creative solutions? It was described most colourfully by Dennett (1987), who summarises the problem as "A walking encyclopedia will walk over a cliff, for all its knowledge of cliffs and the effects of gravity, unless it is designed in such a fashion that it can find the right bits of knowledge at the right times, so it can plan its engagements with the real world" (p.53).

The Frame problem has tended to sit as a rather esoteric little problem for researchers in the area of AI to do with "planning", but it actually raises a much more fundamental problem about the nature of our understanding of cognition. If we cannot think of a way to solve this problem in open-ended problem domains, this means that our current understanding of human cognition, which clearly circumvents the Frame problem somehow, is fundamentally limited. If we had any idea at all how we bring (mostly) the right information to play at the right moments, we could have a stab at building a machine to do the same things. However, although the Frame problem remains unsolved at present, we are now beginning to understand the neurological underpinnings of aspects of planning and decision with the recent flurry of research into the patterns of deficit found in frontal lobe patients (see Monsell, Chapter 4 of this volume, for detailed examples).

If we agree with Fodor (1983), the prospects for progress in understanding core issues in cognition with our present theoretical tools are pretty bleak (see also Fodor, 1994). However, in the present book, some of these core issues of control, consciousness, emotion, and belief are raised with more notes of optimism than despair. The scientific study of cognition is probably sufficiently young for optimism to be allowed, as least for a decade or two longer.

STRUCTURE OF THE BOOK

My motivations for choosing these particular mysteries were various. On the one hand, for a tutorial book to accompany more conventionally ordered course texts in cognition, it seemed important to sample the territory of the contemporary Cognition text. In these traditional terms, the different chapters here can be seen as tutorial companions to course sections on Perception (Chapter 2: "Visual illusions"), Visual Cognition and Memory (this chapter, and Chapter 3: "Reality and imagination"); Attention and/or Skill (Chapter 4:"Control of mental processes"); Cognitive Neuropsychology (Chapter 5: "Consciousness"); Cognition and Emotion (Chapter 6: "Why do we need emotions?") and Thinking (Chapter 7: "Can animals think?"). In these terms there are undoubtedly some gaps—we don't have anything much relevant to Language, for example. I have also sampled mysteries of different kinds and of different scales. In Chapters 2 and 3 we describe research in the areas of visual perception and visual imagery where progress has been dramatic in recent years, through the convergence of cognitive, neuroscientific, and computational research. Nevertheless there are still a set of curious phenomena of visual perception that seem to defy simple explanation but provoke flurries of scientific activity. The Müller-Lyer and Moon illusions were on Newell's list in 1973. Are we any further on with understanding these phenomena today? Michael Morgan suggests that we should be, in Chapter 2. In Chapter 3 I take a subject—visual imagery—that would itself have been a candidate mystery only a dozen or so years ago, but for which we now seem to have an emergent theoretical understanding built on just the kind of converging methods and evidence that have been successful in other domains (e.g. see Kosslyn, 1994). However, here we have an example of how one area of progress spawns a new mystery, and in the second part of Chapter 3 I explain how our understanding of the imagery process seems to open up the deeper question of how we can tell reality from imagination. In Chapter 4, Stephen Monsell explores the mystery of how we arrange our cognitive processes to perform one task rather than another, and addresses the tricky issues raised by boxes with labels like "central executive" in other cognitive models. This chapter also bridges the gap between the study of modular sub-systems, such as face recognition, phonological encoding, and other aspects of perception (Chapters 1, 2, and 3), and the study of possibly more pervasive or central aspects of cognition which is covered in Chapters 5, 6, and 7.

Consciousness, the greatest mystery of all, has hardly been neglected by psychologists. It's just that we don't seem to have got very far in understanding what it is or what it is for. Andy Young and Ned Block explore some of the reasons for this in Chapter 5, and suggest that modest progress is being made. In contrast, emotions were neglected, quite deliberately, by cognitive psychology until remarkably recently. Research on mood and memory only really got started in the early 1980s (e.g. Bower, 1983; Teasdale, 1983) and seemed radical even then. Now the relationship between cognitive and affective psychology is productive and important in clinical and other pathological contexts, but, as in the case of consciousness, we don't really understand what emotions are, or what they are for. Philip Smith and Susan Kemp-Wheeler review these questions in Chapter 6. The final chapter explores a further fundamental question—that of what it is to be intelligent. Philosophers and scientists addressing the question of whether a machine can think sometimes appeal to the biological basis of thinking and consciousness (e.g. Searle, 1980). According to Searle, the essence of real cognition—the representational mind—must be biologically based. To understand characteristics of intelligence in general, and human intelligence in particular, we should explore cognition in non-human animals. In Chapter 7, Stephen Lea and Marthe Kiley-Worthington investigate the criteria that would be needed to attribute intelligence and creativity to other animals.

In the course of these chapters we will discuss a number of phenomena that everyone would immediately accept as "mysteries"—such as illusory perceptions, hallucinations, confabulations, delusions, and consciousness—although we will as it happens omit some other popular mysteries, like hypnosis and dreams. But we will also be examining many aspects of mental life that are usually taken for granted, and only become mysterious when a psychologist poses the question, "how is it done"? Face recognition is just such a topic; its mysteries attracted me into research and I hope that this collection of essays will stimulate the curiosity of a new generation of students.

REFERENCES

Allport, A., Styles, E.A., & Hsieh, S. (1994). Shifting intentional set: Exploring the dynamic control of tasks. In C. Umilta & M. Moscovitch (Eds.), *Attention and performance XV*. MIT Press.

Anderson, J.R. (1993). *The rules of the mind*. Hillsdale, NJ: Lawrence Erlbaum Associates Inc.

Atkinson, R.C. & Shiffrin, R.M. (1968). Human memory: A proposed system and its control processes. In K.W. Spence (Ed.), *The psychology of learning and motivation: Advances in research and theory, Vol 2* (pp.89–195). New York: Academic Press.

Baddeley, A.D. (1978). The trouble with levels: A re-examination of Craik and Lockhart's framework for memory research. *Psychological Review, 85,* 139–152.

Baddeley, A.D. (1986). *Working memory*. Oxford, UK: Oxford University Press.

Baddeley, A.D. (1990). *Human memory: Theory and practice*. Hove,UK: Lawrence Erlbaum Associates Ltd.

Baddeley, A.D. (1992). Is working memory working? The fifteenth Bartlett lecture. *Quarterly Journal of Experimental Psychology, 44A* 1–31.

Baddeley, A.D. (1993). Verbal and visual systems of working memory. *Current Biology, 3,* 563–565.

Baddeley, A.D. & Hitch, G.J. (1974). Working memory. In G.A. Bower (Ed.), *Recent advances in learning and motivation, Vol 8*. New York: Academic Press.

Baddeley, A.D., Papagno, C., & Vallar, G. (1988). When long term learning depends on short term storage. *Journal of Memory and Language, 27,* 586–595.

Baddeley, A.D. & Warrington, E.K. (1970). Amnesia and the distinction between long- and short-term memory. *Journal of Verbal Learning and Verbal Behavior, 9,* 176–189.

Baron-Cohen, S., Leslie, A.M., & Frith, U. (1985). Does the autistic child have a "theory of mind"? *Cognition, 21,* 37–46.

Bartlett, F.C. (1932). *Remembering*. Cambridge University Press.

Bartlett, J.C. & Searcy, J. (1993). Inversion and configuration of faces. *Cognitive Psychology, 25*, 281–316.

Bower, G.H. (1983). Affect and cognition. *Philosophical Transactions of the Royal Society of London, B302*, 387–402.

Broadbent, D.E. (1958). *Perception and communication*. New York: Pergamon Press.

Brooks, L.R. (1968). Spatial and verbal components in the act of recall. *Canadian Journal of Psychology, 22*, 349–368.

Brown, E., Deffenbacher, K., & Sturgill, W. (1977). Memory for faces and the circumstances of encounter. *Journal of Applied Psychology, 62*, 311–318.

Bruce, V. (1982). Changing faces: Visual and non-visual coding processes in face recognition. *British Journal of Psychology, 73*, 105–116.

Bruce, V. (1994). Stability from variation: The case of face recognition. The M.D. Vernon memorial lecture. *Quarterly Journal of Experimental Psychology, 47A*, 5–28.

Bruce, V. & Humphreys, G.W. (1994). Recognising objects and faces. *Visual Cognition, 1*, 141–180.

Bruce, V. & Langton, S. (1994). The use of pigmentation and shading information in recognising the sex and identities of faces. *Perception, 23*, 803–822.

Bruce, V. & Valentine, T. (1985). Identity priming in the recognition of familiar faces. *British Journal of Psychology, 76*, 373–383.

Bruce, V. & Valentine, T. (1986). Semantic priming of familiar faces. *Quarterly Journal of Experimental Psychology, 38A*, 125–150.

Bruce, V. & Young, A.W. (1986). Understanding face recognition. *British Journal of Psychology, 77*, 305–327.

Bruyer, R., Laterre, C., Seron, X., Feyereisen, P., Strypstein, E., Pierrard, E., & Rectem, D. (1983). A case of prosopagnosia with some preserved remembrance of familiar faces. *Brain and Cognition, 2*, 257–284.

Burgess, N. & Hitch, G.J. (1992). Toward a network model of the articulatory loop. *Journal of Memory and Language, 31*, 429–460.

Burton, A.M., Bruce, V., & Johnston, R.A. (1990). Understanding face recognition with an interactive activation model. *British Journal of Psychology, 81*, 361–380.

Burton, A.M., Young, A.W., Bruce, V., Johnston, R.A., & Ellis, A.W. (1991). Understanding covert recognition. *Cognition, 39*, 129–166.

Cohen, G. & Burke, D. (Eds.) (1993). *Memory for proper names*. Hove, UK: Lawrence Erlbaum Associates Ltd.

Craik, F.I.M. & Lockhart, R.S. (1972). Levels of processing: A framework for memory research. *Journal of Verbal Learning and Verbal Behavior, 11*, 671–684.

De Haan, E.H.F., Young, A.W., & Newcombe, F. (1991). A dissociation between the sense of familiarity and access to semantic information concerning familiar people. *European Journal of Cognitive Psychology, 3*, 51–68.

Dennett, D.C. (1987). Cognitive wheels: The frame problem of AI. In Z.W. Pylyshyn (Ed.), *The Robot's Dilemma: The Frame Problem in artificial intelligence*. Norwood, NJ: Ablex.

Devlin, Lord P. (1976). *Report to the secretary of state for the home department of the departmental committee on evidence of identification in criminal cases*. London: HMSO.

Ellis, A.W. & Young, A.W. (1988). *Human cognitive neuropsychology*. London: Lawrence Erlbaum Associates Ltd.

Ellis, H.D., Ellis, D.M., & Hosie, J.A. (1993). Priming effects in children's face recognition. *British Journal of Psychology, 84,* 101–110.
Ellis, H.D. & Young, A.W. (1989). Are faces special? In A.W. Young & H.D. Ellis (Eds.), *Handbook of research on face processing.* Amsterdam: North Holland.
Flude, B.M., Ellis, A.W., & Kay, J. (1989). Face processing and name retrieval in an anomic aphasic: Names are stored separately from semantic information about familiar people. *Brain and Cognition, 11,* 60–72.
Fodor, J.A. (1983). *The modularity of mind.* MIT Press.
Fodor, J.A. (1992). A theory of the child's theory of mind. *Cognition, 44,* 283–296.
Fodor, J.A. (1994). Concepts: a pot-boiler. *Cognition, 50,* 95–113.
Frith, C. (1992) *The cognitive neuropsychology of schizophrenia.* London: Lawrence Erlbaum Associates Ltd.
Frith, U. (1989). *Autism: Explaining the enigma.* London: Blackwell.
Frith, U. & Happe, F. (1994). Autism: beyond theory of mind. *Cognition, 50,* 115–132.
Goldstein, A.G. & Chance, J.E. (1971). Visual recognition memory for complex configurations. *Perception & Psychophysics, 9,* 237–241.
Hanley, J.R., Young, A.W., & Pearson, N.A. (1991). Impairment of the visuo–spatial sketch pad. *Quarterly Journal of Experimental Psychology, 43A,* 101–125.
Hay, D.C. & Young, A.W. (1982). The human face. In A.W. Ellis (Ed.), *Normality and pathology in cognitive functions.* London: Academic Press.
Kosslyn, S.M. (1994), *Image and brain.* MIT Press.
Kurucz, J. & Feldmar, G. (1979). Prosopo-affective agnosia as a symptom of cerebral organic disease. *Journal of the American Geriatrics Society, 27,* 225–230.
Kurucz, J., Feldmar, G., & Werner, W. (1979). Prosopo-affective agnosia associated with chronic organic brain syndrome. *Journal of the American Geriatrics Society, 27,* 91–95.
Laming, D.R.J. (1988). Multiple book review of sensory analysis. *Behavioural and Brain Sciences, 11,* 275–339.
Landauer, T.K. & Bjork, R.A. (1978). Optimum rehearsal patterns and name learning. In M.M. Gruneberg, P.E. Morris, & R.N. Sykes (Eds.), *Practical aspects of memory* (pp.625–632). London: Academic Press.
Logie, R.H., Gilhooly, K.J., & Wynn, V. (1994). Counting on working memory in arithmetic problem solving. *Memory and Cognition, 22,* 395–410.
MacLeod, C.M. (1991). Half a century of research on the Stroop effect: An integrative review. *Psychological Bulletin, 109,* 163–203.
Martin, R.C. (1993). Short–term memory and sentence processing: Evidence from neuropsychology. *Memory & Cognition, 21,* 176–183.
Mathews, A. (1993). Biases in processing emotional information. *The Psychologist: Bulletin of the British Psychological Society, 6,* 493–499.
McClelland, J.L. & Rumelhart, D.E. (1981). An interactive activation model of the effect of context in perception, Part I. An account of basic findings. *Psychological Review, 88,* 375–406.
Meyer, D.E., Abrams, R.A., Kornblum, S., Wright, C.E., & Smith, J.E.K. (1988). Optimality in human motor performance: Ideal control of rapid aimed movements. *Psychological Review, 95,* 340–370.
Miller, G.A. (1956). The magical number seven plus or minus two: Some limits on our capacity for processing information. *Psychological Review, 63,* 81–97.

Monsell, S. (1984). Components of working memory underlying verbal skills: A distributed capacities view—A tutorial review. In H. Bouma & D.G. Bouwhuis (Eds.), *Attention and Performance, 10* (pp.327–350). Hove, UK: Lawrence Erlbaum Associates Ltd.

Morton, J. (1969).Interaction of information in word recognition. *Psychological Review, 76,* 165–178.

Neisser, U. (1967). *Cognitive psychology.* New York: Appleton-Century-Crofts.

Newell, A. (1973). You can't play 20 questions with Nature and win. In W.G. Chase (Ed.), *Visual information processing.* New York: Academic Press.

Newell, A. (1991). *Unified theories of cognition.* Cambridge, MA: Cambridge University Press.

O'Toole, A.J., Deffenbacher, K.A., Valentin, D., & Abdi, H. (1994). Structural aspects of face recognition and the other-race effect. *Memory & Cognition, 22,* 208–224.

Plug, C. & Ross, H.E. (1994). The natural moon illusion: A multifactor angular account. *Perception, 23,* 321–333.

Premack, D. & Woodruff, G. (1978). Does the chimpanzee have a theory of mind? *Behavioural and Brain Sciences, 4,* 515–526.

Pylyshyn, Z.W. (Ed.) (1987), *The Robot's Dilemma: The Frame Problem in artificial intelligence.* Norwood, NJ: Ablex.

Rhodes, G., Brake, S., & Atkinson, A.P. (1993). What's lost in inverted faces? *Cognition, 47,* 25–57.

Rips, L.J. (1989). The psychology of knights and knaves. *Cognition, 31,* 85–116.

Rolls, E.T. (1992). Neurophysiological mechanisms underlying face processing within and beyond the temporal cortical visual areas. *Philosophical Transactions of the Royal Society of London, B335,* 11–21.

Scoville, W.B. & Milner, B. (1957). Loss of recent memory after bilateral hippocampal lesions. *Journal of Neurology, Neurosurgery and Psychiatry, 20,* 11–21.

Searle, J.R. (1980). Minds, brains and programs. *The Behavioral and Brain Sciences, 3,* 417–457.

Sergent, J., Ohta, S., MacDonald, B., & Zuck, E. (1994). Segregated processing of facial identity and emotion in the human brain: A PET study. *Visual Cognition, 1,* 349–369.

Shallice, T. (1988). *From neuropsychology to mental structure.* Cambridge, UK: Cambridge University Press.

Shallice, T. & Warrington, E.K. (1970). Independent functioning of verbal memory stores: A neuropsychological study. *Quarterly Journal of Experimental Psychology, 22,* 261–273.

Shepard, R.N. (1967). Recognition memory for words, sentences and pictures. *Journal of Verbal Learning and Verbal Behavior, 6,* 156–163.

Standing, L. (1973). Learning 10,000 pictures. *Quarterly Journal of Experimental Psychology, 25,* 207–222.

Standing, L.G., Conezio, J., & Haber, N. (1970). Perception and memory for pictures: Single trial learning of 2500 visual stimuli. *Psychonomic Science, 19,* 73–74.

Stroop, J.R. (1935). Studies of interference in serial verbal reactions. *Journal of Experimental Psychology, 18,* 643–662.

Tanaka, J.W. & Farah, M.J. (1993). Parts and wholes in face recognition. *Quarterly Journal of Experimental Psychology, 46A,* 225–245.

Teasdale, J.D. (1983). Affect and accessibility. *Philosophical Transactions of the Royal Society of London, B302*, 403–412.

Wimmer, H. & Perner, J. (1983). Beliefs about beliefs: representation and constraining function of wrong beliefs in young children's understanding of deception. *Cognition, 13*, 103–128.

Young, A.W. (1994). Recognition and reality. In E.M.R. Critchley (Ed.), *Neurological boundaries on reality.* London: Farrand Press.

Young, A.W. & Bruce, V. (1991). Perceptual categories and the computation of Grandmother. *European Journal of Cognitive Psychology, 3*, 5–49.

Young, A.W., Hay, D.C., & Ellis, A.W. (1985). The faces that launched a thousand slips: Everyday difficulties and errors in recognising people. *British Journal of Psychology, 76*, 495–523.

Young, A.W., McWeeny, K.H., Ellis, A.W., & Hay, D.C. (1986a). Naming and categorising faces and written names. *Quarterly Journal of Experimental Psychology, 38A*, 297–318.

Young, A.W., McWeeny, K.H., Hay, D.C., & Ellis, A.W. (1986b). Matching familiar and unfamiliar faces on identity and expression. *Psychological Research, 48*, 63–68.

Young, A.W., Newcombe, F., De Haan, E.H.F., Small, M., & Hay, D.C. (1993). Face perception after brain injury. *Brain, 116*, 941–959.

CHAPTER TWO

Visual illusions

Michael J. Morgan University College London

PREAMBLE

One of the great "unsolved mysteries of the mind" is how we see. The challenge is to understand how we form a three-dimensional representation of objects in the outside world on the basis of an image on the retina of the eye, which is merely a two-dimensional distribution of shading and colour. Simply forming an image, whether in the eye or later in the brain, is not the same as seeing. A camera forms an image, but does not understand it. Seeing involves using the image to understand the world. Some appreciation of the magnitude of the problem can be gained from two facts. First, in the cerebral cortex of the most-studied primate (the Macaque monkey) as many as 50% of all neurones have a visual input. (In the human brain the proportion is probably somewhat smaller, because of the expansion of the prefrontal cortex.) Second, attempts to make computers recognise objects (such as human faces) from images have so far had very limited success. Even the problem of finding the boundaries of an object from a cluttered image presents a host of difficulties which machine vision has not yet solved (Marr, 1982; Watt, 1991).

It is not generally realised that vision is a complex mental activity. Unlike algebra, "seeing" seldom requires any conscious mental effort. Only when our visual system appears to make errors does it excite comment. "Errors" of perception are commonly called "illusions". A typical example would be the "moon illusion", in which the moon low on the horizon appears larger than the moon high in the sky. Illusions have played an important part in the history of visual science, because they have stimulated thought about underlying mechanisms. An example to which we shall return is the illusion of movement described by Exner (1888) which occurs when two flashes of light are presented at different times in different places (apparent movement).

Important though illusions have been historically in stimulating interest in vision, I shall argue in this chapter that the term "illusion" is not a particularly helpful one. There are some genuinely mysterious visual phenomena, where we do not yet understand the underlying physiological mechanisms. As soon as these are explained, the need to talk about an illusion disappears. The history of colour vision offers many examples. On the other hand, there are other cases where we talk about illusions only because of mistaken assumptions about the way in which the visual system works. Scientific problems can arise both from empirical ignorance and from conceptual confusion. We find visual illusions puzzling partly because the underlying physiological mechanisms are unclear, but also because of mistaken general ideas about vision. One of the key confusions in the history of visual science has been between optical images and visual representations, also confusingly called "images". Confusion between these two has spawned many of the mysteries that we refer to as "illusions". I shall use the term "picture theory of vision" to refer to the mistaken idea that seeing involves having an image in the head, rather than the extraction of information from an image.

THE PICTURE THEORY OF VISION

The eye forms an image on the light-sensitive retina. The retinal image can be completely described by the luminance (L) at each point on a two-dimensional surface(x,y). Luminance is a measure derived from light intensity (radiance) that takes into account the effectiveness of different wavelengths of light. To include colour in the image we would need a separate description for each visible wavelength, giving a four-dimensional quantity. To bring home the physical nature of an image, it is useful to present the image as a surface, in which luminance is given by the height of the surface above the x,y plane (Fig. 2.1). The landscape representation contains all the information in the conventional image but in a form not readily interpretable by the eye, thus serving to remind us how complex the image is, when considered as a purely physical object.

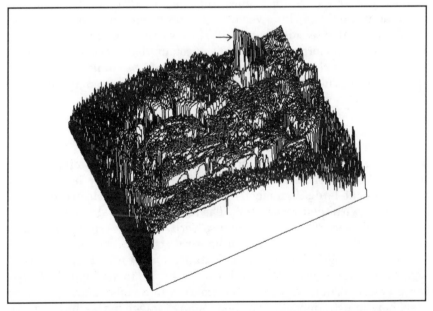

FIG. 2.1.   A conventional image (top) and its "landscape" representation in which the intensity of each point is represented by its height (bottom). The blacker a point in the original, the higher it is in the landscape. The arrow points to the region of the image containing the handlebar. The landscape representation contains the same amount of information as the conventional image, but not in a form that allows the visual system to recognise objects. The landscape representation could also be taken to represent the activity levels of photoreceptors to the conventional image, and the task of the visual system to extract information about the world from this array, not to reconstruct the original image.

The picture theory of vision considers the task of vision to be the building up of another kind of image, the *perceptual image*, somewhere in the brain. The perceptual image resembles the outside world in the same way that a colour photograph resembles the real world. In particular, there is a point-by-point resemblance between each part of the retinal image and each part of the perceptual image. A relatively intense point in the retinal image maps onto a relatively intense point in the perceptual image; the longer of two lines in the retinal image will map onto the longer of two lines in the perceptual image; and so on. When this resemblance obviously fails, as for example when a line looks bent but is "really" straight, we are said to be suffering from an illusion.

Of course, everyone knows that this theory is wrong in cases like the perception of colour: since Newton, philosophers have known that colours are not properties of objects, but effects that they have on us. In 1795, 200 years ago, John Dalton read a paper to the Manchester Literary and Philosophical Society describing some unusual features of his own perception of colours. A recent analysis of the DNA in one of Dalton's preserved eyes has shown that he lacked the normal gene for manufacturing the medium wavelength absorbing cone pigment (Hunt, Dulai, Bowmaker, & Mollon, 1995). It is worth spending a little time reviewing the modern understanding of colour vision, because it carries some important clues about the way we should be thinking about the spatial metric. The following is a brief and necessarily dogmatic account.

COLOUR VISION

The purpose of colour vision in primates is not to give us a pretty picture, but to convey information about the surfaces of objects, by means of which they can be distinguished from neighbouring objects in the image, and to help with their recognition. The relevant physical property of the surfaces of objects for colour is their *surface reflectance spectrum*, which represents the relative amount of light reflected rather than absorbed at each wavelength. The surface reflectance spectrum is a characteristic signature of an object, which will usually suffice to distinguish it from other objects. There is a lot of information in a reflectance spectrum: just how much depends on how many wavelengths have to be independently specified. Luckily, it turns out that natural reflectance spectra are quite smooth, so that a complete description would be highly redundant. In other words, the reflectance at a given wavelength is in general highly predictable from its neighbours in the spectrum. Statistical analysis reveals that over 99% of spectra can be distinguished by just three numbers. Our colour vision capitalises on this physical simplicity in the input by making do with just three classes of cone, which, by signalling the quantum catch in three overlapping regions of the spectrum, provide the three numbers needed to distinguish the great majority of natural spectra.

This is not the end of the story, however. The retinal image does not contain the surface reflectance spectrum of objects directly, but rather the product of the spectrum and the spectrum of the illuminating source, for example, the sun. The image of a banana illuminated by candlelight has a different wavelength composition from its image under a clear blue sky. To recover the fact that it is "yellow", we have to take account of the illuminant. This is the celebrated problem of "colour constancy", which is still far from solved, although it is suspected that the solution makes use of the fact that illuminants, like reflectance spectra, typically vary rather smoothly over wavelength.

We could, if we wished, say that colour is "a great illusion". Having only three classes of cone makes us vulnerable to metamerism—the sensory confusion between physically different mixtures of wavelengths. For example, we confuse a mixture of red, green, and blue with the flat spectrum of white light: luckily so, for this is how colour printing and colour television work. But if the consequence of possessing specialised filters such as cones is called an "illusion", it is also an illusion that we, unlike some animals, do not perceive ultraviolet light, hardly a useful description. I shall argue later on that spatial illusions arise because of specialised processing of the image, and that they are no different in this respect from colour vision.

There are two main points to be gained from the example of colour. First, the purpose of vision is to give us *information* about the outside world, not to provide a picture; and second, in order to understand a particular visual function, we have to understand the physics of natural objects. Vision has evolved under natural selection to give us information about our particular world. Colour is not an illusion, once we have understood its function; and so it may eventually prove for all so-called illusions.

APPARENT MOVEMENT

Another example of the need to understand the true physical nature of the image is seen in the phenomenon of "apparent movement". A sequence of frames taken of a moving object, such as we see in the cinema or on television, gives us a compelling impression of continuous movement. When this phenomenon was first discovered it was widely considered as a marvellous visual illusion. However, a mathematical analysis of movement gives us a deeper understanding. A series of frames representing the uniform movement of an object can be considered as a set of samples of the space-time trajectory of that object (Fig. 2.2a), as if the moving target were illuminated by a stroboscope. The fact that we see such sampled motion as if it were continuous suggests that the visual system *interpolates* between these samples to give a continuous representation of the change of target position over time[1].

The accuracy of interpolation can be measured by the technique of vernier alignment (Fig. 2.2b)[2]. A moving vernier target is presented as a series of discrete frames, and the observer has to judge whether the bottom bar is shifted to the left or the right of the top. When the relative positions of the two bars in each frame are such that the top bar is shifted slightly forwards in the direction of motion, then not surprisingly this is what the observer sees and reports. This is what the picture theory would expect, because the vernier offset is "really there" in each frame. More surprisingly, however, exactly the same misalignment is seen if the bars are exactly aligned in each frame, but one of them is delayed relative to the other for a few milliseconds (Fig. 2.2c): in this case, the delayed bar is seen as if it were displaced backwards along the motion trajectory. The effect of a temporal delay can be cancelled by a spatial misalignment in the opposite direction, and vice versa. This exact equivalence between a spatial misalignment and a temporal delay is comprehensible if the visual system is using the discrete samples in each frame to construct the continuous target trajectory, for then shifts in space and time become equivalent.

It turns out to be very simple to interpolate between discrete samples, provided certain conditions are met in the input. All we need is a filter that is insensitive to very rapid changes of its input in time, and an input in which the target trajectory is relatively smooth (as in the case of colour spectra, and their sampling by cones). The mathematical technique of *Fourier analysis*[3] reveals that a discretely-sampled uniform motion trajectory contains within it a signal corresponding to the original trajectory. The effect of the sampling process is to *add* a set of other trajectories corresponding to different real velocities (Fahle & Poggio, 1981; Morgan, 1979, 1980). Thus, whether we consider the continuous movement we see in the cinema and on television as an "illusion" or not depends on our description of the physical nature of the signal. The part of the signal corresponding to continuous motion is actually there, so our perception of it is not an illusion. On the other hand, we are failing to perceive the spurious additional signals due to the discrete sampling, and this could be considered an illusion, except that we should then have to say the same about colour metamerism, and even our inability to perceive ultraviolet radiation.

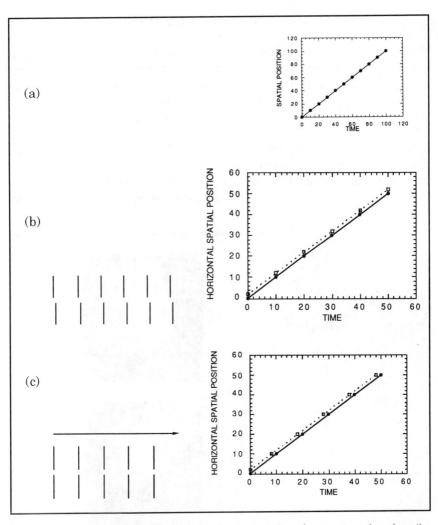

(a)

(b)

(c)

FIG. 2.2.   The top panel (a) is a graphical representation of a target moving along the trajectory shown by the continuous line, but made visible only at the space-time points represented by circles. With sufficiently small temporal and spatial intervals between its instantaneous positions, the target appears to move continuously. The circles can be considered samples of the continuous trajectory, between which the visual system interpolates by spatio-temporal filtering. The middle panel (b) shows a vernier target in sampled motion, with the stations drawn on the left and the space-time diagram on the right. The vernier offset is present in each station, and the observer sees the top target as lagging behind the right. Spatial offsets of as little as 5 arcsec can be reliably perceived. The bottom panel (c) also shows a vernier target in sampled motion, but as the space-time diagram illustrates, the two lines are now presented at spatially aligning positions with a slight relative temporal delay. The two trajectories are identical to those in (b) and are merely being sampled at different times. Once again, observers see the top bar as lagging, and temporal delays of 1 msec can be reliably perceived as an equivalent spatial offset.

ILLUSORY BANDS OF LIGHTNESS

There are numerous examples in which our perception of the relative lightness of two parts of the scene does not depend in any obvious way on the relative intensities of light in the image. The most famous example is the "Mach Bands" observed by the physicist Ernst Mach at the edges of a region where light intensity was changing linearly (Mach, 1906; Morrone, Ross, Burr, & Owens, 1986; Watt & Morgan, 1985). Mach bands are not easy to illustrate, so I shall consider instead a more dramatic version: in the "pyramid illusion", a set of concentric squares with luminance increasing towards the centre appears as if it has bright rays running through the corners of the squares (Fig. 2.3). It is tempting

FIG. 2.3. The image at the top consists of a series of concentric squares increasing in intensity towards the centre. A cross-like pattern is seen apparently radiating from the centre, with the arms of the cross joining the corners of the squares. The cross would not be visible to a simple photocell scanning the image, but the following two images show how they would be seen by a more complicated scanner with an aperture, as illustrated in Fig. 2.4.

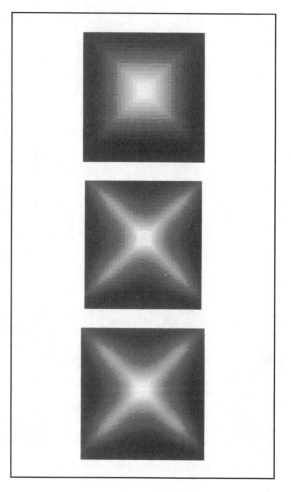

to say that these rays are illusory, in the sense that a point-by-point description of the light intensity in the image would not reveal any structures corresponding to them. But if they are illusory, does this mean that they would not be registered by a physical instrument? The answer is "no". To be concrete about this, we need to consider what kind of physical measuring instrument we would use to obtain a point-by-point description. For example, we might use a photoelectric cell with a pinhole aperture in front of it, which is scanned across the image, and take the output of the cell at each point to represent the intensity of the image at that point. But several practical questions immediately arise. How large should the pinhole be, and how far apart should the "points" be in the point-by-point description? It is easy to see that if the pinhole is the same size as the whole image, all spatial detail will be lost; a pinhole one tenth the size of the whole image will still transmit some coarse spatial detail, but not fine features. Thus, different sizes of pinhole will transmit different representations of the image: which of these corresponds to reality, and which are illusory?

SPATIAL SCALE IN IMAGES

The answer is that all these descriptions correspond to real physical structures present in the image: this must be so, because they are obtained by physical measuring instruments. But each is only a partial description, depending on the *spatial scale* to which the instrument is tuned. A quite close analogy can be made with the way in which filters on an audio amplifier can be changed to emphasise some parts of the tonal range at the expense of others. Indeed, the technique of Fourier analysis (see Note 3) can be used with both audio and visual images, and the conclusion in both cases is the same: a complex image can be considered as the sum of components at different spatial scales, which can be revealed by appropriately tuned physical measuring instruments, each of which emphasises a different set of physical structures actually present in the original image.

But is there any physical device that will reveal the ray-like structures in the pyramid illusion? The answer is given in Fig. 2.4 which shows how the rays can be emphasised by scanning the original image with a special kind of aperture. This device actually consists of two apertures: a central circle, in which all the light is summed, surrounded by a ring or annulus. All the light falling in the annulus is subtracted from the summed light falling in the central aperture, and the final

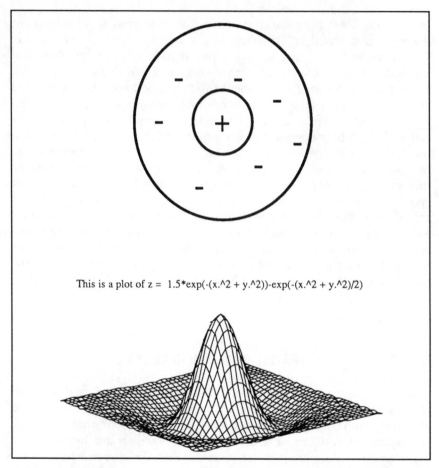

This is a plot of z = 1.5*exp(-(x.^2 + y.^2))-exp(-(x.^2 + y.^2)/2)

FIG. 2.4.   The scanner illustrated at the top adds light falling in its central region (+) and subtracts light falling in the surround (-). If the spatial weighting function of both centre and surround has a Gaussian profile (bottom), the scanner resembles the receptive field of a retinal ganglion cell.

output of the device is thus the difference between the light falling in the centre and the surround. This may seem a rather peculiar and arbitrary device, but it is no less tuned to extract structures that are actually in the image than is the simple circular aperture. The different pictures in Fig. 2.3 show what happens as the size of the centre aperture is increased, keeping the ratio between centre and surround constant. Apertures that are tuned to different spatial scales are called "spatial filters".

WHAT NEURAL MECHANISMS CORRESPOND TO SPATIAL FILTERS?

The filtering device we have used to produce these images is similar in some ways to the receptive field of retinal ganglion cells, and also of cells in the lateral geniculate nucleus (LGN), the main sensory relay station between retina and visual cortex. The receptive field of a visual neurone is defined as the region of the retina from which it receives its input (Hartline, 1940) The receptive fields of retinal ganglion cells are roughly circular, and receive opponent signals from cones in their centre and surround, with the result that they respond maximally to a light spot exactly filling their centre, and hardly at all to a uniform light filling their receptive field. They act as *spatial frequency filters*, with a low sensitivity to images of uniform light intensity and with a maximal sensitivity to wavelengths $w/2$, where w is the width of the receptive field centre. As the early stages of spatial vision are dominated by spatial filters of this type, and because filtering the pyramid image with an engineering approximation to such filters produces images in which the illusory features are enhanced, it is tempting to think that the illusion has been explained and that no further discussion is necessary.

But that conclusion would be mistaken, and the real message is somewhat different. The filtered images in Fig. 2.3 are still images, and they no more explain perception than the fact that the retinal image is coloured explains colour perception. It would be perfectly possible for visual processing beyond the LGN to reverse the effects of earlier bandpass spatial frequency filtering, in the same way that the effects of diminishing retinal image size with distance are corrected to achieve size constancy. The physiological fact that retinal ganglion cells remove low spatial frequencies from the image is not the real issue here, but rather the formal insight that images contain structures at multiple spatial scales, and that none of these scales has a right to be considered as any more veridical or less illusory than another. The interesting questions that emerge from the pyramid illusion are ones like the following, in which there are no references to "illusions":

- How are features like bars and edges extracted from the spatially distributed firing rates in retinal ganglion cells?
- How are the results of filtering at different spatial scales subsequently combined to yield a unified percept?
- At what level, if any, of visual processing does the firing rate of single cells make explicit the brightness of surfaces in objects?

THE "CAFE WALL" AND MUNSTERBERG ILLUSIONS

A similar set of questions, and some further ones, arise from analysis of the "Cafe Wall" illusion illustrated in the top panel of Fig. 2.5. In the Cafe Wall illusion (so-called because it was first seen on the wall of a Cafe in Bristol) the alternating rows of black and white squares are separated by a line of "mortar" mid-way between the black and white squares in intensity. In the weaker Munsterberg illusion the mortar lines are black.

Spatial filtering with receptive fields similar to those of retinal ganglion cells gives some insight into the causes of the apparent bending of the mortar lines (Morgan & Moulden, 1986). In the centre panel of Fig. 2.5 a region of the Cafe Wall has been filtered by scanning it with a filter similar to that used in the case of the Pyramid illusion. The scanning is carried out by placing the filter in turn at each point (x,y) in the image, multiplying the intensity of that point in turn by each point in the filter, adding up (integrating) all the products, and then using the value of the sum to determine the intensity of the corresponding point in the new image. This process of pointwise multiplication and integration is referred to as *convolution*, and convolution can be considered formally as the process by which the array of intensity values in an image is transformed into an array of firing values in a sheet of retinal ganglion cells to make a *neural image* (Robson, 1980.) Removal of low spatial frequencies from the image by circular bandpass filters results in an image in which the straight grey "mortar" lines are replaced by alternating tilted black and white strips. The white strips represent areas of positive activity in the filtered output, and the black strips represent areas of negative activity; in physiological terms, these would correspond to activation of on-centre and off-centre retinal ganglion cells respectively. But why should *local* tilts in the filtered mortar lines produce an impression that the lines themselves are tilted? To understand this we have to consider another well-known "illusion": the Fraser twisted cord.

FRASER'S TWISTED CORD

Fraser's "twisted cord" effect is illustrated in the right-hand panel of Fig. 2.5 which demonstrates that horizontal lines composed of locally-tilted alternating black–white segments appear tilted in the same direction as their components. Historically, the Fraser phenomenon has been considered as an illusion, but if one thinks more deeply about it, it is not clear why. The temptation is to say that the

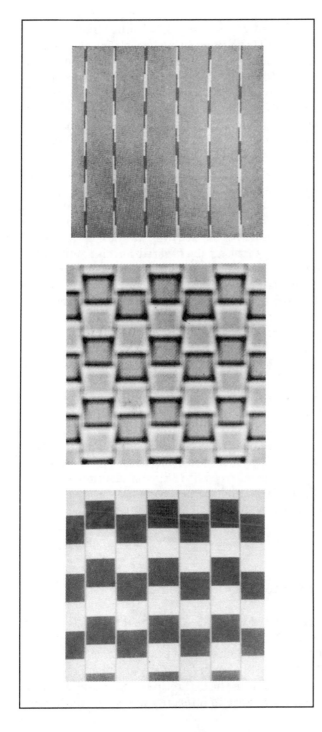

FIG. 2.5 The left panel illustrates the "Cafe Wall illusion", in which the horizontal grey "mortar lines" appear tilted and non-parallel. The illusion is probably related to the weaker "Munsterberg illusion" in which the mortar lines are black. If the mortar lines are either much whiter or blacker than the white and black squares respectively, the illusion disappears (Morgan & Moulden, 1986). The centre panel shows the effect of filtering the Cafe Wall image with a scanning aperture similar to that illustrated in Fig. 2.4 (a Difference-of-Gaussians aperture). Note that in the filtered image, the horizontal mortar lines are replaced by alternating tilted regions of black and white stripes. These could provide the basis for the appearance of tilt via the Fraser "twisted cord" effect, illustrated in the right panel. The horizontal parallel lines appear tilted. Locally, the lines are indeed composed of alternating, tilted regions of black and white. Each tilted segment would provide a stimulus for an orientationally specific cortical cell: presumably the local reports of tilt provided by these mechanisms are being integrated into a global impression of tilt, perhaps by higher-level "collector units" as described by Morgan and Hotopf (1989)

41

twisted cords are locally tilted but globally horizontal, and that our visual system is making a mistake in ignoring the global in favour of the local. This may be true, but it is not obvious why we should talk of this outcome as an illusion. The problem once again is the picture theory of vision, which thinks of perception as another kind of image. In this hypothetical picture, lines that are horizontal are seen as horizontal, and so on. The issue of why the horizontal should be represented at all, and how it is represented, is finessed by the picture theory. A more profitable approach is to consider the general computational problems in detecting and representing long lines in natural images: would local orientation- specific filters suffice, or is a second stage of filtering required in which local reports of orientation are integrated? Would it be sensible to have long oriented filters, or would these be too vulnerable to partial occlusion along the length of the line? Is the key to under-standing the Fraser effect the fact that the twisted cord is composed of alternating polarity lines that would render it invisible to long oriented filters? Certainly the effect is much less strong with tilted elements all of the same polarity. We do not have the answers to these questions yet, but at least they make no reference to the concept of an illusion.

"ILLUSIONS" OFTEN HAVE MULTIPLE CAUSES

The "Cafe Wall" illustrates another point that is likely to apply generally to visual illusions. To make any progress in understanding the pheno-menon, we had to invoke at least two quite independent explanatory principles: bandpass spatial frequency filtering in on- and off-centre recep-tive fields, which produces the "twisted cord", and then the Fraser effect, which is in turn not very well understood. It is the combination of several causes into a single "illusion" that makes these perceptual phenomena so hard to penetrate. It may also be the case that quite different mechanisms are operating in parallel to produce what we call a single "illusion". A well-established instance of this is seen in the "Poggendorff effect".

THE POGGENDORFF EFFECT

The Poggendorff effect is illustrated in Fig. 2.6a. One theory of the effect, elaborated by Gillam (1971), from a more general theory of Gregory (1963, 1966) attributes it to misplaced 3-D processing of the image. Gregory pointed out that one of the important goals of vision is to derive the 3-D structure of the world from the 2-D retinal image, and that our visual system has a strong tendency to interpret any scene in this way,

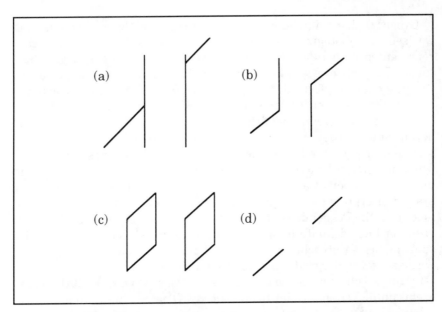

FIG. 2.6.   The top-left panel (a) shows the conventional version of the Poggendorff effect. The two oblique segments are collinear, but do not appear so. The apparent misalignment is reduced, but not abolished, if the figure is rotated so that the traversing lines are vertical or horizontal and the parallels are oblique. Panel (b) shows an obtuse-angle version often said to rule out the cross-orientation inhibition theory (but see the text). The obtuse-angle phenomenon may depend upon quite different mechanisms from the classical Poggendorff effect. A possible depth interpretation of the phenomenon is illustrated in panel (c), which suggests that the line higher in the picture plane is automatically interpreted as being higher above the ground plane, and thus not as being collinear with the lower line. A number of constraints must be invoked to bolster this interpretation, viz.: (i) vertical lines in the picture plane are interpreted as gravitationally vertical (ii) lines meeting at a point are interpreted as defining an occluding surface, not as being a chance conjunction of unrelated events (a version of the "general viewpoint constraint") and (iii) an oblique line meeting a vertical at its upper termination in the picture plane is necessarily raised above the ground plane. Panel (d) may or may not persuade the viewer that there is also a small "Poggendorff effect" without the parallels, but this is actually a different phenomenon (the "Obenai effect") with quite different properties (Hotopf, 1989).

even when the actual scene is 2-D. This is why we recognise photographs and paintings as 3-D scenes. We do not, unless trying to be deliberately obscure, refer to the appearance of depth in a perspective painting as an "illusion". Likewise, according to Gregory, many cases where observers report metrical relations between lines and angles in the image which would not result if they were making a direct physical measurement with a ruler on the image itself, are to be explained by the automatic tendency to represent the image as originating from a 3-D structure. The geometric illusions, on this view, are not idle mistakes, but the reflection of the rules by which the visual system processes two-dimensional images.

Gregory's theory undoubtedly applies to many of the phenomena that we see in photographs and paintings. It explains why objects represented by perspective as being more distant appear larger than "nearer" objects of the same retinal size. But is it a correct account of the Poggendorff effect? Gillam (1980) points out that lines which are collinear in the picture plane are not necessarily collinear in 3-D, and that in fact they cannot be if they are tilted away from the observer in depth and if they meet a fronto-parallel plane such that their termination points on that plane are collinear with the lines themselves. This rather complicated argument is illustrated in Fig.2.7a. Clearly it makes a number of assumptions about the way in which the visual system interprets the 2-D picture. The simplest way to test the theory is to see if the Poggendorff effect is still seen in a 3-D scene in which the observer has adequate information that the tilted lines are not in the same plane as the occluding surface. I have carried out this experiment with several undergraduate classes and the answer is quite clear: the Poggendorff effect is still seen in a real 3-D scene (Fig. 2.7b). It therefore seems unlikely that it is due to misplaced 3-D processing of a flat picture.

THE ANGLE EXPANSION THEORY AND CROSS-ORIENTATIONAL INHIBITION

The most widely canvassed alternative explanation of the Poggendorff effect is the "angle expansion theory", which proposes that nearby lines of different orientation mutually repel one another in the orientation domain. The "cross-orientation inhibition" theory is a physiological one based on the coding properties of orientation-specific cells in the visual cortex. The cells in cortical area V1 described by Hubel and Wiesel (1959) have preferred orientations, but they also respond to a wide variety of oriented lines around their most-preferred value. It is evident then, as in the case of cones and colour, that a single cell is not sufficiently precise to encode orientation. This is the fundamental problem, which has to be answered before we speculate about "illusions". A way around the problem of broad receptor tuning, which seems to apply very generally in sensory systems, is to use *population encoding*, in which the response of the whole set of oriented mechanisms is taken into account. A single oriented line will give rise to activity widely distributed across differently oriented cells, but the cells with a most-preferred orientation corresponding to that of the line will be stimulated marginally more than any others, and this could be recognised at a higher level. The line could be encoded as having that orientation corresponding to the most-stimulated cell or set of cells, or as an alternative, to the mean of

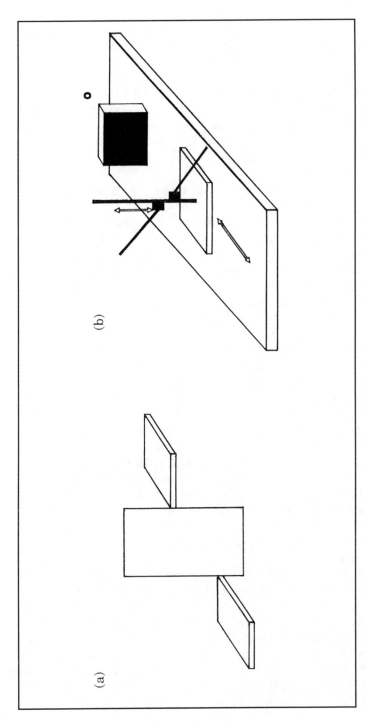

FIG. 2.7.   Gillam's depth processing explanation of the Poggendorff effect is illustrated in Panel (a). According to the theory the traversing lines are not interpreted as being occluded by a nearer surface, but as receding perspective lines abutting a nearer fronto-parallel plane defined by the parallels. In this interpretation, they cannot be collinear in the third dimension. However, the Poggendorff phenomenon survives in a real 3-D scene where the observer has abundant information that the traversing lines are in a different depth plane from the parallels (Panel b). The observer (marked o) viewed the oblique rods behind an opaque occluder so that only their ends were visible. One of the rods was moved vertically until the observer saw the two as collinear. In an experiment on 124 Psychology students, the Poggendorff illusion was still found in these circumstances, and it did not vary in magnitude with the distance of the rods behind the occluder.

45

the population response. Now add to this model the proposition that oriented cells mutually inhibit one another, the strength of this inhibition declining with the difference between their preferred orientations. (In other words, a cell with an orientation preference of 0° inhibits one of 5° more than it does one of 20°). This *cross-orientational inhibition* will change the population response of a set of cells to a single bar if there is another bar nearby. The two bars will set up a population response that has two peaks, which are further apart than the actual orientation difference between the two bars (Blakemore, Carpenter, & Georgeson, 1970).

It has to be admitted that this is an incomplete explanation, because there exists no formal computational model showing that it will work. A properly specified model would have to specify the orientational bandwidths of the initial array of detectors; their spatial sampling density; the exact rule used to derive orientation from the population response (peak of population response? centroid?); the spatial properties and orientational bandwidth of cross-orientation inhibition; and the rules for encoding line orientations from multi-peaked population responses. The model would have to agree with psychophysical data on the strength of the Poggendorff effect as a function of angle, length of line and so on. But despite these present shortcomings there are several lines of evidence suggesting that the cross-orientational inhibition may provide at least part of the mechanism for Poggendorff-type effects.

First, there is direct psychophysical evidence for angular-repulsion effects between spatially resolved lines (see Howard, 1986, for a review). A recent experiment (Westheimer, 1990) used forced-choice methodology to measure the amount of real tilt to a 12min near-vertical line needed to make it appear vertical when it was surrounded by a hexagonal array of inducing lines. Results showed an induced orientation shift opposite to that of the inducing lines: in other words, when the inducing lines were tilted, say, 10° clockwise from the vertical, the observer needed an anti-clockwise shift to the target lines in order to respond "clockwise tilt" and "anti-clockwise" with equal probability. When the separation between target and inducing lines was 20arcmin and the inducing lines were tilted at 15–40°, an induced orientation shift of 1–2° (in different observers) was found. The induced tilt effect decreased both at smaller and at larger inducing tilt angles. No effect was found at 50°, and (to anticipate the later discussion) this is a bit worrying, because Poggendorff effects are still found at angles greater than 45°.

Second, there is physiological evidence for cross-orientation inhibition. The most relevant to the present discussion comes from an experiment by Gilbert and Wiesel (1990) which was explicitly based on Westheimer's stimulus technique. Gilbert and Wiesel studied the orientation preferences and orientation bandwidth of single cells in the cat striate cortex using test bars inside the classically-defined receptive field of the cell, and then measured the responses of the same cell to the test stimulus when it was surrounded by an array of lines outside the classical receptive field. (In other words, the surround stimuli by themselves had no discernible effect on the cell.) They found that the surround stimuli could either increase or decrease the response of a cell to the test line, depending on the orientation of the surround stimulus. In some cells, the effect of the surround was to change the "tuning curve" of the cell, so that its optimal orientation was shifted. Orientation tuning shifts were seen in 9 out of the 27 cells which were isolated for a sufficient period of time to collect the necessary data. For 7 of the 9 the shift was "repulsive" (as in Westheimer's experiment) and in the remaining two it was "attractive". Gilbert and Wiesel speculate that the effect of the surround is mediated by long-range horizontal connections in the superficial layers of cortex, which allow communication between cells with non-overlapping receptive fields and similar orientation preference. More recent work by Gilbert (1994) has extended these results.

It is not possible to map Gilbert and Wiesel's results directly onto the psychophysics, and even the relevance of Westheimer's data to the classical Poggendorff effect is not clear. But the cross-orientational inhibition theory would seem to be worth pursuing. It attempts to explain "illusory" phenomena from a more basic theory of sensory encoding. If it is correct, the origin of the angular illusions is to be found in the broad bandwidth of the first layer of orientationally specific mechanisms, in the same way that metamerism in colour vision is an inevitable consequence of the broad wavelength-tuning of the cones.

PROBLEMS WITH THE ANGLE-EXPANSION THEORY

There are two possible objections to deal with. First, it is known that an effect in the same direction as the Poggendorff exists if the acute angles of the figure are eliminated (Fig. 2.6). Quite correctly, this is often said to rule out the idea that the effect is due to "acute angle expansion", a psychological generalisation often put forward to account for angular illusions. But the cross-orientational inhibition theory asserts not acute angle expansion, but mutual inhibition in the orientational domain. The vertical and oblique lines composing the Poggendorff figure will continue to inhibit one another, according to this account, even if they do not meet at an acute angle. However, it must be acknowledged that inhibition between cells so widely different in their orientation tuning has not been demonstrated, and that Westheimer's data show no "repulsive effect" beyond 50°. We must bear in mind the possibility that the "Poggendorff effect" with obtuse angles may depend on a different mechanism from orientational contrast. It would be interesting to see if the "obtuse effect" survives in a real 3-D scene (cf Fig. 2.7).

A second objection is that there is a small "Poggendorff" effect when the vertical lines are replaced by "subjective contours" or even when they are absent entirely (cf Fig. 2.6). But as Hotopf (1989) has convincingly shown, the effect here is due to a quite different phenomenon (the "Obenai effect") depending on absolute orientation of the lines on the retina. The Obenai effect disappears if the lines are vertically oriented; the Poggendorff is weakened if the obliques are vertically oriented, but by no means abolished. The red herring of the "parallel-less Poggendorff" shows the dangers of supposing that a perceptual phenomenon has a single cause.

OTHER FACTORS THAT MAY BE OPERATING IN THE POGGENDORFF EFFECT

One contribution to the Poggendorff effect may be neural blur in circular filters, similar to those that we considered in relation to the "pyramid illusion." The effects of blur can be conveniently introduced by the photograph shown in Fig. 2.8, which shows the very large shift in apparent angle of small line segments bounded by oblique contours. The same effect can be seen, and psychophysically measured, in the H stimulus shown in Fig. 2.9 , which also illustrates the relation between this and the classical Zöllner stimulus. When the H stimulus is progressively reduced in size, it becomes increasingly hard to discriminate it from a stimulus in which the "crossbar" is at right angles to the "goal posts", and this can be demonstrated by a forced-choice psychophysical technique (Morgan, Medford, & Newsome, 1995). A simple model, in which the H stimulus is subjected to optical blurring and further blurring by concentric receptive fields of the retinal-ganglion cell type, shows that this confusion is inevitable (Morgan & Casco, 1990). The origin of the effect is that the response of circular receptive fields to a line intersection is strongly influenced by both lines, in such a way that the maximum response is found not at the actual point of intersection, but shifted into the acute angle. Assuming that the response pattern of retinal ganglion cells is inherited by cortical simple cells (Hubel & Wiesel, 1959) it can be shown that the effect will be to shift the population response of cortical simple cells in the direction of the perceived shift.

FIG. 2.8.   The photograph was taken of a continuous piece of string behind a venetian blind. The visible segments of the string are seen as tilted in the direction at right angles to the slats of the blind, with the result that the different segments of the string are no longer seen as collinear.

The H-stimulus model cannot account for the "obtuse effect" or for the induction effects between spatially separated stimuli in the Westheimer experiment. On the other hand, the orientation shifts seen in Westheimer's experiment are far too small to account for the dramatic (as much as 40°) shifts seen in small H stimuli. In the end we shall probably have to settle for a wide variety of explanation for the orientation shifts seen in different classes of stimuli. There would seem little point in measuring more and more psychophysical "illusions" of orientation: the failure of this approach over the last 100 years is clear. What we need is a fundamental understanding of the process of orientation encoding itself, both at the level of computational theory and of physiology.

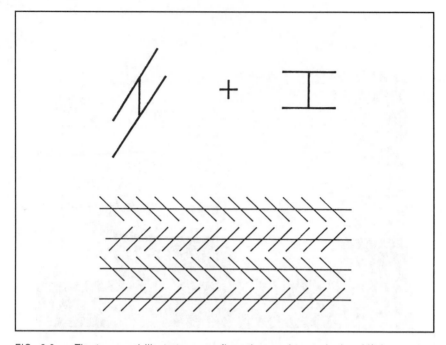

FIG. 2.9.   The top panel illustrates a configuration used to study the shift in apparent orientation of a small line segment enclosed within two obliques. At a suitable viewing distance, when fixating the cross, the vertical line segment in the figure on the left appears tilted anti-clockwise relative to the line to the right of the cross. It also appears shorter (the Judd effect: cf Morgan & Casco, 1990). The lower figure shows the classical Zollner figure, which can be considered to be composed of a stack of *H* segments, in which the individual tilts are combined to give an impression of global tilt, as in the Fraser "twisted cord" (q.v.).

ILLUSIONS OF LENGTH

The Müller-Lyer and associated illusions of length raise a different set of issues (Fig. 2.10). The usual way of introducing the Müller-Lyer illusion is to say that the horizontal line bounded by outgoing arrowheads "looks longer" than the line bounded by in-going arrowheads. But how do we know? The naive assumption behind the "looks longer" assertion is that the image can be fragmented into horizontal lines and surrounding context, and that the observer can measure the length of just the lines. But if we carry out forced-choice psychophysics on the figure we find that this is just what the observer cannot do. There is a bias causing the figure containing the outgoing arrows to be seen as longer. The judgment is no less precise than one made on lines without arrowheads, but there is a bias (Morgan, Hole, & Glennerster, 1990). Plainly, then, the observer cannot abstract the line from the surrounding context. We ask the observer to make a judgment

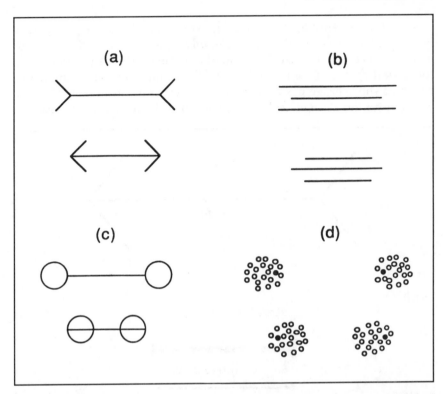

FIG. 2.10.   The figure shows several configurations producing geometrical illusions of the averaging or assimilation variety: (a) the traditional textbook version of the Müller-Lyer illusion; (b) an earlier version of the Müller-Lyer—the line flanked by two longer lines appears longer than the one flanked by shorter lines; (c) The Baldwin figure; (d) similar to Baldwin's figure with the elements replaced by dots. Psychophysical experiments show that the distance between the black dots in the upper figure is overestimated relative to the same distance in the lower figure. It is as if the position of the black dots seems to be shifted towards the centroids of the dots clusters (reproduced with permission from Harris & Morgan, 1993).

based only the line, ignoring the context, and imagine that this should be easy, because it would be easy to do with a printed image using scissors. But we are actually addressing our question to a highly specialised piece of machinery: the visual cortex of the primate brain, which has been adapted by natural selection to carry out tasks like allowing us to run over broken ground, to swing from branches, to avoid obstacles and so on. The amazing thing is that we can communicate with this machine *at all* by verbal instructions: not that there is the occasional breakdown in communications which causes the machine to deliver a slightly different answer to the one intended by the experimenter.

The observer encodes the outgoing-arrow figure as longer because it *is* longer. There is no illusion here, only a failure to respond to the instructions to abstract the line from the context. I shall show later that the visual system is very well adapted to make metrical judgments based on the average position of a large number of features; but poorly adapted to make metrical judgments based on relations between

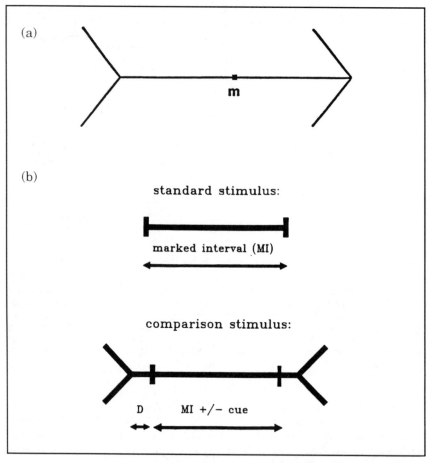

FIG. 2.11.   The top panel (a) illustrates a variant of the Brentano figure, in which the mid-point (m) of the horizontal line is apparently shifted away from the outgoing arrowheads. This is difficult to reconcile with Gregory's size constancy theory, because the figure is ambiguous in 3-D. The bottom panel (b) shows a stimulus configuration for demonstrating that the apparent expansion of the line in the outgoing-arrowhead figure is not global, but due to a local effect at the arrowheads. The distance between the two markers in the arrowhead figure (bottom) is only judged as larger than the control interval (top) when the markers are near to the arrowheads (reproduced with permission from Morgan, Hole, & Glennerster, 1990).

arbitrarily   abstracted   features.   But   first,   some   preliminary ground-clearing.

The theory of Gregory (1966) that the Müller-Lyer depends on displaced depth processing encounters difficulties with the Brentano version of the Müller-Lyer (Fig. 2.11) in which the figure is entirely ambiguous with respect to a 3-D interpretation, but in which the apparent displacement of the mid-point towards the "in-going" arrowhead end of the figure is stable (Morgan, 1969). Furthermore, if the line in the traditional "outgoing arrowhead" version is being expanded by size constancy, as Gregory conjectures, then any segment marked off along it should appear expanded (Fig. 2.11) and this is not true: only if the target segment is close to the arrowheads is there any effect (Morgan et al., 1990).

To deal with difficulties such as these Gregory (1963) proposed that the geometric illusions do not depend on the familiar mechanism of size constancy, which operates after the computation of depth; but on a more basic process of "primary scaling" which is driven by local features. In other words, the outgoing arrowheads are recognised as a local perspective cue, and lines in their vicinity, and only in their vicinity, are expanded. The problem with the "primary constancy scaling" theory is that so far the only evidence we have for the process is the existence of the illusions themselves (Humphrey & Morgan, 1965). This does not mean that the theory is wrong, and it is quite possible that a determined search for the features that trigger local scaling will reveal new phenomena; but in the meantime it is not obvious why local constancy scaling should be triggered by circles (as in the Baldwin illusion), and by flanking lines (Fig. 2.10).

The idea that the Müller-Lyer effect is caused by neural blurring was advanced by Ginsburg (1984) and has recently received some support from Rogers and Glennerster (1993). Ginsberg's theory is that after blurring the outgoing-arrowhead figure, the ends of the line will extend into the acute angle formed by the arrowhead. Optical blurring is not sufficient to produce the effect but very heavy blurring in low-spatial frequency neural channels (i.e. those with very large receptive fields) might be. One objection to this account is that the illusion is still present when the illusory figure is composed of small dots containing only high-spatial frequencies. Each one of these dots has a difference-of-Gaussian (DoG) profile (see Fig. 2.4), with the result that the figure as a whole now contains only high spatial frequencies, and indeed, disappears when only slightly blurred. However, this argument ignores the fact that these small DoGs ("puppies"?) will be perfectly visible to retinal ganglion cells, for which they are indeed the ideal stimulus. The low spatial frequency filters in Ginsberg's model could be second-stage filters, elaborated in the cortex from an input provided by ganglion cells of the same polarity[4]. The fact that the illusion survives in a figure composed of "puppies" is thus not necessarily fatal to Ginsberg's theory.

A more serious objection is that the theory is not based on any explicit model of length encoding, so it is not obvious why merely blurring the outgoing-arrow figure should make it appear longer. Does optically blurring a single line make it appear longer? If so, why? Glennerster and Rogers (1993) greatly refined Ginsberg's theory by applying a well-known theory of edge detection, the "zero-crossing" model of Marr and Hildreth (1980). In this theory the location of an edge (or line termination) is placed at the zero-crossing of its second spatial derivative[5]. Merely blurring an edge, according to this model, will not change its location, and this prediction has been verified, at least for the case where early luminance transduction nonlinearities were taken care of (Morgan et al., 1984). Rogers and Glennerster found that outgoing arrowheads did indeed cause a small shift in the position of the line-termination zero-crossings in the Müller-Lyer figure. Unfortunately, the effect was found with very small arrowheads, which cause only a weak Müller-Lyer effect; and further increases in arrowhead size, although they caused a larger Müller-Lyer effect, did not result in any further change in the position of zero-crossings. The neural blurring theory, then, although it may account for one component of the Müller-Lyer effect, is not by any means the whole story.

THE BASIC PROBLEM: HOW ARE LENGTHS AND DISTANCES ENCODED?

The real problem in explaining the Müller-Lyer illusion is that we do not have a satisfactory theory of length encoding to start with. Even if we were to agree that a necessary preliminary to length encoding is the location of features, such as zero-crossings, we should be none the wiser about the mechanisms that then make the distance between such features explicit. In such circumstances, it is useful to forget about "illusions" for the moment and to ask what kinds of metrical tasks the visual system can and cannot perform. It turns out that one task carried out with surprising ease is the location of the centroids (the "centre of gravity") of clusters of features such as those illustrated in Fig. 2.10. If asked to compare the distances between two such clusters to a standard distance, observers perform as well as they do in judging the distance between single dots, subject only to the statistical constraints inherent in the task (Morgan & Glennerster, 1991). In fact, their statistical relative efficiency (Barlow, 1978) for the task of cluster centroid location with modest number of dots is the same as that for single dot location. This skill does not depend on a simple blurring mechanism, because thresholds are the same when all the dots of the cluster have the same polarity as when half are white and half are black (on a grey background). Thus the visual system is efficient at encoding the centroid of a set of objects arranged in a cluster.

What if the task is to pick out two elements, one in each cluster, and to encode the distance between them? As one might suspect from the Müller-Lyer illusion, this is a task that the visual system performs badly. If the target dots are black and the other dots in the clusters are white, the targets are clearly discriminable, but observers do not accurately encode the distance between them. Instead, they seem to base their judgments on the distance between the centroids of the cluster. Apparently, then, the tendency towards centroid extraction is automatic and hard to override.

We can speculate about the functional reasons for this. To see effectively, we need to encode the distances between objects in space in order to form a map in which we can navigate. But a map in which the distances between every possible pair of features in the image was encoded would be impossibly cumbersome. A strategy to overcome this problem would be to postpone the making explicit of spatial relations until after the image has been segmented into objects. In this way, only a relatively small number of metrical relations has to be made explicit; those between objects. If we then wish to consider a single object, and make explicit the relations between its component parts, in order to compute its 3-D shape, we could home in on that object and make a more detailed map. This is the essence of the hierarchical encoding scheme proposed by Watt (1991). There may, however, be fundamental constraints making it difficult to form a map that makes explicit the metrical relations between component parts of different objects. To do so would mean reversing the initial scene segmentation, potentially leading to a huge combinatorial explosion of the relation between all possible feature pairs. Thus, in asking the observer to report the distance between two specific dots in two different dot clusters, or asking for a judgment of the length of the Müller-Lyer figure independently of its arrowheads, we may be setting tasks that the visual system is ill-adapted to perform. Ask the wrong question, and you get the wrong answer.

I suggest, then, that the Müller-Lyer will in the end seem no more of an "illusion" than colour metamerism. The outgoing arrowhead figure is judged as longer because it really is longer, according to the encoding scheme used by the visual system. When we ask the observer a question, we are not speaking directly to a visual system. Some version of our instructions converges (we don't know how) with the output of visual mechanisms, and a decision is made. If the decision is not the one we expected, too bad. The purpose of the visual system is to allow us to get around in the world, not to conform to our arbitrary linguistic conventions.

CONCLUSION

The mystery of the visual illusions is thus subsumed under the much greater mystery of how we see at all. Although much progress has been made in understanding the early stages of vision, the student need not share the anxiety of Alexander the Great that "there are no worlds left to conquer". It is still a mystery what kind of brain activity we should be looking for as the basis for our experience of an apparently continuous, three-dimensional world. And what kind of neural activity could possibly explain the quality of "greenness" that we see in grass? If the history of other scientific questions is any guide, the solution to the problem of seeing will depend crucially on technical advances; but it may also involve some basic re-thinking of our fundamental assumptions. Dennett (1991) cogently argues that many claims made by philosophers about the nature of visual experience are just plain wrong. It may seem paradoxical to say that we are capable of profound errors in describing what happens when "we see", but the history of "illusions" shows that such errors have been made.

NOTES

1. The procedure of interpolation will be familiar from graph plotting. Most graphs start out as a series of discretely separated points, which can be considered as samples from an underlying continuous function. When we draw a continuous line between them we are "interpolating". One method of interpolating involves making each point on the graph the weighted average of the samples to either side. This corresponds exactly to the process of low-pass spatial frequency filtering.
2. Vernier alignment as in the Vernier scale, which is based on the fact that we are very accurate at determining whether two lines are colinear or not. Misalignments can be detected when they are as small as one tenth of the diameter of a cone in the retina. Vernier alignment is thus a sensitive probe for the apparent position of a line.
3. Fourier analysis splits a waveform into simple components called "sine waves". The technique is most familiar in acoustics, where a complicated sound pressure wave, for example, the sound from an orchestra, is split into pure tones. The technique can be applied to vision if we consider an

image as a signal in which luminance varies over space. Equally, it can be applied to motion by considering the motion signal as one in which position varies over time. A motion signal in which the position of an object oscillated sinusoidally like a pendulum would correspond to a "pure tone" in acoustics.

4. Retinal ganglion cells are either "on" centre with an "off" surround, or vice versa. The "on centre" class respond best to bright spots on a darker background; the off-centre class respond best to dark spots on a lighter surround.

5. The derivative of a function expresses the difference of a point from its neighbours. The first derivative is the difference from the neighbours on one side only; the second derivative is the difference from the average of the neighbours to either side. If the function represents movement, the first derivative corresponds to velocity, and the second to acceleration. Exactly the same concepts can be applied to the profile of light in images (the luminance profile). The second derivative of a luminance profile is positive when light values are accelerating, and negative when they are decelerating. A zero-crossing is the point where acceleration changes to deceleration. A dark–light boundary in an image will always be somewhat blurred by the optics of the eye, and the resulting blurred edge will always have a zero-crossing.

REFERENCES

Barlow, H.B. (1978). The efficiency of detecting changes of density in random dot patterns. *Vision Research, 18,* 637–650.

Blakemore, C., Carpenter, R. H. S., & Georgeson, M. A. (1970). Lateral inhibition between orientation detectors in the human visual system. *Nature, 228,* 37–39.

Dennett, D.C. (1991). *Consciousness explained.* London: Allen Lane; The Penguin Press.

Exner, S. (1888). Einige Beobachtungen uber Bewegungsnachbilder. *Centralblatt fur Physiologie, 1,* 135–140.

Fahle, M., & Poggio, T. (1981). Visual hyperacuity: spatiotemporal interpolation in human vision. *Proceedings of the Royal Society of London, B 213,* 451–477.

Gilbert, C.D. (1994). Circuitry, architecture and functional dynamics of visual cortex. In G.R. Bock & J. Goode (Eds.), *Higher-order processing in the visual system.* London: Wiley.

Gilbert, C.D., & Wiesel, T.N. (1990). The influence of contextual stimuli on the orientational selectivity of cells in the primary visual cortex of the cat. *Vision Research, 30,* 1689–1701.

Gillam, B. (1971). A depth processing theory of the Poggendorff illusion. *Perception and Psychophysics, 10,* 211–216.

Ginsburg, A. P. (1984). Visual form perception based upon biological filtering. In L. Spillman & B.R. Wooten (Eds.), *Sensory experience, adaptation and perception.* Hillsdale, NJ: Lawrence Erlbaum Associates Inc.

Glennerster, A., & Rogers, B.J. (1993). New depth to the Müller-Lyer illusion. *Perception, 22,* 691–704.

Gregory, R. (1966). *Eye and Brain.* New York: McGraw-Hill.

Gregory, R.L. (1963). Distortions of visual space as inappropriate constancy scaling. *Nature (London), 199*, 678–680.

Harris, J., & Morgan, M. J. (1993). Stereo and motion disparities interfere with positional averaging. *Vision Research, 33*, 309–312.

Hartline, H. K. (1940). The receptive fields of optic nerve fibers. *American Journal of Physiology, 130*, 690–699.

Hotopf, N. (1989). The role of angles in inducing misalignment in the Poggendorff figure. *Quarterly Journal of Experimental Psychology, 41a*, 355–383.

Howard, I.P. (1986). The perception of posture, self-motion and the visual vertical. In R.K. Boff, L. Kaufman, & J.P. Thomas (Eds.), *Handbook of perception and human performance (Ch. 18)* New York: Wiley.

Hubel, D.H., & Wiesel, T.N. (1959). Receptive fields of single neurons in the cat's striate cortex. *Journal of Physiology, 148*, 574–591.

Humphrey, N.K., & Morgan, M. J. (1965). Constancy and the geometrical illusions. *Nature (London), 296*, 744–745.

Hunt, D, Dulai, K.D., Bowmaker, J., & Mollon, J.D. (1995) The chemistry of John Dalton's Color Blindness. *Science, 267*, 984–988.

Mach, E. (1906). Uber den Einfluss rumlich und zeitlich variierender Lichtreize auf die Gesichtswahrnehmung. In F.R. (Eds.), *Mach bands: Quantitative studies on neural networks in the retina* (pp. 321–332).

Marr, D. (1982). *Vision*. San Francisco: WH Freeman & Co.

Marr, D., & Hildreth, E. (1980). Theory of edge detection. *Proceedings of the Royal Society of London, B 207*, 187–217.

Morgan, M.J. (1969). Estimates of length in a modified Müller-Lyer figure. *American Journal of Psychology, 82*, 380–384.

Morgan, M.J. (1979). Perception of continuity in stroboscopic motion: A temporal frequency analysis. *Vision Research, 19*, 491–500.

Morgan, M.J. (1980). Analogue models of motion perception. *Philosophical Transactions of the Royal Society, London, B 290*, 117–135.

Morgan, M.J., & Casco, C. (1990). Spatial filtering and spatial primitives in early vision. *Proceedings of the Royal Society of London, B 242*, 1–10.

Morgan, M.J., & Glennerster, A. (1991). Efficiency of locating centres of dot clusters by human observers. *Vision Research, 31*, 2075–2083.

Morgan, M.J., Hole, G.J., & Glennerster, A. (1990). Biases and sensitivities in geometrical illusions. *Vision Research, 30*, 1793–1810.

Morgan, M.J., & Hotopf, N. (1989). Perceived diagonals in grids and lattices. *Vision Research, 29*, 1005–1015.

Morgan, M.J., Medford, A., & Newsome, P. (1995). The orthogonal orientation shift and spatial filtering. *Perception*, in press.

Morgan, M.J., & Moulden, B. (1986). The Munsterberg figure and twisted cords. *Vision Research, 26*, 1793–1800.

Morrone, M.C., Ross, J., Burr, D.C., & Owens, R. (1986). Mach bands are phase dependent. *Nature, 324* (20 November), 250–253.

Robson, J.G. (1980). Neural images: The physiological basis of spatial vision. In C.S. Harris (Ed.), *Visual coding and adaptability* (pp. 177–214). Hillsdale, NJ: Lawrence Erlbaum Associates Inc.

Watt, R.J. (1991). *Understanding vision*. London: Academic Press.

Watt, R.J., & Morgan, M.J. (1985). A theory of the primitive spatial code in human vision. *Vision Research, 25*, 1661–1674.

Westheimer, G. (1990). Simultaneous orientation contrast for lines in the human fovea. *Vision Research, 30*, 1913–1921.

CHAPTER THREE

Reality and imagination

Vicki Bruce University of Stirling

INTRODUCTION

Imagine a dinner plate. Around the top rim of the plate there is some spaghetti. Just below the spaghetti there are two fried eggs, side by side. In the middle of the plate there is a carrot, pointing down towards the bottom rim. And below the carrot is a banana with its curved side parallel to the lower rim of the plate. Not a very appetising sight, is it—but what else can you see in the imaginary meal you have constructed? Can you see the colours of the pieces of food? Can you see a face?

Most people have little difficulty in following instructions like those I have just given, and, with varying degrees of clarity, report doing something that feels like constructing a picture "in the mind's eye". Moreover, for many people such imaginings form an everyday and central part of their thought processes. They may "hear" their thoughts with an inner voice, as well as seeing with the mind's eye. What does contemporary psychology have to say about such phenomena?

In recent years there has been a considerable revival of interest in mental imagery, and particularly visual imagery. The need for a revival is itself quite mysterious. As Thomas (1989) points out, for most of history the mental image was regarded by scholars as the primary, if not the sole, medium of human thought, and this might lead us to expect that imagery would find a central role in any curriculum in psychology.

During this century, however, the concept of imagery has itself come under scrutiny, and research into the topic was abandoned for many years. Prior to the neglect of the topic, the problem that scholars tackled at the turn of the century concerned whether imageless thought was possible—i.e. was it possible to maintain an idea in the absence of an image of any sort, whether visual, auditory or whatever? Much later, when interest in imagery was revived, scholarly debate concerned the nature of mental images, contrasting particularly the "picture" metaphor with the "propositional" analysis of their content. Here I will review some of the controversial issues that have surrounded mental imagery, but conclude that contemporary theories of imagery, expressed in computational terms, render these debates obsolete. A new consensus framework for interpreting visual imagery seems to have emerged from a combination of empirical study of imagery and theoretical developments in the related field of visual perception and memory. The first and larger part of this chapter reviews the developments in cognitive psychology that have led to this position.

However, the new theoretical framework for imagery seems to raise a larger question, of how we distinguish reality from imagination, which has not been granted the same attention. In the theoretical account of imagery that I will introduce, imagery and perception both involve the activation of representations in a temporary storage system, but this raises the question of how we distinguish internally generated (imagined) from externally generated (perceived) activity. Remember that plate of food we discussed earlier? Are you remembering something real, or something you imagined? How can you tell? In the second part of this chapter I will consider contemporary approaches to the problem of reality monitoring, and consider how an understanding of this process may allow us to explain certain psychiatric symptoms.

HISTORY OF MENTAL IMAGERY

Philosophers and scholars throughout history have commented on the creative powers evoked by our ability to maintain and manipulate mental images. Shepard and Cooper (1982) describe a number of scientific discoveries that seem to have been facilitated by the powers of imagery. One well-known story is Kekule's dream of the ring structure of benzene, where he claims to have dreamed of a writhing chain whose head, like a snake, turned to swallow its tail. A more deliberate strategy of mental rotation was apparently employed by James D Watson in thinking up the double helix solution to the structure of DNA, while his colleague Crick went through a parallel set of physical manipulations with pieces of cardboard. Roger Shepard himself claims (Shepard & Cooper, 1982) that he imagined the classic mental rotation experiments (see later) while lying half awake one morning, and that from his spontaneous images of block shapes transposed in space, constructed the experiments that subsequently proved so influential in the revival of interest in the imaginal state (Shepard & Metzler, 1971).

Until this century, speculation about the basis of such powers of the imagination was the province of philosophers rather than psychologists. Many philosophers maintained that images are like mental "pictures" (Tye, 1991)—a view that has strongly influenced contemporary psychological theory. The evidence on which philosophers based their analysis of mental imagery was largely introspective. Some remarkable insights were achieved in this way. For example, Descartes drew a distinction between conceptual thought and imagination by using the example of telling the difference between polygons with different numbers of sides. Descartes argued that we can easily imagine the difference between a pentagon and a hexagon, but we cannot imagine the difference between a figure with 1000 sides and another with 999 sides, even though we have no difficulty in conceiving of a 1000-sided and a 999-sided figure as distinct entities. According to Tye (1991) this example demonstrates Descartes' anticipation of an analogy between mental imagery and perception, as the force of the example seems to be that we could not apprehend in a single glance the difference between two such figures even if these were real rather than imaginary. Thus visual imagery may be subject to the same limitations as visual perception. The analogy between mental imagery and *perception* is an important advance on the idea that mental images are like pictures, as we shall see later.

Although the Descartes example is powerful, the reliance on introspection to study unobservable mental acts such as imagery led to the neglect, if not damnation, of the concept during the middle half of this century when the predominant paradigm was behaviourism. Through the 1940s and 50s, *Psychological Abstracts* records only five references to imagery (Kessel, 1972). Thomas (1989) charts the curious demise of imagery from the mental life, as well as the science, of J.B. Watson. As a younger scientist Watson apparently professed to having strong mental imagery, which he reported using in the construction of his experimental apparatus. By 1913, however, he was intent on debunking the myth of mental imagery. Indeed he was adamant: "there is a need for questioning more and more the existence of what psychology calls imagery—I should throw out imagery altogether and attempt to show that practically all natural thought goes on in terms of sensori-motor processes in the larynx" (1913/1961, p.816). This is rather an interesting quote, because it indicates that Watson was happy enough to consider an "inner voice", as long as this was underpinned by some neurological processes to do with speaking, but he was clearly unable to contemplate anything analogous in the visual domain. According to Thomas, Watson's attempt to explain all thought in terms of muscle action was influenced by the ideas of his contemporary and colleague Dunlap who attempted to explain imagination in terms of the activation of muscular reflexes. However, rather than attempt to *interpret* imagery in such mechanistic ways, Watson sought to dispense with the notion altogether. Indeed, in 1914 he claimed that imagery was "the most serious obstacle to the establishment of a thoroughgoing behaviourism" (1914, pp.16ff).

REINSTATEMENT OF MENTAL IMAGERY
1: MENTAL ROTATION

Mental images regained respectability during the early 1970s as a direct result of two related developments. First, the revival of the study of cognition generally was aided by the new "machine" metaphor for mysterious inner thought processes. The invention of the digital computer lent respectability to psychological notions of "memories", "buffers", and "processors", even though computers were probably designed in the image of their inventors rather than the other way round. At about the same time as cognitive psychology became established, a powerful range of new methods began to be developed which used mental chronometry (Posner, 1978) to deduce the information processing operations involved in different tasks by examining how long people took to perform under different conditions. This approach appeared to provide an objective way to investigate cognitive processes that could not be directly observed, and has provided a productive scientific technique for the study of imagery.

An early and extremely influential example of the chronometric approach to the study of mental imagery was the "mental rotation" paradigm of Roger Shepard and colleagues. The original experiments are well known: subjects were requested to decide whether or not two depicted shapes showed the same 3D object (Fig. 3.1) and were found to take longer to make their decision the further away one member of the pair was rotated from the other. It was as though the decisions could only be made once one shape had been mentally rotated into coincidence with the other: the further the required mental rotation, the longer the decision took. Similar results were found if the subject's task was to decide whether a familiar shape (e.g. a letter) was presented normally

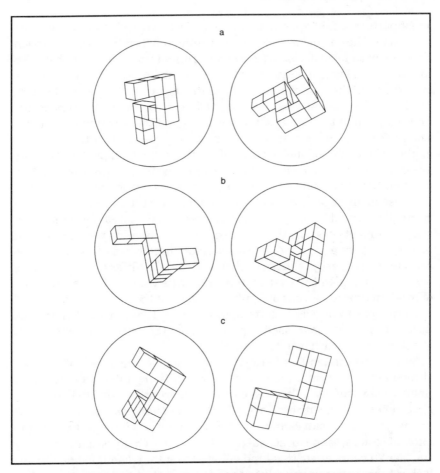

FIG. 3.1.   Examples of the shapes used by Shepard and Metzler (1971). The pair at a) differs by a 90 degree rotation in the picture plane; at b) they differ by an 80 degree rotation in depth, and at c) they differ by a reflection as well as rotation. Reprinted with permission from "Mental rotation of three-dimensional objects" by Shepard and Metzler, *Science, 171,* p.701. © 1971, the American Association for the Advancement of Science.

or mirror-reversed. The further away from the upright the character was presented, the longer the decision took (Cooper & Shepard, 1975).

Shepard and Metzler's (1971) original experiments differed from much later work in imagery, as subjects were not invited or instructed to perform the task in this way—the experimenters inferred an internal process of imagery to account for the data they obtained in their experiments, rather than assuming that it occurred. In order to verify their theory of how such visual problems were solved, however, later experiments warned the subjects in advance of the orientation in which a test pattern would appear, to which subjects would then have to make a decision. The earlier the advance warning, the flatter was the function obtained in a plot of decision time against orientation difference between the presented letter and the target orientation, (for example, the upright orientation in the case of an alphanumeric character, Cooper & Shepard, 1973, see Fig. 3.2). It was as though subjects could start to rotate the first shape in anticipation of the second, given the warning of required orientation. Given long enough, the first shape would mentally "arrive" at the orientation of the second before the second shape was actually presented—thus eliminating the time required for mental rotation from decision times measured to the onset of the second shape.

Subsequent experiments tested the mental rotation hypothesis even more directly. Mental rotation rates were calculated for individual subjects in a pre-test. In the main experiment, subjects were instructed to begin rotating a shape in a particular direction as soon as it was presented. The test pattern was then presented at different orientations from that in which the first pattern *would be imagined*, given the rate of rotation typical for that individual subject, at the time that the second pattern appeared. The results showed an orderly effect of increased decision time with increased departure from the orientation of the first shape in imagined space (Cooper, 1976).

These experiments illustrate quite nicely the use of mental chronometry to probe mental imagery, initially in a way in which imagery was the hypothesised cause of the results, but later in a way that relied on the direct instruction of subjects to use imagery in particular ways. Images moved from being intervening events used to explain results, to the direct subject of the research investigations. Over the last 20 years or so, this kind of experimental technique has become well established, particularly in the United States, and has produced an empirical base of findings about mental imagery which have, in turn, stimulated different theoretical perspectives on the imagery process.

REINSTATEMENT OF MENTAL IMAGERY
2: DUAL CODING THEORY

As well as the seminal work of Roger Shepard on mental rotation, an early and important influence in the imagery field came from the work of Allan Paivio (1969, 1979). Paivio was initially concerned to explain the "pictorial superiority" effect—that people were better at remembering pictured concepts than the same concepts expressed as words, and better at remembering imageable than abstract nouns. He accounted for such findings by proposing that there were two parallel

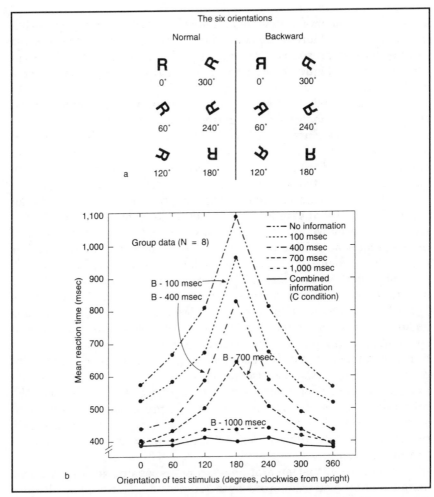

FIG. 3.2.   a) Examples of the letter shapes used in Cooper and Shepard's (1973) study in which subjects decided whether test letter shapes were normal or backward. b) With no prior information, the times to make these decisions were a function of the orientation from the upright (top curve). The more the test shape departed from upright, the longer the subjects took to decide whether the shape was normal or backward. In the B conditions, subjects were pre-warned with an upright letter shape and an arrow indicating the orientation of the test letter shape. The longer the arrow was shown before the test letter (from 100 to 1000ms), the more time subjects had to prepare for the orientation of the test letter, by mentally rotating the upright letter to the orientation in which the test shape would appear, and the flatterthe functions become. In the "combined information" condition (bottom curve) subjects were shown the upright letter and the arrow together in advance of the test stimulus. Original figure from Cooper and Shepard (1973). ©1973 by the Psychonomic Society, Inc. This adaptation from J.B. Best (1995). *Cognitive Psychology*. Fourth Edition. West Publishing Company. Used by permission.

systems of memory—the verbal/linguistic system and the pictorial/ imaginal system. Moreover, in considering the difference between these two systems he presumed that coding in the imaginal system was, in some sense, analogue or picture-like in contrast to that in the verbal system.

In support of his argument—common among earlier philosophical treatments of imagery—that images were pictorial in nature, he conducted experiments on the "symbolic distance" effect. Moyer's (1973) original demonstration was that, when asked to judge the relative size of two members of the same category, people were slower the closer the actual sizes of the two objects to be compared. So people are slower to decide that a cat is smaller than a dog, than that an ant is smaller than a dog. Paivio (1975) extended this research to show that the effect is maintained even when the comparisons are made between members of different categories. Thus people are slower to judge that a cat is smaller than a chair than that an ant is smaller than a chair. This effect is obtained whether the questions are asked using pictures or words, but decisions are usually made more quickly when interrogation is made with pictures. Paivio's explanation of these findings was that decisions about relative size are made by reference to representations stored in the imaginal system. Because pictures access this system directly, but words must be translated, decisions can be made more quickly to pictures than to words. Because the representations within the imaginal system are analogical in form—mirroring properties of the world—the relative size of objects must in some way be preserved in the imaginal system. Using a perceptual analogy, it must then be easier to compare two things of quite different size than to compare two things that are similar in size.

The conclusion that mental images are responsible for the symbolic distance effect was reinforced by a later study by Kosslyn, Murphy, Bemesderfer, and Feinstein (1977), who taught people novel stick figures of varying sizes, which were drawn from two different categories labelled "large" and "small". When these categorical labels were overlearned, subjects were able to judge the relative sizes of objects drawn from different size categories without showing any effect of the actual difference in their sizes. Within a category, however, the normal effect of relative size was observed. This shows that the effect does not arise when an alternative to the imaginal mode is available to form the basis of the judgement.

The interpretation of the symbolic distance effect as arising from Paivio's "imaginal" system, wherein are stored concrete object properties, is slightly muddied by the observation that much more abstract judgements about objects are also made more quickly when probed by pictures rather than words; for example, judgements of monetary value (Paivio, 1978) and ferocity (Kerst & Howard, 1977). Moreover, Kerst and Howard (1977) showed that judgements of ferocity showed a symbolic distance effect, but it seems difficult to argue that "fierceness" is represented analogically. Controversy also surrounds some of the other findings on which the dual coding framework was built. For example, it is not clear how the imageability of words, and imagery instructions, enhance verbal recall, with researchers such as Bower (1970) and Begg (1982) claiming that at least some effects arise because of more general organisational principles rather than through the evocation of a qualitatively different code. On the other hand, as I mentioned in Chapter 1 of this book, the basic finding that recognition memory for pictures is so accurate remains unexplained. Despite these complexities, Paivio's dual coding theory was influential in re-opening the debate about visual imagery. Firmer evidence about the "spatial" properties of imagery was obtained in a series of experiments by Kosslyn, which are described next.

IMAGE-SCANNING EXPERIMENTS

Similar conclusions about the pictorial nature of images seemed forced by the results of a programme of research conducted during the 1970s by Steve Kosslyn and associates. Kosslyn's experiments showed that when subjects were asked to scan images, or to answer questions on the basis of imagery, the time taken to perform the task was a direct function of the distance that needed to be traversed in the image in order to perform the task. For example, Kosslyn (1973) found that people were slower to answer questions about a part of an imagined drawing that was a long way from their current mental fixation point than one that was close to it. In these experiments, subjects might be asked to focus to the left or to the right of an imagined picture of a boat, and then verify whether or not the boat had an anchor. Time to verify the object parts was a direct function of the distance between the imagined fixation location and the part to be verified. Similar results were found in experiments on the time taken mentally to scan imagined maps (Kosslyn, Ball, & Reiser, 1978). Subjects learned the locations of a set of objects on a map, and they were required to focus on one object before verifying whether or not a second named object, at varying distances from the first, was present on the same map. Verification times were again a direct function of distance between the two objects, and the map-scanning experiments avoided any confound between distance scanned and number of objects encountered, a criticism of the earlier experiments of Kosslyn (1973) (Lea, 1975). However, although the results of the map-scanning experiment seemed to provide strong evidence for the mental scrutiny of images, it is also true that subjects were strongly directed to perform in exactly that way—to verify whether the named object was present by imagining a small black speck moving across the map in a direct, straight-line path from the first object towards the second. Under these conditions of instruction, it is difficult to see how results other than those obtained could have occurred, a point taken up most vociferously in Pylyshyn's (1973, 1981) criticisms of the picture-like properties of mental images.

More convincing evidence for spatial properties of images was obtained in a later experiment by Kosslyn (1976), where he found a dissociation between the kinds of object features that were easy to verify, depending on whether or not the instructions encouraged the use of imagery. Without imagery instructions, the easiest properties to verify were those of high associative strength (e.g. "does a bee have a sting?" "does a cat have whiskers?"). When subjects were instructed to use imagery to help answer questions, however, the properties that were easier to verify were those that were larger in size (e.g. "does a bee have wings?", "does a cat have a head?"). Such results would be accommodated within the dual coding theory, which would see different representations as forming the basis of the performance under each different kind of instruction.

THE IMAGERY DEBATE

This kind of dual coding theory was strongly challenged by Pylyshyn (1973) who argued that visual images could not be *pictorial* in nature. The main arguments levelled against the pictorial nature of images were that images are interpreted wholes, whereas pictures must be interpreted. This need for interpretation is important if access and retrieval of images is to occur in a sensible way. Information is lost from images in meaningful chunks, not in spatial chunks (i.e. we forget what a person looks like, we don't lose the image of one side of their body as in a ripped photograph). Moreover, Pylyshyn argued that storage of picture-like images was unparsimonious—and might use up the storage capacity of the brain.

To account for what appears to be a respectable body of data showing that mental images had spatial qualities, like pictures, Pylyshyn (1981) argued that the results of experiments such as Kosslyn's arose not because of intrinsic spatial properties of the medium of imagery, but because of the demand characteristics of the task and subjects' knowledge of what it is to manipulate objects in physical space. According to Pylyshyn, imagery phenomena are "cognitively penetrable"—they are influenced by subjects' beliefs and expectations—rather than reflecting the properties of a special imagery *medium*. Thus, for example subjects take longer to scan further distances on imagined maps because they are familiar with the relative time taken to travel different distances. Pylyshyn argues that mental images can only *represent* distance, and cannot have distance as an intrinsic property. Do we really want to argue that an image of an elephant is bigger than an image of a flea? The debate between the "imagery" and "propositional" theorists raged for some 10 years or more (Tye, 1991). However, during that same period the imagery theorists subtly shifted their arguments about the nature of imagery, and at the same time our understanding of other aspects of visual perception and cognition increased, to the point that it became much less controversial to posit a form of representation in which *space* was represented in some "analogue form". However, Pylyshyn's arguments about other aspects of images retain their force. If a mental image is a mental picture, are we claiming that an image of a tomato is red? (a picture of a tomato would be). Clearly this is absurd—the "picture" metaphor for imagery must be replaced by a *perceptual* analogy.

COMPARISONS BETWEEN IMAGERY AND PERCEPTION

Contemporary psychological research has provided overwhelming evidence that imagery shares some resources with visual perception. I now review this evidence before considering critically exactly what may be shared between perception and visual imagery.

The first kind of evidence comes from some classic experiments of Rodney Brooks, showing interference between visual perception and visual imagery. In these experiments (Brooks, 1968), subjects were asked to make a series of decisions about a spatial pattern, or about a sentence, that they were actively maintaining in short-term memory. Decisions about spatial patterns required subjects to state whether each corner of an imagined block letter touched the sides of an imaginary box within which the letter was drawn. Decisions about sentences required that subjects mentally rehearse the sentence and decide whether each word in it was an article ("a", "the") or not. Decisions could be made either by saying "yes" or "no" out loud as each corner or word was encountered, or by pointing to the correct letter (Y or N) from a spatial array of Ys and Ns. Brooks found that subjects were faster and more accurate at pointing when responding to the sentence, but at speaking when responding to the stored spatial pattern. Pointing responses were particularly difficult in the spatial imagery condition. It was as though storing the pattern to which a response had to be made was disrupted by the process of visually scanning the response sheet.

Similar results were found subsequently by Baddeley and colleagues while exploring the properties of the short-term memory system that they termed the "visuo-spatial sketch pad". Subjects who were required to remember sequences of items by using a spatial array (another task devised by Brooks, 1967) were much less accurate in their performance if they were also required to perform a pursuit rotor task, which requires tracking a target spatially (Baddeley, Grant, Wight, & Thomson, 1975). The same results were found even when subjects were blindfolded and the spatial tracking task required them to try to track a sound source that moved in front of them (Baddeley & Lieberman, 1980). These experiments, together with the older ones of Brooks, suggest that visual imagery shares resources with *spatial* rather than necessarily *visual* perception. Indeed, Baddeley and Lieberman (1980) found that spatial memory was not affected by the purely visual task of making brightness judgements.

If imagery shares resources with perception, how similar are the two processes? Is imagining just like seeing, but fainter? A programme of research by Finke and collaborators (reviewed by Finke, 1989) has clarified which properties are shared by imagery with visual perception. Finke and Kosslyn (1980) reported that in visual imagery, like perception, acuity decreased towards the periphery of the visual or imaginal "field". To measure acuity, subjects either imagined, or actually saw, a pair of dots in the centre of a stimulus field, and used a moveable fixation point to indicate the point at which the two dots could no longer be resolved as they mentally, or visually, scanned towards or away from the periphery of the visual field. Imaginary fields as plotted using this acuity task were the same shape as visual fields—roughly elliptical with a horizontal elongation, with the extent of the field greater below than above the horizontal axis of the field. Control subjects who were asked to guess what the findings should have been were unable to anticipate these rather subtle aspects of the shape of the visual and imaginary fields, suggesting that the results did not arise as a result of subjects' expectations.

Finke and Kurtzman (1981) extended this investigation by using bar gratings to measure the sensitivity to different "spatial frequencies". The spatial frequency of a stripe pattern (known as a "grating") describes the width of the spacing of the stripes. The higher the spatial freqency of the grating, the more narrowly spaced are the stripes.

Grating patterns constructed from intensities that vary sinusoidally across space have commonly been used to probe visual sensitivity, because responses to more complex patterns can be predicted from a knowledge of responses to simpler ones (see Cornsweet, 1970, for a more extensive introduction). Finke and Kurtzman (1981) showed that the measured visual or imagined field sizes showed similar sensitivity to the spatial frequency of the stimulus. Low spatial frequencies could be resolved at greater eccentricities than higher spatial frequencies, whether the gratings were real or imagined. Moreover, Kosslyn (1980) reports that the "oblique" effect is observed with imagined as well as perceived spatial gratings: subjects are less sensitive to gratings oriented obliquely than to those oriented horizontally or vertically. Again, such findings are particularly interesting as it is unlikely that subjects are aware of the differential sensitivity to horizontal or vertical gratings, and it seems unlikely that the results arise because of subjects' explicit knowledge, in the way that Pylyshyn (1981) suggested.

Neither of these sorts of experiments is easy to explain in terms of cognitive penetrability, as the basic effects are not ones of which subjects have any explicit knowledge. However, Intons-Peterson (1983) was able to show that some aspects of these results may be influenced by *experimenter* effects, as she showed that the imaginal field sizes revealed by naive experimenters were of smaller extent than those revealed by knowledgeable experimenters, and that manipulating experimenter expectations could influence the pattern of results obtained. However, as Finke (1989) points out, Intons-Peterson's studies did not manage to manipulate experimenters to produce results where the imaginal field extended beyond the size of the visual field, suggesting that experimenter effects may contribute, but are unlikely to account for the entire pattern of data obtained in such experiments.

The investigations of the size and shape of the imaginal field show that the mental territory of imagination may be the same as that of visual processing. Thus visual imagery appears to involve at least one component of the processing that occurs when subjects look at real patterns. The next set of experiments we will review attempts to go further and explore which stages of visual analysis are implicated in the imagery process. After-effects and adaptation to prolonged stimulation provide a technique to study low levels of visual processing. Prolonged exposure to a red light, for example, produces a transient adaptation of the colour processing system with the result that a white surface seen soon afterwards looks green. Exposure to a grating of a particular spatial frequency similarly adapts the visual system such that an observer is less sensitive to gratings of that same frequency shortly afterwards. If visual imagery involves the mental activation of some of the same processors involved in early colour or form processing, then adaptation should be observed following prolonged imagining of such stimuli just as with actual exposure.

Rhodes and O'Leary (1985) explored this by asking subjects to visualise horizontal or vertical bar gratings, and examined whether this imagined exposure altered sensitivity to visually presented gratings. They found that such imagined gratings had no effect on sensitivity to visual gratings, in contrast to the adaptation effects observed after visual exposure to real gratings. This study suggests that imagery does not activate low-level feature analysers.

An apparent exception to this is found with a study by Finke and Schmidt (1978) which seemed to show that the McCullough contingent colour after-effect could be obtained following an imagined adaptation period. The McCullough effect involves adaptation to alternate patterns of black vertical stripes on a red background and black horizontal stripes on a green background. After several minutes of such adaptation, subjects are shown a complex pattern containing some horizontally striped and some vertically striped regions, now on a uniform white background. Subjects report seeing the white horizontal bars tinged with pink, and the vertical bars tinged with green, and this after-effect can be remarkably persistent. Finke and Schmidt showed that when bar gratings of different orientations were imagined on uniform coloured fields that were actually seen, a McCullough effect was observed, although this did not happen when different colours were imagined superimposed on actually presented gratings. This result might suggest that imagery does involve the activation of oriented feature detectors early in the visual pathway, although not of colour detectors. However, there are a number of peculiarities about these findings which urge caution over this interpretation. Finke (1989) describes how, for example, the imagery McCullough effect transfers between eyes in contrast to the visual McCullough effect which does not, and also how the imagery effect cannot be demonstrated in all the test situations that give rise to the visually based after-effect. On balance, none of the experiments on imaginary after-effects gives any strong support to the involvement of *low-level* visual feature detectors, or receptors, in imagery.

A number of other strands of research (see Finke, 1989) reinforce this conclusion, and suggest that the resources or mechanisms shared between visual perception and visual imagery are not those of low-level visual processing but of later stages of object perception and attention.

Closely related to the question of whether imagined stimuli can cause adaptation that affects the perception of subsequent stimuli is the question of whether imagined items can produce priming that affects the identification of subsequent visual stimuli. Repetition priming is the facilitation given to the identification of an item by its earlier occurrence. Repetition priming is interesting because it seems to reflect *perceptual* rather than *conceptual* memory, because it does not cross "domains". For example, identification of a picture of an object is facilitated by earlier exposure to a picture of that object, whether the same or different from that presented at test, but is not facilitated by exposure to the name of the object compared with an unprimed control condition (Warren & Morton, 1982). This is in contrast to explicit memory where subjects will recognise seeing a picture of a dog, when probed with the word "dog", or vice versa, due to the common conceptual and linguistic knowledge that is activated by a picture and by a word. Given that repetition priming reflects perceptual facilitation, does an imagined event prime recognition of a visually presented item? Stadler and McDaniel (1990) report data that shows that imagining the appearance of words in lower case does not facilitate later decisions made to those words when actually presented in lower case (although imagining words does prime later decisions made to imagined words). However, seeing the words in lower case does facilitate decisions made to imagined word shapes. Thus imagery does not prime perceptual decisions, although perception does prime imagery. We have found similar results in unpublished experiments on repetition priming and face recognition, where making decisions based on imagined facial appearance does not prime later familiarity decisions to faces, but making a familiarity decision to a face does facilitate a later decision based on imagined appearance (Cabeza & Burton, in prep.; Gould, 1992).

More recently, McDermott and Roediger (1994) have shown that imagining the referents of words presented in a study phase does facilitate recognition of fragmented pictures of these items in a later test phase, compared with an unstudied control condition. Although this finding could be interpreted as an effect of imagery priming perception, McDermott and Roediger also suggest that the effects may depend crucially on the use of a fragment completion task in the test phase. It is possible, for example, that the process of completing a partial pattern itself requires imagery. Consistent with this, Cabeza and Burton (in prep) find priming of face recognition by imagery when the test phase requires recognition of part faces but not when it involves recognising whole faces. Thus imagery processes appear to overlap with the processes needed for perceptual completion of fragmented patterns or objects, an idea elaborated in Kosslyn's most recent (1994) theory of the role of visual imagery in object recognition.

A further way in which imagery appears to differ from perception is in the potential for reinterpretation that is possible from an image. Chambers and Reisberg, (1985) showed that if subjects memorised one of the classic ambiguous figures, such as the duck-rabbit (see Fig. 3.3), which they had interpreted in only one of its possible ways, they were subsequently unable to inspect their image of the item and provide the alternative interpretation. If asked to draw the item from memory, however, they could then reinterpret the figure. Chambers and Reisberg argue that images carry with them their interpretations and thus are very unlike raw sensory data on which such interpretations are based. Similarly, other experiments have shown that subjects find it difficult to detect hidden parts of patterns from imagery, such as the parallelogram shape formed when two equilateral triangles are superimposed to form a star shape (Reed, 1974) (see Fig. 3.3). However, Finke, Pinker, and Farah (1989) have shown that reinterpretation of images is possible in some circumstances. For example, subjects can correctly report the emergent forms that arise when two different shapes are mentally superimposed and/or manipulated (remember the fried egg face we made earlier?). They argue that reinterpretations at the level of low-level grouping and depth perception is probably needed in order to reverse figures such as the duck-rabbit or Necker cube, and that this is why imagery does not support such reversal. However, mentally conjoining a hemisphere and a J shape to reveal an umbrella does not require any changes at the lower levels, but a redescription at higher levels of object identification.

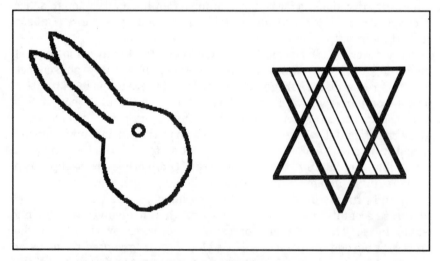

FIG. 3.3.   Figures which give rise to alternative interpretations in perception but not in imagery. In the classic duck-rabbit shape, the rabbit's ears become the duck's beak when the figure reverses. When two triangles overlap to form a star, several parallelogram shapes can be found in the resulting figure. One of these is shaded in this example.

A further piece of evidence that imagery involves higher, but not lower levels of perception comes from some clever experiments by Martha Farah (1989). She examined how subjects' sensitivity and criterion for detecting a point stimulus was affected when a shape was imagined at the location where the stimulus was projected. In her tasks, subjects saw a spatial matrix within which a shape was actually drawn, or imagined. Subjects then had to decide whether, and where, a faint point stimulus was presented. She found that where parts of the matrix were mentally filled by part of an imaginary matrix, subjects' detection criterion, but not their sensitivity, was altered. This contrasted with what was found with patterns that were perceived rather than imagined on the matrix, where sensitivity rather than bias was affected. In a final experiment, Farah was able to show that visual imagery produced results that were more like those obtained when subjects were asked to attend selectively to a shape, than when they merely perceived a shape. This was achieved by having subjects pay attention to one of two overlapping patterns that were physically present on the matrix. This selective attention to one of two patterns again affected bias but not sensitivity to the point light targets. This similarity between imaginal and attentional rather than low-level perceptual processes suggests that imagery shares something with higher rather than lower levels of visual perception.

From the evidence so far, it seems that imagery overlaps with some, but not all, of the processes involved in visual object recognition. Recently, additional evidence for the extent and nature of the overlap between perception and imagery has come from neuropsychological patterns of impairment following brain damage, and from patterns of cortical activation observed using electrophysiology and cerebral blood flow (see Farah, 1988 and Kosslyn, 1994 for details). Studies of regional cerebral flood flow compare the cortical activation observed during a task involving imagery, with the activation for a task of similar complexity that does not involve imagery. By subtraction, the activation due to imagery alone can be obtained. Using this logic and procedure, several studies have shown that visual imagery produces activation of the occipital lobe which includes the areas in which low level visual features are analysed, as well as activation in areas of the temporal lobe known to be involved in higher-level visual processing. Electrophysiological studies of event-related potentials (ERPs) have also shown activation in the occipital area during imagery. Furthermore, difficulty with visual imagery is often associated with varieties of visual agnosia following brain damage, and this association does not appear to be confined to higher levels of object interpretation. For example, patients with damage to the visual cortex that leads to acquired colour blindness are generally unable to imagine colours or to report the colours of objects from memory. These studies of activation and effects of brain damage in the occipital cortex suggest that imagery may share the neural structures of quite early levels of visual processing, whereas the behavioural studies reviewed earlier suggest that imagery shares characteristics of higher, but not low-level visual perception. All the studies converge on the overlap between imagery and perception. What is yet to be resolved is the extent of the overlap.

VISUAL BUFFER THEORY OF VISUAL IMAGERY

The results summarised earlier can reasonably well be explained by a computational account of visual imagery developed by Steve Kosslyn (1980) and extension of this account to encompass more of what is known about object recognition by Farah (1984) (see also Humphreys & Bruce, 1989, Chapter 6). Kosslyn distinguishes short-term from long-term memory components of imagery. The short-term component is the "visual buffer", which forms the medium within which images may be constructed or maintained. It is the medium within which the imagined maps, animals, or block letters would be maintained in typical experiments on image scanning, or within which imagined items of food can be arranged to form a face. The buffer is held to be spatial, and in format it is an array of locations. When an image of an object is *generated*, its long-term memory representation is translated into the spatial coordinates of the short-term visual buffer, within which it can be *inspected*, or *transformed* (as in mental rotation).

Long-term memory houses lists of facts about objects and stores of the appearances of objects. Kosslyn suggests that these appearances are literal, and are coded in terms of their spatial placement within the short-term buffer. A schematic outline of the imagery model as adapted by Farah (1984) is shown in Fig. 3.4.

According to this model, imagery shares several of the representations and processes of visual perception. When an object is seen, its appearance is encoded from the retinal images into the visual buffer. It may then be matched with an appearance stored in long-term memory, and hence recognised by virtue of this match, so that associated facts about the object may be retrieved. Moreover, a representation in the visual buffer derived from perception can be inspected or transformed—just like one that has been generated from memory. According to this model, then, the difference between a percept and imagination lies in the route by which activity in the buffer is generated. Imagery is merely the reactivation of a spatial sequence of code that

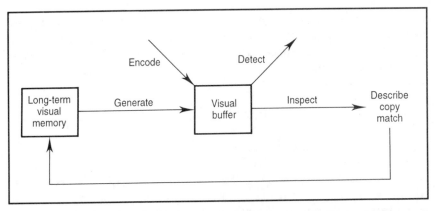

FIG. 3.4.   Schematic diagram of the stores and processes involved in visual imagery and visual perception. The visual buffer is the common medium into which visual images are generated from long term visual memory, and where descriptions of perceived images are constructed. Adapted by Humphreys and Bruce (1989) from Farah (1984).

would have been created by perception. On this account, imagery and perception share their end-point (visual buffer) but not their routes, and this could explain why imagery appears to share properties with the higher levels, but not lower ones, of visual perception. Moreover, the account of the visual buffer furnished by Kosslyn bears a strong resemblance to the account of a temporary visual store needed to assemble descriptions of objects prior to identification offered by Treisman (1988) in developing her account of visual attention and object recognition (see Humphreys & Bruce, 1989).

Kosslyn (1994) has subsequently developed and elaborated his theory of the relationship between visual perception and visual imagery, and accommodates the observations of visual cortical activation during imagery that we mentioned earlier. In his 1994 book, he locates the visual buffer in the occipital lobe, consistent with the electrophysiology and blood flow studies described earlier. He suggests that the process by which an image is constructed in the buffer in an imagery task involves a process that more usually forms an integral part of visual object recognition. On Kosslyn's account, in visual object recognition, partial information (e.g. from a occluded object) may lead to the access of a stored model whose appearance is then copied to the visual buffer to facilitate matching. Note that this explanation is consistent with McDermott and Roediger's observation that prior imagining helped the identification of picture fragments, a situation where the "top-down" route from object memory to the visual buffer might be particularly important. Kosslyn's most recent version of his theory is very much more complex and ambitious than this, however, and attempts to integrate phenomena of visual attention, memory, and action alongside object recognition. However the central notion—that perception and imagery both involve activation within a shared visual buffer—remains.

DOMAINS OF IMAGINATION

One difficulty with much of the recent work on imagery, is that although it provides a plausible, spatially based medium within which to explain visual imagery, rather little is said about imagination in other domains. We have already noted that, although visual imagery has been controversial this century, there has been rather little argument about the psychological basis of an "inner voice", which has been legitimised by an appeal to an articulatory basis. Baddeley and Hitch's (1974; Baddeley, 1986) framework for working memory spells out more clearly the current understanding of the basis for our "inner voice", and in so doing links this quite neatly with Kosslyn's visual buffer theory of visual imagery.

Working memory is a model of short-term memory, which developed as a result of problems that arose within the "modal" model of short- and long-term memory developed during the 1960s (Atkinson & Shiffrin, 1971). In Baddeley and Hitch's model, and its subsequent development (1986), the system that allows active manipulation and maintenance of information in the short term comprises three main components: a general central executive system and two modality-specific slave stores; the visuo-spatial sketch pad and the articulatory loop. The visuo-spatial sketch pad (VSSP) appears to be synonymous with the visual buffer that we outlined earlier—what differs is that Baddeley and his colleagues have focused their work on the role played by this store in short-term memory and imagery tasks of a particular type, and have not considered the relationship between the representations generated in the VSSP and long-term memory. This means that the working memory framework does not deal with the relationship between imagery and object recognition. Nevertheless the proposed properties of VSSP overlap so closely with those of Kosslyn's visual buffer that it is reasonable to equate the two. The articulatory loop system itself comprises two components—the phonological store and the articulatory control process. The phonological store is a short-term, limited capacity store of speech sounds, to which spoken speech has direct access, and into which written words may be translated. Maintenance of this store depends on the articulatory control process which recycles the speech sounds. The evidence on which the theory of the articulatory loop was built is extensive, and I will not attempt to review it here (see Baddeley, 1986). The important point to convey is that there does appear to be a good candidate system in contemporary cognitive theory to play the role of "inner ear" and "inner voice".

Recently, Daniel Reisberg and his associates have conducted some interesting experiments which lend some support to this suggestion. Smith, Reisberg, and Wilson (1992) examined the processes involved in interpreting a printed string such as "NE1 4 10S" as a heard phrase "anyone for tennis". They reasoned that to translate the printed symbols to this auditory interpretation without saying the words out loud required auditory imagery, and set out to examine how engaging either the "inner ear", or the "inner voice", or both, in secondary tasks, affected the interpretation process. In the absence of interference, subjects interpreted 73% of such printed strings correctly, but when they heard concurrent auditory input their performance dropped to 40%; with concurrent articulation it dropped to 21%; and with both it dropped to 19%. These results suggest that both the phonological input store and the articulatory control process are involved in the kind of auditory imagery that mediates such a process. Similar conclusions were reached in experiments where subjects had to imagine the melodies associated with popular tunes (e.g. "White Christmas") and indicate whether the third note of the tune went up or down in pitch. Again, performance on this task dropped if there was concurrent auditory distraction, or concurrent articulation, or both. Thus the phenomena of auditory imagery for materials that can be spoken or sung fit rather neatly within the model of auditory short-term memory, providing a pleasing symmetry with the case of visual imagery.

In drawing analogies between the processes of visual and auditory imagery, Reisberg, Smith, Baxter, and Sonenshine (1989) examined whether ambiguous auditory images were reversible (recall that visual images of ambiguous objects such as the Necker cube do not reverse). They exploited Warren and Gregory's (1958) auditory analogue of the visual reversing figures, where rapid repetitions of a word such as "stress" may appear to change into repetitions of a different word, in this case "dress". Reisberg et al. found that subjects did experience such reversals when invited to imagine repetitions of such words, in contrast to the apparent irreversibility of ambiguous visual images. However, preventing articulation by having subjects chew a sweet, or by clamping their jaws, prevented such reversals. Subsequently Wilson, Smith, and Reisberg (discussed in Smith et al., 1992) found that presentation of an irrelevant message via headphones also abolished the effect, again suggesting that auditory imagery makes use of both the phonological and the articulatory components of the articulatory loop.

This all seems very neatly to set up a framework for explaining some of the phenomena of imagery as the temporary activation of representations within buffer storage systems dedicated to space and speech. However, there are other phenomena of everyday imagery that seem to find no place within such a framework. Many of us experience the persistent memory of a tune that we can't get out of our heads, but it is not clear how such musical imagery can be accounted for. Although there have recently been some interesting comparisons between musical imagery and visual imagery (e.g. Halpern, 1988; 1992) there is little theoretical understanding of the locus of such effects, although Baddeley and Logie (1992) have suggested that the articulatory loop might be used for non-speech as well as speech sounds. Similarly, people experience imaginary tastes—wine buffs report imagining the taste of particularly excellent wines. There is no difficulty, in principle, in accommodating such phenomena within a generalised theory of imagery, where imagery is seen as the reactivation of some of the same neural processes invoked by perception—the main problem is that our understanding of music, or wine, perception is much less developed than our understanding of visual perception or speech understanding. Nevertheless, I feel optimistic that a satisfactory account of such imaginings will emerge from cognitive research into the perception of music and taste, because: "The imagining of a thing is, on this view, no more mysterious than the perceiving of that thing" (Shepard, 1990).

REALITY TESTING AND REALITY MONITORING

However, there is a deeper question that arises once an acceptable computational account of imagery is on the agenda. If both visual perception and visual imagery involve attentional allocation to relevant attributes at spatial locations in the visual buffer, how can we distinguish reality from imagination? The same question can be raised about audition—if heard words and imagined words activate some time-coded phonologically based code in the articulatory loop, how can we discriminate a real from an imagined voice? The question gets even deeper than this, as noted by Johnson (1988), because other things follow from our interpretation of an event as real or imagined. Real perceptual events are located "out there" in the world, whereas imagined events are located "inside" our heads. Indeed it has sometimes been suggested that the defining criterion for an hallucination is that an inner event is wrongly projected into external reality (although see Bentall, 1990). The mystery is that we do not, on the whole, make false attributions on the basis of computational events that must be similar internally, given the shared resources and representational medium that seems to underlie our phenomenal experiences of visual and auditory imagery. Although there is a problem of accounting for how we distinguish currently perceived from imagined events, this becomes even greater when the task is to know whether a memory is of a real or imagined event. All of us day-dream of achieving our ambitions, only rarely do people subsequently mistake the reverie for actual achievement. According to Johnson (e.g. 1988) our normal ability to make distinctions between actually experienced and imagined events, whether ongoing or in memory, requires us to monitor the balance between different kinds of mental events—those to do with perception and action, and others to do with planning and strategy. In this closing section of the chapter, I outline what is currently known about such "metacognitive" processes.

This question of distinguishing reality from imagination has been strangely neglected during the revival of interest in mental imagery. However, recent pockets of research suggest that in thinking clearly about such questions, we can begin to get a handle on some of the cognitive mechanisms that are affected by organic brain diseases such as schizophrenia. Understanding how a cognitive system fails can give important clues about its normal functioning, and the new "cognitive neuropsychiatry" has provided some clues that will help us to consider this question.

HALLUCINATIONS

According to the account developed here, the difference between a perception and an imagination lies in the source of the contents of the appropriate perceptual buffer store. The source of the perception is external sensation and that of the imagination lies with self-generation. Clearly some other cognitive system must be able to monitor the routes to very similar endpoints (cf Fig. 3.4). This indeed is the basis of Frith's cognitive account of the nature of hallucinations in schizophrenic patients. According to Frith (1992), schizophrenic hallucinators who report hearing voices may have a failure in "self-monitoring"—i.e. failure to distinguish information in articulatory loop derived from self rather than outside events. What they are "hearing" are their own internal thoughts in their own inner voices, but through the failure to self-monitor they wrongly attribute the source of articulatory loop information and falsely project the result to the outside world.

Mintz and Alpert (1972) suggested that hallucinations in schizophrenia might arise as a result of failed reality monitoring combined with vivid imagery. They screened hallucinating schizophrenic patients, non-hallucinating patients, and normal controls on Barber and Calverley's (1964) "White Christmas" test. In this test, subjects are invited to close their eyes and imagine "a record with words and music playing White Christmas". They are asked afterwards to decide which of four descriptions best matched their experiences:

A. They heard the record clearly and believed it was playing.
B. They heard the record clearly but knew that no record was playing.
C. They had a vague impression of a record.
D. They heard nothing.

Mintz and Alpert found that 17 of 20 hallucinating schizophrenics opted for A or B, but only 1 out of 20 non-hallucinating subjects did so. Rather less than 50% of control subjects opted for B (none for A), a slightly lower proportion than had been reported by Barber and Calverley in their original study, though this may be explained by slightly different instructions issued in the original study.

Mintz and Alpert then went on to test the same patients in a speech perception experiment where subjects had to report what words were played in different amounts of white noise, and report their confidence in their reports. For normal subjects and non-hallucinating patients there was a clear correlation between confidence and accuracy—when the words were most difficult to hear, people reported most uncertainty in their reports. The hallucinating group showed a much less strong correlation. This suggested to Mintz and Alpert that this group were failing properly to monitor reality, and it was this combined with their vivid imagery that created the combination of factors promoting hallucinations.

The suggestion is therefore that misattribution of the source of information in the articulatory loop, or visual buffer, is the cause of an illusion. If so, then the prediction follows that filling up the articulatory loop with real, externally generated material should lead to fewer opportunities for hallucination, as the externally generated material should leave less room for the "inner voice". One rather neat piece of evidence for this hypothesis comes from the effect of auditory shadowing on schizophrenic hallucination. Slade (1974) found that the frequency of reported auditory hallucinations declined in two patients as the rate of presentation of letters increased in a shadowing task. Margo, Hemsley, and Slade (1981) compared the rated duration, clarity, and loudness of hallucinations in seven schizophrenic patients, exposed to different kinds of external stimulation for periods of two minutes. When the patients were reading aloud, or listening to speech, their reported hallucinations dropped the most; listening to "vocal music", a passage of Africaans (an unfamiliar language), or electronic blips had less of an effect on the reported hallucination. If the articulatory loop hypothesis is correct, we would expect any phonological material to reduce frequency and any non-speech material to have little effect. The results are roughly, but not entirely in line with this hypothesis, because vocal music and a foreign language might have been expected to be more effective. However, given the crudity of the measures available in this study, the results are actually remarkably good.

The articulatory loop hypothesis is intriguing, and is a considerable advance over the idea that schizophrenic illusions arose from faulty *sensation* rather than faulty *interpretation*. Nevertheless, the case is not water-tight (see Smith, 1992 for a detailed review) and considerable further research is needed. I here note just one of the hypotheses that this kind of theory of hallucination suggests. Hallucinations in schizophrenic patients are usually auditory (Bentall, 1990) but where visual hallucinations are reported, it should be the case that visual imagery tasks should also reduce the reported incidence of visual hallucinations. This hypothesis awaits investigation (Bentall, 1990).

Confusions between reality and imagination can occur without any more deep-rooted mental disorder, as evidenced by anecdotal experiences of people under the influence of psychoactive drugs, or extreme fatigue. However, even normal subjects tested in ambiguous circumstances can be shown to fail to discriminate reality from imagination, as in the situation described by Perky (1910). In Perky's (1910) experiments, subjects were asked to imagine a particular object (e.g. a yellow banana, or a green leaf) projected onto a smoked glass screen. While engaged in imagining these objects, pictures of the same objects were projected onto the screen, very faintly and with fuzzy outlines. Under these conditions, some subjects reported seeing clear visual images of the objects but they did not think they were really seeing the objects, even though they were.

Why did subjects in these experiments confuse reality with imagination in this way? I think this confusion is explicable when we consider other constraints that usually allow us to distinguish whether the source of a representation in the visual buffer is real or imaginal. Usually we can tell whether something is "real" or not by seeking other sensory evidence: we can reach out and touch a real but not an imagined object. Moreover, certain systematic changes in viewpoint occur as we move our eyes and head when viewing a real but not an imaginary object—indeed certain illusory phenomena (as opposed to imaginary ones), such as the hollow face, are revealed as illusory because they violate normal expectations when movements are made. Real objects occlude other objects in the background appropriately, and are invisible when the eyes are closed. The Perky experimental result is important because the image was to be projected onto a uniform field, thereby removing the main obstacle (occlusion) to distinguishing the real from the imagined.

In experiments that followed up the Perky effect, Segal and colleagues produced some evidence to support the idea that the effect depends on the limited opportunity and information to confirm the perceptual hypothesis. Segal and Nathan (1964) replicated the Perky phenomenon, but a much smaller percentage of subjects confused the projected images with their own perceptions. This percentage increased with a change of apparatus so that subjects looked into a translucent cylinder that restricted their field of vision, and thereby their opportunities to seek better perceptual evidence. Moreover, circumstances that provided better perceptual evidence, where stimuli were more intense, of longer duration, less fuzzy in outline, or presented with a background, were less likely to be confused with imagination (Segal, 1970).

The availability to perceptual confirmation of our everyday visual experiences may explain why auditory hallucinations are so much more common than visual ones among schizophrenic patients, because the experience of an auditory stimulus without any accompanying evidence to confirm its reality is commonplace (for example hearing music or a person in an adjacent room; speaking on the telephone, etc). Moreover, given that there are normally situations where voices or other sounds can be heard but their reality cannot be confirmed, this ought to make it possible to set up the auditory equivalent of the Perky effect quite easily, although I am not aware of any direct attempts to do so.

REALITY MONITORING IN MEMORY

The foregoing discussion suggests that our everyday discrimination of real from thought events requires that we monitor the source of representations. It is also necessary for these different aspects of our ongoing cognition to be retained in memory, or we will be in danger of mistaking, for example, a remembered dream for something that actually happened. On a trip to a local safari park, my husband worried aloud at the possibility that monkeys would get on the car and tear off his windscreen wipers, an event that did not occur—indeed we saw no monkeys except in enclosures. Two years later, as we passed the park, one of the children we had taken with us announced that he remembered going to the safari park: "That was where the monkeys took our windscreen wipers". The child had confused a hypothetical imaginary event with reality.

Marcia Johnson and colleagues have studied the processes that allow us more usually to distinguish real from imagined events in memory (e.g. Johnson, Hashtroudi, & Lindsay, 1993; Johnson & Raye, 1981). The basic assumption underlying the framework developed by Johnson is that memory potentially consists of numerous attributes to do with physical properties, semantic properties, contextual information about time and place of occurrence, and cognitive operations associated with the event, such as acts of image generation or effort after meaning. Johnson sees the attribution of the source of a memory to external or internal events as an act of judgement that depends on a weighing up of the balance between stored perceptual information and stored information about cognitive activities associated with these events. In recent experiments she has shown that this act of judgement takes longer to achieve than simple recognition that an item is familiar (Johnson, Kounios, & Reeder, 1994).

Her framework has been elaborated as a model; the "multiple entry modular memory system" or MEM, where two reflective subsystems (the "executive" and "supervisor") interact with two perceptual subsystems in monitoring and initiating behaviour and thought processes, which in turn deposit records of past activity within the systems themselves. Thus the memory system preserves the results both of perceptual processing (external memories) and of the self-generated or reflective activities (internal memories) that are the properties of the executive and supervisory systems.

This framework is supported by experiments that show that external and internal memories are more likely to be confused by operations that shift the balance of attributes normally associated with external or internal memories, so that the judgement process is more difficult. For example, situations that make an internally generated event have attributes more like an external event increase confusions between the two. One example is provided by Johnson, Foley, and Leach (1988) who found that subjects were more likely to confuse words that they had imagined with ones spoken by someone else, when they were instructed to imagine the words in the speaker's, rather than their own voice. Imagining the words spoken in a voice that was neither their own nor that of the external speaker produced less confusion between imagined and spoken words, suggesting that the confusions arose because of the specific overlap between the "sensory" characteristics of the real and imagined voices, rather than because of the effort required to imagine another voice. In fact, other research has shown that situations that increase the amount of deliberate cognitive effort required to generate an internal thought or image make it less likely that the event will later be misremembered as occurring externally. For example, Johnson, Raye, Foley, and Foley (1981) asked subjects in a memory test to discriminate between category members that had been presented earlier, and those that the subjects had generated from category cues. For some of the generated category members the first letter of the required word was given alongside the cue, whereas for others this was not provided. Subjects were more likely to categorise those items for which a first letter had been provided as having been presented, a result that was interpreted as due to the lesser effort required making the remembered attributes of the cognitive operations less distinctive.

Similarly, Finke, Johnson, and Shyi (1988) showed that subjects were more likely to confuse an imagined object that required little effort to image with an actually studied item, than one which required a lot of effort. Johnson, Finke, Danzer, and Shyi found a similar result using the mental generation of completions of patterns drawn in a 5 × 5 grid. A familiar or unfamiliar shape could be created by filling some squares in the grid, but on some trials a subset of these squares was left empty and had to be mentally filled by the subject to complete the shape. Subjects later had to remember which of the shapes they had seen in whole form and which had been seen in only partial form. They were better at discriminating those that their own mental efforts had completed when these formed novel shapes than when they were familiar alphanumeric patterns. Again, the argument is that the unfamiliar patterns required more cognitive effort to complete, and memory for the effort involved helps to distinguish what was actually present from what was just imagined.

Distinguishing a remembered event from a remembered imagination thus appears to depend on memory for the metacognitive events that surrounded the initial activity. If hallucinating schizophrenic patients are poor at such self-monitoring at the time of an event, and tend to attribute internally generated events to external sources, then they should be bad at remembering their own thoughts. Heilbrun (1981) asked schizophrenic patients to distinguish their own verbatim statements of opinion from similar statements generated by other people, one week after the original statements were generated. Hallucinating patients were worse at this task than non-hallucinating patients. Consistent with this, Harvey (1985, cited in Frith, 1992) showed that schizophrenics were normal at distinguishing whether the source of a memory was speaker A or speaker B but impaired at distinguishing whether the source was self or external, compared with normal subjects.

Moreover, there are further disorders that seem to arise from failures or disorders in reality monitoring in memory, which can also be considered within the MEMS framework of Johnson and colleagues. The first kind of disorder is that of confabulation, where patients will elaborate with great conviction memories that are quite clearly false. Here it seems that patients are confusing a current or past imagination with the record of an actually experienced event. For example, Stuss et al. (1978) describe a frontal patient who falsely remembered that one of his children had been drowned in an accident and that he had himself sustained his head injuries as a result of trying to rescue the child. As in this case, confabulation often occurs in patients who have bilateral damage to the frontal lobes, often associated with temporal lobe damage that affects memory. The involvement of both these areas in cases of persistent and prolonged confabulation is consistent with the disorder arising primarily from a failure of the reflective processes that normally help monitor the source of memories (Johnson, 1991)

A further phenomenon that may arise from inappropriate reality monitoring is that of *déjà vu*, an experience that most people report occasionally but which can become a persistent feature of some pathological conditions. *Déjà vu* was defined by Neppe (in Sno & Linszen, 1990) as "any subjectively inappropriate feeling of familiarity of a present experience with an undefined past". As a pathological condition (it occurs within a range of psychiatric disorders) it appears to involve a disturbance of memory and attention. The temporal lobe has been implicated in *déjà vu* experiences—it can be a feature of epilepsy, and stimulation of the temporal lobes in awake patients gives rise to the feeling.

This review of reality monitoring and its failures illustrates the kind of approach that has been taken to the question of how we distinguish reality from imagination in memory. The work of Johnson and her colleagues has rightly focused on some of the consequent difficulties that arise once a cognitive framework for imagination is developed, and the MEM framework goes some way towards providing an explanation of how real events may be distinguished from thoughts in memory. There do seem to me to be some problems with the framework as presented by Johnson, however. For example, suggesting that discriminating memory for real from imagined events depends on the balance of external and internal aspects of the trace is fine when making comparisons between different mental circumstances surrounding roughly similar events, but it seems less easy to apply to the comparison between very different kinds of events. For example, we might read the word "justice" but *imagine* eating an ice-cream. The sensory attributes associated with the imaginary ice-cream might be quite strong compared with the abstract word that was actually presented—but is it the case that abstract words are more likely to be misremembered as resulting from thought and concrete words as arising in the real world? Moreover, because the MEM framework is deliberately agnostic about the kinds of domain-dependent and time-limited memories that we discussed when considering the visual buffer and articulatory loop theories of visual and auditory imagery, it is difficult to use the framework to make very specific predictions about the interaction between events occurring internally and externally in, say, hallucinations. The MEM framework shares with the working memory model a further deficiency, which is the relatively poor definition of the "executive" and "supervisory" systems on which so much of the burden of reality testing and monitoring is placed. Although the neuropsychology of frontal lobe symptoms and of ("frontal") psychiatric disorders such as schizophrenia is promising, there is still a considerable way to go to develop a theory of executive functioning. In the next chapter, Stephen Monsell examines how psychologists have approached this mystery.

To sum up, in this chapter I have reviewed recent research that has led to a coherent and elaborated theoretical framework for understanding visual imagery; a topic that only regained respectability some 20 or so years ago, and which has been remarkably controversial in the recent past. Now, with our better understanding of the computational demands and neural substrate of visual cognition, this controversy has subsided. However, this conceptual framework itself raises a whole new set of questions about how we distinguish reality from imagination, questions that have not yet attracted the same amount of attention, but which appear to be central to our understanding of a number of psychiatric symptoms. Related to the specific topics mentioned in this chapter are a number of other questions with practical consequences, such as whether it is possible to distinguish a memory of a real event from a "false" memory suggested through leading questions or hypnosis. I hope this chapter may stimulate more research by cognitive psychologists on these intriguing and important questions.

REFERENCES

Atkinson, R.C. & Shiffrin, R.M. (1971). The control of short-term memory. *Scientific American, 225,* 82–90.

Baddeley, A.D. (1986). *Working memory.* Oxford: Oxford University Press.

Baddeley, A.D., Grant, W., Wight, E., & Thomson, N. (1975). Imagery and visual working memory. In P.M.A. Rabbitt & S. Dornic (Eds.), *Attention and performance V*, pp. 205–217. London: Academic Press.

Baddeley, A.D., & Hitch, G.J. (1974). Working memory. In G.A. Bower (Ed.), *Recent advances in learning and motivation, Vol. 8.* New York: Academic Press.

Baddeley, A.D. & Lieberman, K. (1980). Spatial working memory. In R. Nickerson (Ed.), *Attention and performance VIII*, pp. 521–539. Hillsdale, NJ: Lawrence Erlbaum Associates Inc.

Baddeley, A. & Logie, R. (1992). Auditory imagery and working memory. In D. Reisberg (Ed.), *Auditory imagery*. Hillsdale, NJ: Lawrence Erlbaum Associates Inc.

Barber, T.X., & Calverley, D.S. (1964). An experimental study of "hypnotic" (auditory and visual) hallucinations. *Journal of Abnormal and Social Psychology, 68*, 13–20.

Begg, I. (1982). Imagery, organization and discriminative processes. *Canadian Journal of Psychology, 36*, 273–290.

Bentall, R.P. (1990). The illusion of reality: A review and integration of psychological research on hallucinations. *Psychological Bulletin, 107*, 82–95.

Bower, G.H. (1970). Imagery as a relational organiser in associative learning. *Journal of Verbal Learning and Verbal Behavior, 9*, 529–533.

Brooks, L.R. (1967). The suppression of visualisation by reading. *Quarterly Journal of Experimental Psychology, 19*, 289–299.

Brooks, L.R. (1968). Spatial and verbal components in the act of recall. *Canadian Journal of Psychology, 22*, 349–368.

Cabeza, R. & Burton, A.M. (1995). Manuscript in preparation.

Chambers, D. & Reisberg, D. (1985). Can mental images be ambiguous? *Journal of Experimental Psychology: Human Perception and Performance, 11*, 317–328.

Cooper, L. (1976). Demonstration of a mental analog of an external rotation. *Perception & Psychophysics, 19*, 296–302.

Cooper, L. & Shepard, R.N. (1973). The time required to prepare for a rotated stimulus. *Memory & Cognition, 1*, 246–250.

Cornsweet, T.N. (1970). *Visual perception.* New York: Academic Press.

Farah, M.J. (1984). The neurological basis of mental imagery: A componential analysis. *Cognition, 18*, 241–269.

Farah, M.J. (1988). Is visual imagery really visual? Overlooked evidence from neuropsychology. *Psychological Review, 95*, 307–317.

Farah, M.J. (1989). Mechanisms of imagery-perception interaction. *Journal of Experimental Psychology: Human Perception and Performance, 15*, 203–211.

Finke, R.A. (1989). *Principles of mental imagery.* Cambridge, MA: MIT Press.

Finke, R.A., Johnson, M.K., & Shyi, G.C.W. (1988). Memory confusions for real and imagined completions of symmetrical visual patterns, *Memory & Cognition, 16*, 133–137.

Finke, R.A. & Kosslyn, S.M. (1980). Levels of equivalence in imagery and perception. *Psychological Review, 87*, 113–132.

Finke, R.A. & Kurtzman, H.S. (1981). Mapping the visual field in mental imagery. *Journal of Experimental Psychology: General, 110*, 501–517.

Finke, R.A., Pinker, S., & Farah, M.J. (1989). Reinterpreting visual patterns in mental imagery. *Cognitive Science, 13*, 51–78.

Finke, R.A. & Schmidt, M.J. (1978). The quantitative measure of pattern representation in images using orientation-specific colour aftereffects. *Perception & Psychophysics, 23*, 515–520.

Frith, C. (1992). *The neuropsychology of schizophrenia.* London: Lawrence Erlbaum Associates Ltd.

Gould, C. (1992). *Image generation, face recognition and repetition priming.* Unpublished undergraduate project, University of Nottingham.

Halpern, A.R. (1988). Mental scanning in auditory images for familiar songs. *Journal of Experimental Psychology: Learning, Memory and Cognition, 14,* 434–443.

Halpern, A.R. (1992). Musical aspects of auditory imagery. In D. Reisberg (Ed.), *Auditory imagery.* Hillsdale, NJ: Lawrence Erlbaum Associates Inc.

Heilbrun, A.B. (1980). Impaired recognition of self-expressed thought in patients with auditory hallucinations. *Journal of Abnormal Psychology, 89,* 728–736.

Humphreys, G.W. & Bruce, V. (1989). *Visual cognition.* London: Lawrence Erlbaum Associates Ltd.

Intons-Peterson, M.J. (1983). Imagery paradigms: How vulnerable are they to experimenters' expectations? *Journal of Experimental Psychology: Human Perception and Performance, 7,* 833–843.

Johnson, M.K. (1988). Discriminating the origin of information. In T.F. Oltmanns & B.A. Maher (Eds.), *Delusional Beliefs,* pp. 34–65. New York: Wiley.

Johnson, M.K. (1991). Reality monitoring: Evidence from confabulation in organic brain disease patients. In G.P. Prigatano & D.L. Schacter (Eds.), *Awareness of deficit after brain injury* (pp. 176–197).

Johnson, M.K., Finke, R.A., Danzer, A., & Shyi. G.C.W. (1991). Ease of imaging and reality monitoring. Manuscript in prep.

Johnson, M.K., Foley, M.A., & Leach, K. (1988). The consequences for memory of imagining in another person's voice. *Memory & Cognition, 16,* 337–342.

Johnson, M.K., Hashtroudi, S., & Lindsay, D.S. (1993). Source monitoring. *Psychological Bulletin, 114,* 3–28.

Johnson, M.K., Kounios, J., & Reeder, J.A. (1994). Time-course studies of reality monitoring and recognition. *Journal of Experimental Psychology, 20,* 1409–1419.

Johnson, M.K. & Raye, C.L. (1981). Reality monitoring. *Psychological Review, 88,* 67–85.

Johnson, M.K., Raye, C.L., Foley, H.J., & Foley, M.A. (1981). Cognitive operations and decision bias in reality monitoring. *American Journal of Psychology, 94,* 37–64.

Kerst, S.M. & Howard, J.H. (1977). Mental comparisons for ordered information on abstract and concrete dimensions. *Memory & Cognition, 5,* 227–234.

Kessel, F.S. (1972). Imagery: A dimension of mind rediscovered. *British Journal of Psychology, 63,* 149–162.

Kosslyn, S.M. (1973). Scanning mental images: some structural implications. *Perception & Psychophysics, 14,* 90–94.

Kosslyn, S.M. (1976). Can imagery be distinguished from other forms of internal representation? Evidence from studies of information retrieval times. *Memory & Cognition, 4,* 291–297.

Kosslyn, S.M. (1980). *Image and mind.* Cambridge, MA: Harvard University Press.

Kosslyn, S.M. (1994). *Image and brain.* Cambridge, MA: MIT Press.

Kosslyn, S.M., Ball, T., & Reiser, B.J. (1978). Visual images preserve metric spatial information: Evidence from studies of image scanning. *Journal of Experimental Psychology: Human Perception & Performance, 4,* 47–60.

Kosslyn, S.M., Murphy, G.L., Bemesderfer, M.E., & Feinstein, K.J. (1977). Category and continuum in mental comparisons, *Journal of Experimental Psychology: General, 114,* 311–341.

Lea, G. (1975). Chronometric analysis of the method of loci. *Journal of Experimental Psychology: Human Perception and Performance, 1,* 95–104.

Margo, A., Hemsley, D.R., & Slade, P.D. (1981). The effects of varying auditory input on schizophrenic hallucinations. *British Journal of Psychiatry, 139,* 122–127.

McDermott, K.B. & Roediger, H.L. (1994). Effects of imagery on perceptual implicit tasks. *Journal of Experimental Psychology: Learning, Memory and Cognition, 20,* 1379–1390.

Mintz, S. & Alpert, M. (1972). Imagery vividness, reality testing, and schizophrenic hallucinations. *Journal of Abnormal Psychology, 19,* 310–316.

Moyer, R.S. (1973). Comparing objects in memory: Evidence suggesting an internal psychophysics. *Perception & Psychophysics, 13,* 180–184.

Paivio, A. (1969). Mental imagery in associative learning and memory. *Psychological Review, 76,* 241–263.

Paivio, A. (1975). Perceptual comparisons through the mind's eye. *Memory & Cognition, 4,* 635–647.

Paivio, A. (1978). Mental comparisons involving abstract attitudes. *Memory & Cognition, 6,* 199–208.

Paivio, A. (1979). *Imagery and verbal processes.* Hillsdale, NJ: Lawrence Erlbaum Associates Inc.

Perky, C.W. (1910). An experimental study of imagination. *American Journal of Psychology, 21,* 422–452.

Posner, M.I. (1978). *Chronometric explorations of mind.* Hillsdale, NJ: Lawrence Erlbaum Associates Inc.

Pylyshyn, Z.W. (1973). What the mind's eye tells the mind's brain: A critique of mental imagery, *Psychological Bulletin, 80,* 1–24.

Pylyshyn, Z.W. (1981). The imagery debate: Analogue media versus tacit knowledge. *Psychological Review, 88,* 16–45.

Reed, S.K. (1974). Structural descriptions and the limitations of visual images. *Memory & Cognition, 2,* 329–336.

Reisberg, D., Smith, J.D., Baxter, D.A., & Sonenshine, M. (1989). "Enacted" auditory images are ambiguous: "Pure" auditory images are not. *Quarterly Journal of Experimental Psychology, 41A,* 619–641.

Rhodes, G. & O'Leary, A. (1985). Imagery effects on early visual processing. *Perception & Psychophysics, 37,* 382–388.

Segal, S.J. (1970). Imagery and reality: Can they be distinguished? In W. Keup (Ed.), *Origins and mechanisms of hallucinations,* pp.103–113. New York: Plenum Press.

Segal, S.J. & Nathan, S. (1964). The Perky effect: Incorporation of an external stimulus into an imagery experience under placebo and control conditions. *Perceptual and Motor Skills, 18,* 385–395.

Shepard, R.N. (1990). Postscript: On understanding mental images. In H. Barlow, C. Blakemore, & M. Weston-Smith (Eds.), *Images and understanding.* Cambridge University Press.

Shepard, R.N. & Cooper, L.A. (1982). *Mental images and their transformation.* Cambridge, MA: MIT Press.

Shepard, R.N. & Metzler, J. (1971). Mental rotation of three-dimensional objects. *Science, 171,* 701–703.

Slade, P.D. (1974). The external control of auditory hallucinations: An information theory analysis. *British Journal of Social and Clinical Psychology, 13*, 73–79.

Smith, J.D. (1992). The auditory hallucinations of schizophrenia. In D. Reisberg (Ed.), *Auditory imagery*. Hillsdale, NJ: Lawrence Erlbaum Associates Inc.

Smith, J.D., Reisberg, D., & Wilson, M. (1992). Subvocalisation and auditory imagery: interactions between the inner ear and inner voice. In D. Reisberg (Ed.), *Auditory imagery*. Hillsdale, NJ: Lawrence Erlbaum Associates Inc.

Sno, H.N., & Linszen, D.H. (1990). The déjà-vu experience—remembrance of things past. *American Journal of Psychiatry, 147*, 1587–1595.

Spanos, N.P. & Barber, T.X. (1973). Hypnotic experiences as inferred from subjective reports: Auditory and visual hallucinations. *Journal of Experimental Research in Personality, 3*, 136–150.

Stadler, M.A. & McDaniel, M.A. (1990). On imagining and seeing: repetition priming and interactive views of imagery. *Psychological Research, 52*, pp366–370.

Stuss, D.T., Alexander, M.P., Lieberman, A., & Levine, H. (1978). An extraordinary form of confabulation. *Neurology, 28*, 1166–1172.

Thomas, N.J.T. (1989). Experience and theory as determinants of attitudes toward mental representation: The case of Knight Dunlap and the vanishing images of J.B. Watson. *American Journal of Psychology, 102*, 395–412.

Treisman, A. (1988). Features and objects: The fourteenth Bartlett Memorial lecture. *Quarterly Journal of Experimental Psychology, 40A*, 201–237.

Tye, M. (1991). *The imagery debate*. Cambridge, MA: MIT Press.

Warren, C.E.J. & Morton, J. (1982). The effects of priming on picture recognition. *British Journal of Psychology, 73*, 117–130.

Warren, R. & Gregory, R. (1958). An auditory analogue of the visual reversible figure. *American Journal of Psychology, 71*, 612–613.

Watson, J.B. (1913/1961). Psychology as the behaviourist views it. In T. Shipley (Ed.), *Classics in psychology* (pp.798–821). [Reprinted from *Psychological Review, 20*, 158–177,1913.]

Watson, J.B. (1914). *Behaviour: An introduction to comparative psychology*. New York: Holt.

CHAPTER FOUR

Control of mental processes

Stephen Monsell University of Cambridge

INTRODUCTION

Cognitive psychology has made considerable headway, both technical and substantive, over the last 30 to 40 years. We can point both to sophisticated methodologies that have been developed for the analysis of cognitive skills such as reading, face recognition, and remembering, and to impressive examples of analyses of such skills, increasingly often in the form of computational simulations (see Vicki Bruce's Introduction). For all this progress, there remains a somewhat embarrassing zone of almost total ignorance—a heart of darkness—in our understanding: the mystery of how cognitive processes are controlled. To try to capture the mystery in a nut-shell: we can, for many cognitive skills, say something useful about what the component processes are, how they work, and how they are organised; what we are unable to say much about is how that particular organisation, rather than some other, is called into play at a given moment.

Behaviour is directed by a hierarchy of goals. At the top of the hierarchy are the fundamental but abstract goals we inherit as the members of any successful species: survival and reproduction. At the next level we may identify those goals, part biologically, part culturally determined, that in our particular primate species are an individual's vehicles for realising the abstract aims of survival and reproduction: access to nourishment, shelter, social acceptability, social success and dominance, comfort, knowledge of the world, sex, companionship, co-operation, etc. Working our way down the hierarchy from these broad goals with time-spans of many years we arrive at goals with a time-span of days (reading a book), hours (painting a ceiling), minutes (making a cup of tea), and at the lowest level seconds and fractions of a second (recognising a word, dipping the brush, switching on the kettle). In this chapter, I will be concerned with control of cognitive operations lasting seconds and fractions of a second.

At the time-scale of minutes and seconds, the time-scale with which the analysis of cognitive skill has been mostly concerned[1], a natural unit of analysis of mental activity seems to be the cognitive task. Much of the success of cognitive psychology has been manifest in its analysis of the performance of particular tasks, such as comprehension of a spoken sentence, deciding the truth or falsity of a syllogism, deciding whether two visual forms are the same or different, recalling the words in a list, naming a familiar face or object, performing mental arithmetic, searching an array of visual objects for a target, and many, many others. The typical research paper reports a series of experiments which measure the effects on the performance of one such task of variables such as stimulus materials, context, subject population, individual differences, and so on. The aim is to partition the processes underlying performance of the task into components, draw conclusions about the properties of those components, and infer their organisation. Sometimes, more ambitiously, the underlying processing architecture is inferred from comparisons of performance among several related tasks; an example is the analysis of the relation between various word reading tasks: lexical decision, naming, semantic classification (e.g. Coltheart, 1985; Monsell, Doyle, & Haggard, 1989).

At any one time, our processing resources seem to be devoted to performing just one, or at best, two or three tasks at a time. This bland statement immediately prompts some hygienic qualifications. Considered at a coarser time-scale, we are always concurrently performing an almost indefinitely large number of "tasks". As I type these words, the task I am visibly performing may be variously described as: typing; composing a chapter; attempting to inform you, gentle reader; promoting my ideas; furthering my career; earning my salary; fulfilling my contract with the publishers and my promises to the Editor (if a little late!), etc. To acknowledge this is only to recognise that any piece of mental and behavioural activity can trivially be described in relation to any level of a complex hierarchy of goals and sub-goals. Second, on the whiteboard above my desk is an alarmingly long list of "tasks to be done", many of which I have started but not finished: prepare these lectures, review that manuscript, read that essay, and so on. However, while typing this sentence I am not *actively* engaged on these other tasks: they are inactive, in abeyance, "on hold", although they may be triggered into activity by a phone call or some other prompt. Third, whatever else we are doing, we constantly monitor the environment for threats and opportunities relevant to our major life goals: dangers to life, limb, comfort, and esteem; opportunities for material acquisition, sexual or social gratification, etc. This monitoring appears largely unconscious, and I am going to make the possibly rash claim that it can be considered an automatic and essentially passive background process that, except perhaps in cases of pathological anxiety (Eysenck, 1992; Mathews, 1988), consumes no cognitive resources to speak of, unless and until a potentially "significant" cue has been detected.

Granting all these pernickety qualifications, here I am with my cognitive resources and effectors at any moment apparently devoted to just one task: typing, or reading, or reaching for an apple. (Or two or three such tasks: certain pairs of tasks , such as scratching and reading, may be performed concurrently, with no apparent interference; we shall return to this issue later.) The brain is capable of an enormous range of such tasks. For the performance of many of them psychology can give sophisticated analyses. But what causes me to devote my processing resources, organised in a particular way, to this one task rather than another, and when, and how? This is part of the mystery. Before I review what we know about it so far, it will help to distinguish between a "single-step" task and a "multi-step" task.

Single-step tasks
The paradigm case of the sort of single-step task that psychologists like to study is when, in response to a particular stimulus, we respond almost immediately with a particular action, as for example when we name an object, repeat a word, detect a target in an array, or catch a ball—what used to be called "associative reactions". Some input arrives, some chain of processes occurs which results in the emergence of a response, typically with a reaction time of between 200msec and 2sec. Even though there may be iterated operations within these processes (e.g. searching successive positions within an array, as discussed later), or iterative error correction in the on-line control of a movement (as in ball-catching), we are basically talking about a single cycle of processes mapping input to output. Experimentalists like tasks of this kind, with overt input and output, because they can control the presentation of the input and measure the identity and latency of the response precisely. But single-step tasks also include the harder-to-study cases where the "input" is internal: i.e. an idea, a memory, or the internal product of some other operation, evokes an act. And there are tasks where an input

evokes no overt response—as when our response to an experience is merely to "read, mark, learn, and inwardly digest".

Critical control questions that arise in the context of single-step tasks are these. How do we set ourselves to perform one such task rather than another (*task-set configuring*)? As I will elaborate later, configuring has a number of elements: enabling connections between processing modules, setting their operating parameters, preparatory orienting (e.g. of direction of gaze), and readying of effectors (e.g. getting your hands ready). What limits our ability to perform several tasks concurrently (*resource allocation*)? How do we *monitor* and *optimise* our performance?

Multi-step tasks

Making a mug of tea is a multi-step task. One has to locate the container of tea, open it, locate a suitable mug, take out a teabag, bring it and the mug into proximity, put the teabag in the mug, locate, fill, and turn on the kettle[2]; when it has boiled, water must be poured on the teabag; when it has brewed, the teabag must be disposed of, and so on. Like most multi-step tasks, this one has many options. Some of the steps must be performed sequentially in a fixed order (filling the kettle, boiling the water) but others can be performed in a variable order , and, logically at least, in parallel (boiling the water, finding a teabag). Some steps may be left out (when the kettle is already full, for example). The content of the steps may be varied in response to environmental constraints (no teabags, a broken kettle) or internal whim (e.g. use leaf tea, boil the water in a saucepan, move the teabag container to proximity with the mug). Responsibility for selecting among such options, both of organisation (*sequencing*) and of content (*configuring*), is standardly attributed to (mysterious) executive control processes.

A multi-step task may be analysed as a critical-path network of single-step components. An important control issue that arises only when we consider multi-step tasks is the need to suspend the carrying-out of some steps until a future condition is fulfilled; for example, when the mug and teabag are ready, and the kettle switched on, there is nothing more to be done until the kettle boils. Typically we prosecute other tasks during this interval (reading the newspaper, daydreaming, wiping up spills). The control function of placing a task on hold, and then ensuring its resumption when some trigger condition is fulfilled, is a critical one, and quite often goes awry in everyday life. We either neglect to resume the process when the trigger condition occurs (as when we becomes so absorbed in reading that we do not notice that the kettle has boiled and switched itself off) or we detect the trigger condition, but forget what we are then supposed to do (as when one finds oneself having gone upstairs for some purpose, but cannot remember what it is). As this last example demonstrates, the conditions for resumption may be achieved either by some external agency (the kettle boiling), or by some action on one's own part (walking upstairs) that does not (apparently) require continuous executive control.

Another vital pair of control functions required for the performance of multi-step tasks are *monitoring* and *troubleshooting*. Monitoring is the process of checking to see that intended goals and sub-goals are adequately fulfilled. Troubleshooting is doing something about it when they are not. Frequently troubleshooting involves finding a suitable substitute means to a goal (e.g. if the kettle's fuse blows, heat the water on the gas stove instead). Often this will involve evoking, or setting up, a whole new embedded task, with its own goals and subgoals, which, when fulfilled, will enable resumption (suitably triggered) of the original task. When the kettle's fuse blows, one may, for example, decide to replace the fuse (which in turn means finding the spare fuses, a screwdriver etc). An important sub-category of the monitoring function is *termination assessment*: deciding when enough is enough. Without such an assessment process one could end up rewiring the house in order to make a cup of tea, or, when deciding which of several CDs to buy, weighing the evidence and vacillating endlessly. Finally, when two tasks are performed concurrently, available resources need to be allocated between the tasks (as in the case of single-step tasks), with the additional complexity engendered by the possibility of interdigitating steps belonging to each of the tasks and keeping track of where each task has got to when one returns to it.

To illustrate the control functions needed to perform multi-step tasks, it is didactically convenient to pick one like tea-making, in which the steps all involve *overt* actions. However, for many multi-step tasks, most or all of the steps occur covertly inside the head. Each step carries out some operation (searching, matching, deciding, evaluating, translating, transforming) and generates output that is stored, temporarily or permanently, to be used as input by subsequent processes, until the goal is achieved or abandoned. The paradigm case is the solving of tricky logical problems, such as the "cannibals and missionaries" problem, where many minutes of cogitation may be required. When allowed, we often relieve the memory demands posed by such problems by resorting to pencil and paper, so that some of the covert steps become visible. Newell and Simon (1972) famously pioneered the recording of "talking aloud" protocols generated by their subjects as they attempted to solve such problems, to try to track the current guiding hypotheses, sub-goals, back-trackings, blind alleys, etc, of a subject's otherwise private multi-step odyssey through the problem space. (For more recent analyses of reasoning and problem solving in these terms, see Newell,

1980,1990.) I am going to make the (probably rash) assumption that the executive functions involved in covert multi-step tasks are not radically different from those involved in more overt sequences of actions, although they presumably place a greater burden on the ability to manage limited memory resources and set up prospective memory triggers cued by endogenous rather than external events.

The distinction between "multi-step" and "single step" tasks, in the case where the processes are covert, raises once again the slippery issue of levels of control. Consider the task specified by the instructions "Press the right hand button if the display you are about to see contains a square blue object, the left hand button otherwise", when the display always contains some square non-targets and some blue non-targets. Viewed in one way, this is a paradigmatic case of a "single-step" task: an input arrives, a few hundred msec of processing happens, a decision is made, a response emerges. However, many experts on visual search (e.g. Treisman & Gelade, 1980) analyse the search process mediating performance as an iterative cycle in which (a) an attentional "spotlight" is moved to the next object (or region) on the display, (b) that object (or region) is tested for the required conjunction of features, (c) if the test is positive, the search stops, but (d) if it is negative then (a) the spotlight moves to another object (or region) (b) that is tested, and so on until all the candidate locations in the visual field have been inspected. If that is the correct analysis, the sequence of micro-steps (a) through (d) requires "control"—of which object to test next and when to stop. My prejudice here is to assume that these "micro-control" functions are handled within a specialised module whose function is visual-target-finding, and do not call on the same general executive resources that select and organise sequences of steps of which "look for such and such a target" is one. But of course, I may be wrong; ultimately this is an empirical question.

Here is a list of the control functions I have informally identified so far (cf Allport, 1989, p.652):

Control functions for single-step tasks
- Task-set configuration, including:
  § Enabling/disabling of module–module connections
  § Module configuration (target assignment, operation selection, input–output rules, setting of decision criteria, output sufficiency criteria, etc)
  § Perceptual orienting
  § Response mode preparation
- Outcome monitoring
- Optimisation

Additional functions for multi-step tasks
- Step selection
- Step critical path configuration (serial/parallel organisation)
- Setting triggers for delayed operations (a.k.a. "prospective memory")
- Monitoring, including:
  § Termination assessment
- Troubleshooting (by activation of an embedded task)

TASK-SET

Preparation to perform one task rather than another may be described as adopting a *task-set*. Where do task-sets come from? Well-learned task-sets are retrieved from memory. New tasks are often specified by verbal instruction. For example, here is a little task for the reader: When you next read the word *complexity* I want you to think "Aha!". Start now. To specify a task to young children and animals, non-verbal demonstrations, or the more laborious process of shaping behaviour through reinforcement are necessary. It may take some time to figure out how to configure one's processes to achieve the desired result, and a novel task of any complexity must initially be accomplished by, presumably, a general-purpose (slow, effortful) trial-and-error procedure. (Did you? Behold: the mystery!) Once one has figured out how to configure oneself to perform a novel task, the settings applied by the control functions listed earlier (e.g. the manner of connecting and configuring modules to accomplish a single step, or the appropriate sequencing or parallel organisation of steps for a multi-step task) may be stored in memory, and subsequently evoked as part of a task-set "schema". Hence one gets oneself, or finds oneself got, without really thinking about it, into "driving mode", "teeth-brushing mode", "tennis-playing mode", or "squash-playing mode". Of course, most novel tasks share configurational elements with familiar ones, and familiar task-sets often need some modification, so the idea of evoking a task-set as a package does not preclude the immediate retuning of it for changed circumstances.

How, why, and when are task-sets evoked, whether by instruction, or by stored schemata in memory? That is the mystery, so far rather abstractly stated: it will become more concrete as we proceed. We consider first some broad theoretical conceptions—or, really, theoretical metaphors for—the way in which mental processes might be controlled. Then we shall consider three types of evidence that provide windows, albeit small, obscure and, distorting, into the heart of the mystery:

- everyday failures of cognitive control in normal people;
- pathological failures of cognitive control in patients with brain damage;
- laboratory experiments that reveal the operation of control processes, in situations of competition or switching between tasks.

THEORETICAL METAPHORS

The hypothesised executive mechanism has been called many things: The Will (James, 1890); Control Processes (Atkinson & Shiffrin, 1968), the Central Executive (Baddeley, 1986), the Supervisory Attention System (Norman & Shallice, 1986); sometimes the mechanism is, like Jehovah, not named but merely invoked, by distinguishing between Controlled Processes and Automatic Processes (Posner & Snyder, 1975, Shiffrin & Schneider, 1977). Critics refer scornfully to the Homunculus, reminding us that to attribute powers of deciding, intending, monitoring, choosing, and planning to a miniature Person inside the head does not get us very far in explaining how the head accomplishes choosing, intending, etc. As Newell (1980, p.715) states, for example:

A major item on the agenda of cognitive psychology is to banish the homunculus (i.e. the assumption of an intelligent agent (little man) residing elsewhere in the system, usually off stage, who does all the marvellous things that need to be done actually to generate the total behaviour of the subject). It is the homunculus that actually performs the control processes in Atkinson & Shiffrin's (1968) famous memory model, who still does all the controlled processing (including determining the strategies) in the more recent proposal of Shiffrin & Schneider (1977), who makes all the confidence judgements, who analyses all the payoff matrices and adjusts the behaviour appropriately, who is renamed the "executive" in many models (clearly a promotion), ...

In our industrialised culture, the term "executive" pleasingly captures some intuitions about control processes: the lack of concern with domain-specific detail, the idea that low-level "production-line" functions can trundle along with only intermittent intervention from the executive, the major role of executive planning in dealing with novel situations. But labels like "the central executive" tend to carry at least two assumptions along with them: that there is a unitary entity that does the controlling, and that there is a functional distinction between the controller and the controlled. A further assumption is often made: that the controller is anatomically separate from the controlled.

We should be very wary of all these assumptions. Many lower animals exhibit co-ordinated behaviour without a detectable control "centre". A particularly attractive example is the radially symmetrical starfish[3], whose nervous system has the structure of a ring, with branches to each arm. Normally the starfish moves towards things that are good for it and away from things that are bad, by means of (apparently) co-ordinated movements of its five arms. But if a section of the neural ring next to any one arm is isolated, that arm now attempts to act independently, and no longer co-operates with the general "intention" manifest by the others. Clearly the co-ordination of the intact starfish depends on some form of communication among the five segments, but there is no one part of the ring that is "in charge": co-ordination is an emergent property of the interaction among the segments.

The operating system?

When the digital computer on my desk is switched on, it immediately loads a program called The System, whose job it is to act as an interface between the user and particular special-purpose programs. When I then call up a special-purpose program like the word-processing package WORD, the operating system loads WORD and hands over control of the machine to WORD, until WORD quits, fails, or is suspended, at which point control is returned to the operating system. The operating system may also be called into play if some external signal (like a message waiting from another computer or the printer) is detected.

The analogy of the controller of the mind as an operating system (e.g. Johnson-Laird, 1983) is one embodiment of idea of the mind as a hierarchical system in which control is passed "down" and "up" between high-level general-purpose control processes and low-level specialised processes. However, operating systems on digital computers provide an analogy that is inexact in at least one sense: in as much as the mind has an "operating system", it surely runs concurrently, not in alternation, with specialised processes. Notice also that the operating system of a computer is not really a *higher*-level, or more *general*-purpose program, just a program with different functions from the others, but equally specialised. But then perhaps the mind also is not a hierarchy but a heterarchy. To attribute control to general-purpose mechanisms does not seem warranted, except in the sense that one needs strategies general enough to enable us to figure out out how to perform new tasks, and to enable effective troubleshooting when learned routines for particular tasks fail. The task of controlling other processes is just as specialised a function as that of recognising phonological patterns or rotating images. Nevertheless, at the heart of the classical Von-Neumann computer architecture is a command economy principle: every agent does its task because another agent has "passed" control to it, and this may be an inappropriate analogy for the mind. And the ultimate cop-out in this analogy is, of course, that the real controlling agent of a computer is its user. Hence the operating system in a Von-Neumann architecture is an unsatisfactory analogy.

The mind as a production system

A more anarchic, free-market, metaphor for mind control is available from computer science in the so-called "production system" architecture (Newell, 1973, 1990; see Allport, 1980b, for a good introduction). At the heart of a production system is a large set of condition-action demons called "productions", and a "workspace" (or "working memory"), which receives both external information from sensory systems and information generated by the operation of productions. Each production continually scans the contents of the workspace looking for a pattern that fulfils its condition. If the condition is detected, it performs its action, which may be to operate on some contents of the workspace and place the results back into the workspace. Productions may also generate overt actions, including the sampling of sensory input. No "controller" tells productions what to do or when: when their conditions are present, they activate themselves. The information they place into the workspace, coupled with information from the senses, triggers the activities of other productions. Hence the system is entirely driven by the procedural knowledge embodied in productions, and the contents of the workspace. Each production is a specialised agent. There is no general-purpose agent; general goals, such as survival, must be realised presumably in the existence of particular agents which recognise conditions of danger, and place goals such as "withdraw" into the workspace with high priority attached.

Learning may take place as follows (Newell, 1990). If an impasse is reached, the goal of overcoming an impasse is entered into the workspace. Specialist productions for searching the problem space for ways out of the impasse are triggered, and may in turn set up sub-goals whose presence triggers other productions, whose activity may, with luck, get the system out of the impasse. If the impasse is overcome, then the procedure discovered for resolving the impasse is stored as a new production, or set of productions, which will be evoked by any future encounter with the same impasse. Productions may also be organised to perform sequential tasks by the action of one constituting a condition for the next.

However, a control mechanism is needed. One reason is that two or more productions may find their conditions simultaneously satisfied, but generate conflicting actions. For example, the self-preservation demon may detect danger and signal the goal "withdraw", while the curiosity demon may detect interest, and signal the goal "inspect"! Some sort of arbitration is required. In SOAR (Newell, 1990; Newell, Rosenbloom, & Laird, 1989) there is a two-phase decision cycle. First there is elaboration: productions are allowed to fire freely in parallel, until "quiescence" is achieved; among the elements retrieved as a result of this activity will be preferences among the operators retrieved. The decision process then winnows the available preferences, and selects the strongest operator, which moves the system on to the next cycle . Thus a serial, one-step-at-a-time system is enforced by, essentially, forcing the system to choose at each cycle which of the many things bits of it "want" to do at that moment. The application of SOAR has so far been to the accomplishment of single tasks, such as "memory search", so it is unclear what kind of solution, if any, this approach to the control problem will provide to the problem of switching between, or combining, multiple tasks. (See Shallice, 1994, for a further critique of SOAR's treatment of the distinction between "automatic" and "controlled" processing.)

Norman and Shallice (1986, Shallice, 1988) proposed a psychological model based on the production system architecture (see Fig. 4.1). At the lowest level are production-like entities called thought and action *schemata*—"program-like entities, one for each qualitatively distinct basic type of action or thought operations". These are triggered into action by the presence of appropriate conditions in the "trigger-data base". Each operates using special-purpose cognitive resources to generate either overt action or new information in the trigger-data base. Schemata are organised by learning into hierarchies, so that in a skilled action, such as typing or speaking, etc., the elements of a complex act are controlled by "component" schemata which directly operate on special-purpose processing resources, and are triggered into action in part by the activation from the "source" schemata which organise the sequencing of the component operations (Shallice, 1988).

Schemata are activated to different degrees. A schema is selected if its activation exceeds a threshold. Among the things that schemata do when selected are:

- activate component schemata
- "switch in" particular arrangements of transmission routes between processing modules
- modulate the operations of processing sub-systems.

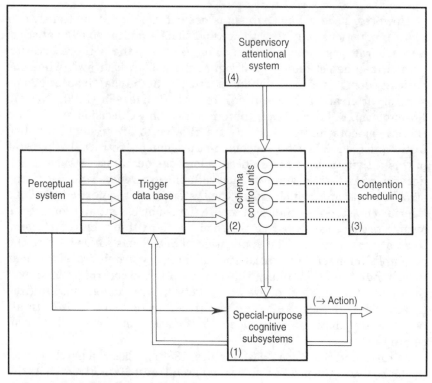

FIG. 4.1.   The Norman-Shallice model. Reproduced from Shallice et al. (1989) by permission. © 1989, Oxford University Press.

- set variables specifying the goal of a schema: e.g. if "catching" is activated, set the parameters of the object to be caught (e.g. ball not butterfly).

There are two mechanisms for preventing anarchy in this free market for control. One is a "contention-scheduling" mechanism, which operates by means of inhibition between activated schemata so that when they are in competition for the use for processing sub-systems only the strongest wins. The degree of activation of a schema is in part determined by the recency and frequency with which it has been activated.

However, a system controlled only by contention scheduling would be a prisoner of habit, tending to produce, in any situation, only the most-practised, and most recently activated, operations of thought and action associated with that context in its repertoire. Hence Norman and Shallice propose a second level of control, called the "Supervisory

Attention System" (SAS), which "has access to a representation of the environment and of the organism's intentions and cognitive capacities" (Shallice, 1988, p.335). It does not directly control the processing modules, but activates or inhibits particular lower-level schemata, essentially biasing the outcome of the contention scheduling process. Norman and Shallice argue that the situations in which this mechanism are needed include: novel situations; those requiring novel actions in a familiar context (including the overcoming of temptation); those requiring "trouble-shooting", those judged to be dangerous or technically difficult; those requiring planning and decision making. It is not specified how the SAS recognises when these conditions apply, and knows which pattern of modulation to transmit to the schema system.

It is clear, I think, that the strength of the Norman and Shallice model is in capturing, in a way for which one can at least imagine a coherent computational architecture in the brain, the automatic content-driven character of much of our cognition and behaviour. The model also captures the way in which habitual patterns of thought and action capture control of our minds and/or behaviour if not overridden in some way (as in action errors and frontal lobe pathology). The idea of the overriding as a *modulation* or *biasing* of the "automatic" part of the system rather than a seizing of direct control is an important advance beyond the mere labelling of "controlled" versus "automatic" processing. The weakness of the account, as in all other accounts of control, is that the mechanism doing the overriding is evoked as little more than a *deus ex machina*, with the usual powers of omniscience about what needs to be done and how to do it. The heart of the mystery of control is how to deconstruct the SAS.

The society of mind[4]

Although we have learned to think about minds in computational terms, our standard metaphors for mind control tend to remain socio-political. And systems of government that are not rigidly hierarchical, with a single "most responsible" agency at the apex, are rare: even modern democracies seem to require a president or prime minister in supreme charge at any moment, as companies require executive directors, committees chairpersons, universities vice-chancellors or provosts, etc. Perhaps it is the dominance of this mode of social control that makes it so hard for us to imagine a mind with no super-ordinate controller at all, no (singular, all-powerful) executive, as such, only a collection of specialised "agents" out of whose interactions coherent behaviour emerges. But there exist analogues elsewhere in the biosphere. I have already mentioned the starfish. An example of even more distributed control is the termite colony (or bee-hive). It behaves as a purposive entity, defending itself, building itself, repairing itself, feeding itself, and reproducing itself with no "chief termite" (or "prime bee"); the apparent coherence of organisation arises out of the interaction of thousands of specialised agents, without any funnelling of choices through a centralised decision process. (The so-called "queen" is merely one agent specialised for reproduction.) It may be objected, however, that although termite colonies show adaptive behaviours in response to damage, attack, etc, they are limited to a set of genetically programmed repertoires of behaviour; they have no way of dealing with (most kinds of) novelty. But it is, at the very least, not obvious that to deal with novelty, trouble-shooting, etc, a mind needs a *single* specialist super-agent or decision mechanism. It is at least as likely that, just as there are different specialised agents for recognising spoken words and transforming spatial patterns, so there is a range of specialised agents for different aspects of control: planning, prospective memory, criterion changing, information-routing, monitoring, problem-space searching, and so on. Indeed, as we will see, there is evidence from both neuropsychology and experiments on normal subjects to suggest fractionation of executive functions. Among those who have suggested that control mechanisms are heterogeneous and distributed are Logan (1985) and Allport (1989, 1993).

What about consciousness?
Only iron self-control has enabled me to avoid mention of this embarrassing beast (or bestiary) so far. To many this will seem odd. Awareness of intention is often thought of as the *sine qua non* of control over our mental processes, and by far the oldest theory of control is that of a non-material conscious mind directing, or attempting to direct, the activities of the material body. My reticence on the topic is only partly motivated by the fact that the mystery of consciousness is ably dealt with by Young and Block elsewhere in this book. My main reason is that, in our present state of ignorance, raising the relationship between control and phenomenal awareness is, I believe, likely to be a distraction in our quest for some understanding of control processes. There may be an additional excuse for avoiding the issue: Humphrey (1992) claims that phenomenal awareness is not intrinsically associated with intentions at all, only with (certain kinds of) sensations, although this is, it has to be said, a contentious view.

To take one example of the trickiness of the relation between consciousness and control, Fehrer and Raab (1962) demonstrated that initiation of a voluntary act does not require awareness of the stimulus that triggers it. The situation is as follows. A briefly displayed shape— the reaction signal—is followed almost immediately by a flanking display whose inner contours are in the same locations as, or very close to, the outer contours of the first display: the simplest example is a circular patch of light followed by a circular annulus that exactly fits around the first patch. It is possible to find conditions (e.g. a 50msec display of the first stimulus, followed by a 50msec gap) under which the first stimulus is not seen. However, this "metacontrast" suppression of awareness does not influence reaction time to the reaction stimulus, compared to the case where no flanking display follows it. Neumann and Klotz (1994) have, in a series of beautiful experiments, further demonstrated that metacontrast-suppressed stimuli that the subject cannot discriminate even by the most sensitive measure, can influence choice as well as simple reactions, even when the stimulus–response mapping changes from trial to trial. In these experiments, the response is not involuntary; the subject is not compelled to press a button when the reaction-time signal is being displayed. If we were to analyse the sequence of events as: detect signal → form intention to press button → initiate button-pressing response, then it would appear that intentions can be unconscious: the subject simply finds that he or she has responded. However, a preferable analysis is that the critical "act-of-intention" does not occur after the signal is detected, but beforehand, in the process of configuring the system (adopting a task-set) so that it is ready "automatically" to release a prepared response, or map a particular discrimination into one of a set of responses, when the signal is detected. The intention lies in the readying of the act, not (necessarily) its release. But if this is so, the conscious intending and the voluntary action can be quite temporally disconnected, and it becomes easier to imagine that they are not necessarily correlated.

Perhaps we should say then that one has intended to perform some task only if one has been conscious of the intention at *some* stage, not necessarily the moment of release of the action? However, it is possible to find in the neurological literature reports of co-ordinated actions by one hand that to an observer may appear intentional, in the sense that they are appropriate to both their target and their context (e.g. grasping a door knob and pulling), but are surprising and upsetting to the patient who feels he or she has not intended them, and therefore disowns them—the "alien hand" (Goldberg, Mayer, & Toglia, 1981). On the other hand, perhaps these should be analysed as actions controlled by external triggers, not the subject's endogenous intentions, and it is only the latter level of control with which awareness is associated.

Frith (1992) has argued that some of the delusions of the schizophrenic are due to a loss of awareness of intention. Intentions are monitored, he argues, to distinguish between the actions caused by our own goals and plans and those triggered by external events. A failure to monitor intentions to act leads to the patient's attribution of his or her own intended action to the control of an external force. "The force moved my lips. I began to speak. The words were made for me." (Frith, 1992, p.66). Frith extends this analysis to delusions of thought insertion, where the patient reports beliefs such as "Thoughts are put into my mind like 'Kill God'. It's just like my mind working but it isn't. They come from this chap, Chris. They're his thoughts." (Frith, 1992, p.66). Frith's proposal is that the patient does not detect or acknowledge his or her own intention to have these thoughts. However, the idea that one "intends" to have thoughts at all, that is to have particular thoughts rather than to "think about X"—is intriguing but tendentious (Henderson, 1994).

These few examples illustrate, I hope, that, although consciousness, or a certain type of consciousness, has been held to be intimately associated with executive function (see Young & Block's chapter), the relationship is sufficiently perplexing that no short cut to an understanding of executive function is likely to be found through introspection. We should be careful, for example, not to be lured into thinking of executive function as unitary merely because consciousness seems unitary, because the both the unitariness of consciousness and its relationship with executive function are moot. Hence it is with some relief that I leave the phenomenal concomitants of control to others, and turn to what observations of behaviour can tell us about how we control our minds.

CONTROL FAILURES IN NORMAL COGNITION

William James, in his chapter on "The Will" in the 1890 *Principles of psychology* (James, 1890), tells a well-known anecdote, which I take the liberty of adapting and dramatising a little. A man goes up to his bedroom at about seven o'clock in the evening to change his clothes to go out for a party. Some minutes later his wife comes up to the bedroom and finds him stepping into bed in his night-shirt. "What are you doing?", she says, "We're due at the Robertsons' in ten minutes". He looks by turns puzzled, confused, chagrined.

What has happened here? Our hero has gone upstairs with the *intention* of carrying out a moderately routine sequence of actions. Instead, he has performed a different—an even more *habitual*—sequence of actions. The sequence is complex, coherent and well-controlled; he hasn't put his leg through an arm-hole, or fallen over. So at one level his actions have been elaborately and appropriately "controlled". But, no matter how beautifully performed, these actions are *inappropriate*, in relation both to the specific intention with which he went to the bedroom, and to his general plan for the evening. When the error is drawn to his attention, he is immediately aware that his actions have not been as intended. He might say something like: "Oh, I wasn't thinking what I was doing, I must have got undressed *automatically*." Typically, he would claim to have been *preoccupied* with an important train of thought. If he did this sort thing often, his wife would doubtless think him characteristically *absent-minded*.

> Those who have stepped into their baths wearing some garment, or struggled to open a friend's front door with their own latch key, or switched on the light as they left the room in the daytime, or attempted to pour a second kettle of water into a pot of freshly made tea, or turned off the television set when they meant to extinguish the gas fire, or said "Thank you" to a stamp machine, will recognise the species. Our daily lives are strewn with such trifling and usually inconsequential blunders. (Reason, 1984, p.517)

Slips of action in everyday life have amused, irritated, terrified, or appalled their victims and observers as long as humans have described the behaviour of their fellows. (Reason, 1984, quotes some particularly charming 17th- and 18th-century accounts). Nor are such errors always trivial in their consequences. Reports on accidents in aviation, shipping, the nuclear industry, etc, not infrequently attribute them, at least in part, to "human error" (see Reason, 1990, for examples). Freud (1901) famously interpreted everyday errors of speech and action as revealing of our covert sexual and emotional desires and intentions. Doubtless some action errors are revealing in this way, but a majority admit of a more mundane interpretation. Their causation is extremely varied. Some errors seem to be clearly failures of control—as when an unintended but habitual act "captures" behaviour, for instance in James' anecdote, or when there is "cross-talk" between two concurrent multi-step tasks—as when a colleague found that she had put a lettuce leaf on the back doorstep and a milk bottle in the rabbit hutch before retiring for the night (M. Broadbent, personal communication). Others, as when we pick up our neighbour's wineglass at a crowded table, clearly arise as errors of recognition or aiming, at a relatively low level of control within specialised perceptuo-motor mechanisms. This is surely not an error of "executive" control (even though the exercise of unusual executive vigilance could, perhaps, have prevented it).

Recently, systematic surveys of action errors been made with a view to developing a taxonomy that might inform us about their causation (Norman, 1981; Reason, 1979, 1984, 1990). The main method has been to ask people to keep diaries; volunteers log instances in which their overt actions or mental operations have deviated from their intentions, specifying the context of the error (Reason, 1979) and answering certain standard questions about each error (Reason, 1984). A related line of research has been to try to relate proneness to action errors, or "cognitive failures", to intrinsic features of the individual (e.g. personality type, age, health) or extrinsic factors (boredom, stress) and their interaction, using questionnaires or diary methods (Broadbent, Broadbent, & Jones, 1986; Broadbent, Cooper, Fitzgerald, & Parkes, 1982).

I shall not belabour the methodological difficulties of relying on people's awareness and later memory of their own slips, and of their intentions, as well as their willingness to report them in an unbiased way. In principle it is possible to study errors in a more experimental way by setting up experimental situations in which errors are very likely, and placing subjects under time pressure so as to increase the error frequency. However, to my knowledge this technique has so far been applied only to rather specific skills like speaking (Baars, 1980), where the focus is not on executive, but on motor, control.

If one examines collections of action errors (e.g. those of Norman, 1981, and Reason, 1984) many can readily be interpreted in terms of the failure of one or more of the control functions listed earlier. Without attempting to be exhaustive, let us consider some examples of error types identified by these authors:

"Capture errors"
Single-step operations are sometimes evoked by habitually associated stimuli, even though they are inappropriate in the particular intentional context, such as when one inattentively shakes a hand proffered for some other purpose, or puts a coin into the coffee vending machine, instead of the cigarette machine (Norman, 1981). In the case of a multi-step task, a common observation is that stronger habits take over at a "choice-point" where a *sequence* of steps must depart from a familiar course *and* "attention" is diverted. Reason (1984) speaks of these as "double-capture" errors: capture of attention by something outside the task resulting in capture of behaviour by an habitual but inappropriate continuation at a choice-point. The capture may be manifest in errors both of commission (as in William James' anecdote) and of omission (e.g. failure to make an intended stop at the fish shop on the familiar way home). But what is this "attention" whose absence seems to be one of the criteria for the occurrence of a capture? In the multi-step case, part of what has gone wrong is presumably the setting of an adequate prospective memory trigger at the choice-point where the intended sequence must diverge from the habitual sequence. Must we not, in

addition, suppose some sort of actively sustained "clamp" on the intended configuration of steps and their constituent processes that, if relaxed sufficiently, allows a stronger learned configuration to reassert itself? Even if that clamp exists, and has relaxed sufficiently to allow the capture, the erroneous sequence would surely not continue so long after the choice-point in the multi-step examples given earlier unless monitoring was also inadequate. Of course, in other cases we notice the error immediately. Hence labelling these errors as "capture", or even "double-capture", errors catches part of their flavour, but should not be allowed to obscure the complex nature of their causation.

Cross-talk errors

These arise when two task sets are concurrently active, or at least contiguously active. I have given an example earlier of a case where the intended objects of two concurrent overt action sequences get swapped (milk bottle, lettuce leaf). An instance familiar to lecturers is that if one attempts to write on the board while continuing to speak, one is quite likely to utter a word one is intending to write, or vice versa. We may also see components of two task-sets being blended, as when, after answering the phone several times, I answered a knock at the office door by opening the door and saying "Stephen Monsell" (my standard office "telephone greeting"). In laboratory experiments on concurrent tasks (see later) the central problem for the subject often seems to be to prevent cross-talk between the tasks, and even when two information streams are successfully processed in parallel most of the time, cross-talk occasionally occurs. Note that, as in the door answering example, cross-talk errors may derive not only from the concurrent, but also the *recent* activation of another similar task-set.

Lost intentions and failed triggers

The case of a lost intention (Reason, 1984) is essentially the familiar "what the hell am I doing here?" syndrome referred to earlier: a prospective trigger has been set and activated in a timely fashion by the appropriate internal or external cue, but the step that is supposed to follow has been forgotten. One must sometimes retrace one's steps to the context in which the intended step was planned in order to retrieve it. The opposite case is where the prospective trigger has been set up in memory but not activated by the relevant cue, in spite of experiencing it, so that one simply fails to perform the intended step. (For example, as I write this, I realise that I have failed to phone someone, as I intended, as soon as I reached my office today. On the other hand, I did remember today, as I failed to yesterday, my intention to pick up some conkers for my son when I passed the horse-chestnut tree near my office.) Lost intentions must surely be the most frequent class of cognitive failure, and have indeed spawned a whole area of research on "prospective memory" or "memory for intentions" (Brandimonte, Einstein, & McDaniel, in press; Ellis, 1988; Kvavilashvili, 1992).

Detached intentions and perceptual confusions

Reason (1984) uses the term "detached intention" to refer to the case where a prospective trigger is activated by the wrong cue. An example given is crossing the room with the intention of shutting the window, but shutting a cupboard door instead. However, this class of errors is hard to distinguish from the case of a perceptual confusion, where appropriate task-set is activated, and in a timely manner, but action is triggered by an object that only partially matches the appropriate input. Is this a control failure? Identifying objects is the job of a low-level perceptual module, not the control processes that bring that module "into play". However, instructing the perceptual identification module how loose a criterion to adopt for identification would seem to be a control function, so the error may be an "indirect control error", although it might equally be the sort of perceptual confusion that sometimes occurs even when the criterion is properly set.

"Program counter failures"

These occur especially when a relatively complex sequence of steps with iterated elements is required, and one loses track of where one is in the intended iteration. The most obvious example is where one intends to do something a set number of times (e.g. put five teaspoons of tea into the teapot), and loses count of how many one has done. I am not asserting here that counting is, per se, a control function. Rather control processes initiate the (automated) process of counting, to keep track of the completion of another process (tea transfer) that is cyclic. The error might arise either through failure to count correctly (not a control error per se) or, more likely, a loss of co-ordination between counting and the cyclic process being counted. More generally, whenever we have a multi-step task, there is the possibility of errors arising through omission of steps, inappropriate repetition of steps, and failure to return to the appropriate step after an interruption.

Dissociations between formulation and execution of intentions

The case of following instructions is an interesting one. There is clearly a gulf between acquiescing in the intention to obey some instructions and putting that intention into effect. An example from Reason's (1984) collection: "I was putting cutlery away in the drawer when my wife asked me to leave it out as she wanted to use it. I heard her, agreed, and yet continued to put the cutlery away." The intuition here is that it is possible to form an appropriate task-plan, have the intention of carrying it out, but somehow fail to send the instructions for reconfiguring task-set to wherever they need to be sent to be acted on: a distinction, perhaps, between conscious intentions, and effective intentions. One may lie in bed intending to get up, but until one "really tries" one has not effectively intended.

Overintrusive control/monitoring

Another common intuition is that errors can occur through a surfeit of executive control, as well as a lack of it. To take one of many possible examples from the self-improvement literature, a book by Galwey (1976) teaches tennis players strategies designed to occupy their attention by focusing it on some feature of the situation that will *orient* their sensory systems appropriately (e.g. concentrating on the exact appearance of the ball) while simultaneously distracting them from attempting to assume control over the perceptuo-motor reactions that will result in *hitting* the ball. The basic intuition underlying such advice seems sound: low-level perceptuo-motor control processes are specialised to do things like track salient parameters of target trajectories, control multijointed limbs, and learn the mapping between these; high-level general-purpose problem-solving procedures are not good at getting these things done. If general-purpose procedures try to take over the tasks of specialised procedures, rather than facilitating their operations, disaster is likely to ensue.

It is worth drawing attention to a common theme running through many types of action error: the tendency of some inappropriate task-set to get in the way is a function of the *frequency* and *recency* with which it has been motivated. The better-practised a task, the more likely it is to intrude: i.e. it is habitual actions that intrude. The more recently one has exercised a task-set, the more likely it is to intrude. Subjects in Reason's (1984) extended diary study were asked to rate the "wrong action" they had performed on a scale of 1 (not performed for a long time) to 7 (performed very recently). They were also asked how often they engaged in this other activity, from 1 (hardly at all) to 7 (very often). In both cases, over 80% of errors scored 6 or 7.

The natural history of action errors is an attractive kind of evidence. Such errors graphically illustrate, in a way that resonates with our own experience, the failure of control functions, and thus highlight the critical role these functions must play when our performance of these everyday tasks is error-free. But it must be obvious that there are serious limitations to what we can learn from such errors. They are an intrinsically qualitative form of data, for which the natural mode of interpretation is essentially post-hoc. Certainly, we can classify and count, and test predictions from theories about the frequencies (as has been widely done for speech errors). But classification is not a theory-neutral activity, and even the recording of errors may be influenced by implicit theories. Perhaps more limiting, it is not clear that further collection of errors will turn up any novel kinds, rather than more graphic or amusing instances of familiar kinds. Science usually starts with natural history, but then proceeds to experimental manipulation. So shall we. But first we look at the effects of Nature's uncontrolled manipulations of the integrity of the system.

PATHOLOGICAL FAILURES OF CONTROL
RESULTING FROM BRAIN DAMAGE

At a neurological hospital in London, a patient LE is brought into a room, and introduced to a psychologist who is going to give him some tests. LE sits at a desk opposite her. On either side of the desk is an array of common objects: a pen, an electric plug, a screwdriver, a pack of cards, a candle, a box of matches, and so on. The psychologist makes conversation pleasantly for a few minutes with LE, who appears in no way confused or demented. She then embarks on a short clinical interview, followed by a set of standard verbal tests in which she gets LE to name pictures, define proverbs, repeat short lists of digits, sort cards and so on. At no point does either the psychologist or LE make any reference to the objects on either side of the desk. However, while being tested, the patient on 13 different occasions picks up one of the objects and performs a set of coherent actions related to its normal use. For example, he twice picks up the candle, checks to see if there are matches, and, finding them, uses them to light the candle; he unscrews the electric plug with the screwdriver (Shallice, Burgess, Schon, & Baxter, 1989).

Did LE simply misunderstand the social demands of the situation, thinking that the objects were there for him to demonstrate his prowess with them? Was he just bored and fidgety? These explanations seem inadequate. The psychologist clearly succeeded in engaging the patient in the various procedures required for the interview and tests. The objects were off to the side of the desk, unmentioned by either party. These odd "utilisation behaviours" (first reported by Lhermitte, 1983), with their strange mixture of appropriateness (to the object) and inappropriateness (to the situation), did not occur only when the conversation flagged, or there was a pause in the testing. Right in the middle of trying to explain the meaning of a proverb, LE picked up the pack of cards and dealt four to the psychologist and four to himself. Nor are these behaviours restricted to the testing situation. Left to his own devices at home, LE makes tea every time he comes across a teabag, and spends much of his time turning taps and lights on and off, opening and closing doors, and so on. LE is suffering from damage to his frontal lobes, and it looks as if the damage has resulted in the inability to inhibit action patterns (stored presumably in an intact part of his brain) from being released or triggered by the sight of the objects with which they are habitually associated.

Utilisation behaviour is but one of many indications that damage to the frontal lobes may result in selective impairments not in any one domain of cognitive activity or behaviour, but in the organisation, control, and monitoring of the whole range of cognitive skills (see reviews by: Duncan, 1986; Shallice, 1982, 1988; Shallice & Burgess, 1991). The function of the frontal lobes was sufficiently mysterious until a few decades ago that some authorities regarded them as essentially "silent". However, Bianchi (1922) observed that experimental monkeys with large frontal lesions exhibited disorganised, fragmentary, and repetitive sequences of action which seemed either purposeless, or terminated short of their apparent goals. And since the 19th century many neurologists have observed clinically that human patients with massive frontal lesions seemed incapable of planned goal-directed behaviour, were distractible, or impaired in dealing with complex situations, and sometimes lacking in spontaneous actions. Luria (1966, p.247) summarises these observations as follows:

> These patients were found to preserve all types of sensation, to have no sign of disturbance of movement, and to have no disturbances of gnosis, praxis and speech; nevertheless, their complex psychological activity was grossly impaired. They were unable to produce stable plans and became inactive and aspontaneous. They could respond to ordinary questions or perform habitual actions, but they were quite unable to carry out complex, purposive and goal directed actions. They were unable to evaluate their attempts, they were not critical of their behaviour, and could not control their actions; they continued to perform automatic actions which had long ceased to be meaningful, without any attempt at correction. They were no longer concerned about their failure, they were hesitant and indecisive, and most frequently of all, they became indifferent or they exhibited features of euphoria, as a result of the loss of their critical awareness of their behaviour.

Here are some examples from Luria's (1966) own clinical observations, to give the flavour of the combination of domain-specific competence with loss of control over cognitive or overt activity:

(i) A patient goes to the station to catch a particular train, and gets on the first one that happens to arrive, though it is going in the opposite direction.

(ii) A patient, seeing a button used to summon a nurse, presses it, but then, when the nurse appears, has nothing to say to her.

(iii) A patient is planing a piece of wood; he goes on "inertly" planing until not only is there nothing left of the piece of wood but he is planing the bench beneath.

(iv) A patient making a speech repeats part of it over and over again.

(v) A patient is asked to press a button each time he hears a tap or a light flashes. He soon ceases to make the necessary movements but says, each time the signal occurs, "I must press", without doing so.

(vi) A patient is asked to draw a square. He does so, but then writes in the centre of the square a word associated with something said in a nearby conversation in the ward

(vii) A patient is asked to signed his name and does so. He is now asked to draw a figure, but instead signs his name again.

Luria's summary of the classical observations, and these examples, read in juxtaposition to the list of control functions I identified earlier, are suggestive. However, we must consider the possibility that these patients were globally intellectually impaired. Were they, to be blunt, just pathologically stupid, confused, and muddled? It seems not. As Hebb and Penfield (1940) first demonstrated and others have since confirmed, many frontal patients are not drastically impaired on conventional measures of IQ, at least those that test rather routine skills. It is insufficient to characterise the "frontal syndrome" as a global intellectual impairment. Indeed, there are cases described in the literature who are in some ways unusually competent intellectually. For example, Eslinger and Damasio (1985) describe a case (EVR), with frontal damage caused by a tumour and its removal, whose IQ was greater than 130, and who performed well on a wide variety of tests, but whose behaviour in everyday life became completely disorganised and indecisive. For example, consideration of which restaurant to go to could take hours, as EVR discussed every conceivable feature of the candidates, even visiting several to see how busy they were, and even then did not reach a decision. Not surprisingly, he was unemployable, and had great difficulty with the management of his everyday life. As

Luria concluded, and many others have agreed, albeit with many terminological variants, frontal patients as a group appear specifically impaired in the programming, initiation, regulation, and monitoring of voluntary mental and behavioural activity, both overt and covert.

Luria's analysis depended heavily on description of single cases whose pathology was often not well described—they may have had more extensive than merely frontal lesions. He also relied heavily on a rather intuitive interpretation of performance in informal and ad hoc tests. More recent work has elaborated his insights through the development of a more formal array of tests in which frontal patients manifest what appear to be deficits in control functions. Let us consider some of the deficits reported in frontal patients in a slightly more analytic way:

Failures of task-set at the "single-step" level

Perseveration, or behavioural rigidity

Clinically this is manifest in the patient persisting in a task-set, although the instruction is changed, as in example (vi) given earlier. The classic test used to bring out this feature of frontal behaviour is the Wisconsin card-sorting test, in which the subject is given a pack of cards on each of which there are between one and four shapes of a particular colour. The patient is asked to place them into piles according to a rule which he must infer from the tester saying "right" or "wrong". After a few trials during which the experimenter reinforces whichever hypothesis the subject happens to adopt first (e.g. classify by colour) the experimenter adopts a different rule (e.g. sort by shape). Frontal patients typically exhibit difficulty in abandoning the first rule in favour of another (Milner, 1963). Owen et al. (1991) have developed a computerised classification test in which frontal patients show difficulty in shifting to classification on the basis of a previously irrelevant dimension (an "extradimensional shift"), although they are not impaired if they must shift to classification on the basis of a new rule based on the same dimension (an "intradimensional shift"). However, both these tasks are quite complex, requiring not only an ability to change the rule for sorting, but also the ability to infer that the rule has changed and what the new one might be.

Luria, Pribram, and Homskaya (1964) describe some simpler cases of perseveration, where a patient goes on performing some simple action inappropriately: asked to shake hands three times, a patient shook hands many times; asked to repeat a sequence of words or movements, the patient repeated the first item over and over again. After a switch of tasks, elements of the previous task may intrude into performance of the new task. For example, asked to draw a cross, then a circle, then a square, a patient complied, but added a cross inside the circle and square (Goldberg & Tucker, 1979).

Failures of voluntary initiation

As well as some patients exhibiting failures to inhibit inappropriate actions, there are patients who fail to initiate appropriate actions, as indicated by Luria's mention (quoted earlier) of patients becoming "inactive" and "aspontaneous". Damasio and Van Hoesen (1983) describe a stroke patient J, with medial frontal damage, who initially lay immobile but alert, producing no spontaneous speech or replies to questions, but who could repeat words and sentences without impairment of articulation and intonation. Although conversational and spontaneous speech recovered, her speech output continued to suggest that her difficulty lay in the lack of a "drive" to speak, not in formulating or articulating the utterance: the patient later described herself as having been able to follow conversations even during the early post-stroke days, but having no "will" to reply to questions. Difficulty in initiating movement is of course a primary symptom of Parkinson's disease, in which projections from the nigrostriatum to dorso-lateral prefrontal cortex degenerate. Parkinsonian patients exhibit some of the same control impairments as patients with other sources of frontal damage, such as a difficulty with extradimensional shifts (Owen et al., 1992).

Capture

Utilisation behaviour, as illustrated earlier, is essentially the pathological analogue of capture errors in normal subjects. The patient loses the ability to overcome the power of a stimulus to evoke a habitual task-set associated with it—a weakening of endogenous relative to exogenous control[5].

Distractibility

Frontal patients are frequently said to be distractible, i.e. unable to control the direction of focal attention. For example, Knight, Hillyard, Woods, and Neville (1981) found that frontal patients were impaired in their ability to detect occasional target signals (longer beeps) among distractors (shorter beeps) in the presence of similar distracting signals in the other ear, and, moreover, they did not show the normal augmentation of the auditory evoked response to signals in the (supposedly) attended ear. Appropriate attentional orienting is one of the components of adopting a task-set. The failure to override the tendency to orient attention to signals in irrelevant channels is another sign of the loss of endogenous relative to exogenous control.

Dissociation between verbally acknowledged intentions and action
Luria's illustrations included a case of a patient acknowledging an intention to act verbally, but failing to carry it out. We may also see patients (apparently) expressing an intention not to act, but acting all the same. For example, Baddeley's (1986) patient, RJ, when asked to measure out a piece of string in order to cut it later, immediately started to cut, and continued to do so when told not to, meanwhile remarking "Yes, I know I'm not to cut it." In these cases the intention appears to be present, but ineffective, and the patients detect the discrepancy. This is of course also true of attempts by normal subjects to carry out (or prevent) movements that they cannot in fact control. What is strange about the frontal patient, is that these are actions of which they appear motorically capable, and, as Duncan, (1986) points out, that they acknowledge a failure of performance without any apparent attempt to improve it. Here the patient appears to be monitoring their intentions and their performance, but the intention is ineffective, and there is no troubleshooting. In many other cases, frontal patients appear simply unaware of their errors (Luria, 1966) as if monitoring too has failed.

Failures in the co-ordination of multi-step tasks

Sequencing
When frontal patients perform even familiar multi-step tasks, we may see a breakdown in the sequencing of the steps. Schwartz et al. (1991) conducted a careful analysis of the sequence in which a patient performed elements of the task of making coffee (moving the instant coffee grounds to the cup, shaking the sugar packet, opening the cream container, etc) or brushing his teeth (wetting the brush, spreading the toothpaste, spitting, etc). Many elements were performed out of sequence, especially early in the recovery period. For example, the patient on several occasions drank before adding anything to the hot water, or after adding the coffee grounds but before adding the milk and sugar. When brushing his teeth he might get locked into a cycle of repetitive actions involving water use—adjusting the tap, inserting the brush or the cup into the water stream—or repeated brushing when he had already completed the cycle. Hence, even for well-practised sequences, it seems that some control mechanism, apparently impaired in this patient, is needed to make and monitor transitions between elements of the sequence.

Goal-maintenance

In his review of frontal lobe damage, Duncan (1986) stresses the importance of setting up and using a list of goals to direct the choice of actions. The behaviour of frontal patients in complex tasks frequently exhibits derailments or insertions of irrelevant activity, suggesting that goals (or their ability to direct the choice of actions) have been lost. For example, a patient asked to recall a short story may go off into a lengthy account of unrelated material. Or, the patient may interrupt performance of a task to engage the experimenter in conversation (Luria, 1966).

Planning

Problem-solving tasks require the subject to work towards a goal state via an unknown path, developing appropriate subgoals, evaluating progress, and revising the subgoals accordingly. This involves the sequential planning, monitoring, and troubleshooting functions. Although it is frequently said that frontal patients are disorganised in their "planning", it is quite hard to get a good measure of it. MacCarthy and Shallice (reported in Shallice, 1982) devised a simplified version of the Tower of Hanoi problem called the "Tower of London", in which a red, a green, and a blue ring are placed on three rods in some initial configuration, and the task is to move one ring at a time onto a different rod, in such a way as to end up in a specified goal configuration. The number of moves required to reach the goal state was substantially increased in a group with left anterior lesions. These patients did not, however, show any deficit in the "Block Design" subtest of the Wechsler Adult Intelligence Scale, which requires mere reproduction of a pattern of blocks, and hence calls on similar spatial and perceptuo-motor, but not planning, skills. Owen et al. (1992) have obtained a similar result with a computerised version of the Tower of London test. Shallice and Burgess (1993) have tested the performance of three frontal patients given a "multiple errands" task, in which they had to achieve certain goals in a shopping centre: e.g. buy a lettuce, find out four pieces of information, write them on a postcard and post it. The patients performed very much worse than controls, with many more inefficient actions, and much "rule-breaking" (e.g. failure to pay for a newspaper). Similar results were obtained in laboratory experiments involving the carrying out of multiple tasks.

Setting and responding to prospective memory triggers

Duncan et al. (in press) had subjects monitoring two streams of random letters and digits, one to the left and one to the right of fixation. They were instructed to begin by repeating out loud any letters that appeared on one side (sometimes the left, sometimes the right). However, after 10 pairs of characters a central symbol appeared, "+" if they were now to repeat digits on the right side, "-" if on the left, followed by three more pairs. Even normal subjects tended to exhibit what Duncan et al. call "goal neglect", failing to switch sides when the cue occurred, especially early in practice, although their later performance or responses to questions often showed that they had understood and could remember the rule. A group of frontal patients showed normal performance on the initial part of the sequence, but a greatly enhanced frequency of goal neglect.

In partitioning these various fragments of data under separate sub-headings, I am of course guilty of two kinds of over-simplification. The various deficits I have listed are not independent, and could doubtless be regrouped under different headings, depending on the theoretical prejudices of the reviewer, as is indeed illustrated in the various papers cited. My purpose has been to give the reader a feeling for the way in which the deficits observed in frontal patients fall under the general heading of "deficits of control", and suggest some of the component functions of "control". The second kind of simplification is to refer to frontal patients as if they were homogeneous in both the locus of their brain damage, and their behavioural symptoms. Of course, they are not. The frontal lobes are large structures, and many different kinds of damage are possible. Recent years have seen the beginnings of fractionation of frontal disorders, and the correlation of different kinds of symptom with anatomical locus (Shallice & Burgess, 1991). For example, Shallice and Burgess's (1993) three patients who are grossly disordered on the "shopping" task, were normal on the Wisconsin card-sorting, and the word fluency test. And EVR, whose real-life decision-making was so disastrously impaired, performed normally on tests such as the Wisconsin card-sorting test, used as diagnostic of executive dysfunction.

EXPERIMENTAL STUDIES OF TASK-SET

Consider the following scenario. A volunteer subject arrives in my laboratory to participate in a typical experiment on word recognition. He is seated in front of a computer screen, a microphone is placed near his mouth, and the experimenter says to him something like the following: "On each trial, there will be a warning beep, and then a word will appear at the centre of the screen. Please read that word aloud as quickly as you can while avoiding errors. Please try to speak clearly and without hesitating or making other noises, so that the equipment can accurately time the moment you begin to speak. When you have responded, the display will disappear, and then another trial will begin after a couple of seconds. There are 30 trials in a block, and the first block is for practice. Ready?". The subject says: "Er, yes, I suppose so", the experimenter touches a key on her keyboard, and then the sequence of trials begins. The subject's first responses are a little hesitant, though accurate. By the middle of the practice block the subject is responding confidently and accurately with a naming latency of around 500msec. Although his performance will improve somewhat through the remaining blocks he will not get a lot faster.

After a dozen blocks of this, and a short rest, the experimenter gives the subject some more instructions. She says: "The rest of the experiment is similar to what you've been doing so far. But instead of naming the word, I want you to press this key with your right index finger if the word describes something that is alive (a person, or an animal, or plant) and this other button if it describes an inanimate object." Again the subject's responses are quite slow on the first few trials, as he gets an idea of what kinds of words he is going to encounter and struggles to remember which key is which, but by the end of the practice block, his responses are fast, confident, and accurate, and although his performance steadily improves thereafter, there are no dramatic or qualitative changes.

This scenario may seem mundane in comparison to the anecdotes of weird pathological failures of control we have already considered, but it is no less rich in the central theme of our mystery, even though the purpose of this experiment has nothing to do with control processes. First, it is clear that, given exactly the same stimulus—a word displayed in the centre of the screen—our subject can readily "set" himself to produce two quite different responses. How? Second we can convey to him what "set" we want him to adopt with a few well-chosen sentences. Third, some experience—of what the words will be like, of how it will feel to speak into the microphone, or to press the keys—seems to be necessary before the performance appears fluent: what is happening in the subject's head during those first few trials? Fourth, everyone has read aloud on numerous occasions ever since childhood. So it is perhaps not surprising to find the subject adapting quickly to the performance of this familiar task in a somewhat novel context. But the inanimate/animate classification task is quite unfamiliar. However the subject is generally able to suppress any tendency to go on naming the words (although we should not be surprised if he did so once or twice, saying "Whoops, I forgot what I was supposed to be doing"). He is able to organise his mind to accomplish this new task effectively and fluently with very little practice.

One part of adopting a "task-set" is getting the right set of "processing modules" linked together. To name an object, for example, we need to chain together low-level sensory analysis of the retinal image ["sensory analysis"] to analysis of object attributes ["structural analysis"], followed by matching of the structural attributes to a stored representation of the object categories we know ["recognition"], followed by retrieval of the learned sound pattern of the object's name ["phonological retrieval"] followed by encoding of this pattern as a sequence of articulatory gestures ["articulatory programming"], followed by execution of programmed gestures ["articulation"] (cf Bruce's introductory analysis of face recognition). Some components of this chain may be permanently connected; many theorists believe, for example, that we *automatically* process visual input to the level of object recognition, regardless of what we are trying to do. At some point in the chain, however, the transmission of information from one module to the next is *optional*, and it is the exercise of this option that is required to adopt a task-set. For example, instead of naming the object, we could set ourselves to count the number of syllables in the word's name (e.g. saying "three" to a picture of an elephant). This would require the same chain of processes up to "phonological retrieval", but then instead of articulating the retrieved pattern, we would have to chain to a process of counting the syllables in the retrieved pattern, which would generate the identity of the number of syllables, followed by the retrieval of the name of the number, and then as before. These two different organisations of the same processes are clearly competing task-sets: they could not be realised simultaneously, because they use the same processes in different ways (although we could set up yet another organisation of processes that would *first* name the object and *then* the number of syllables). The chain of modules required to point to the object, rather than naming it, would begin with the same process of sensory analysis as naming, but then involve a completely separate set of processes (spatial analysis, programming of an arm movement, execution of the arm movement). Unless for some reason the products of early sensory analysis could not be transmitted both to "structural analysis" and to "spatial analysis" simultaneously (unlikely—as these appear to be two major modes of analysis in visual cortex), or unless both tasks required some other common process we have not identified yet (e.g. outcome monitoring?), there is no reason to think of the task-sets for naming and pointing as being in competition: indeed it may well be possible to perform them simultaneously without interference.

Hence adopting a task-set involves, in part, getting the right subset of processing modules from the available repertoire linked together (or, better, *enabling* the existing links between them, and disabling the links to others). But that is not all. We must also "tune" each processing module so that it performs the right mapping between its inputs and its outputs. For example, we can get people to categorise objects in innumerable ways by pressing one of two keys: big/small, edible/inedible, animate/inanimate, etc. Each requires the retrieval of semantic properties to be chained, via a classification, to the same arbitrary response category (e.g. left-index finger, right-index finger), but different rules for mapping semantic space into the two response categories. Two different mappings of this kind specify competing task-sets: we must perform one or the other, although we could also set ourselves to respond to combinations of attributes (e.g. if animate and edible, press the left key, otherwise the right key).

To some extent it is a matter of choice which task-set we adopt at any moment: this is endogenous control. However, we have also seen, in the evidence from pathological failures of control reviewed earlier, that well-practised task-sets can under some conditions be evoked by stimuli. I will conclude the chapter by looking at some experimental paradigms studied in the cognitive laboratory in which issues of control arise, giving some prominence to the idea that, even in normal subjects, exogenous control of task-set is a major factor in determining performance.

Suppressing an unwanted task-set: The Stroop effect

Every psychology student learns about the Stroop effect: subjects take much longer to name the colour in which an incongruent colour word is printed (e.g. RED printed in green ink) than to name the colour of a patch of colour (Stroop, 1935). It appears that the word is involuntarily read, and the retrieval of a colour name or meaning conflicting with that of the ink interferes somehow with the naming of the ink colour. Stroop also compared the naming of words printed in conflicting colours with the naming of words printed in black. He found, as have most subsequent experimenters, no interference to speak of—i.e. no "reverse Stroop" effect, as it is called—unless he gave the subject a great deal of practice at colour naming first.

The Stroop effect is large and robust, as is the asymmetry between the Stroop effect and the small or non-existent reverse Stroop effect. The effect has been very extensively studied and exploited: there are more than 700 studies in the literature according to a recent comprehensive review by MacLeod (1991). Many analogues to the Stroop effect involving stimulus dimensions other than colour have been reported and studied in their own right. For example:

- If one must report the number of characters in a display (e.g. of six 7s), there is interference if the character is a digit whose value is different from the number of characters, but little interference of number with value-naming (Morton, 1969)
- If one must name a pictured object, there is interference if, superimposed on the picture, is the name of a different object. Again, although there may be a small effect of an interfering picture on word-naming, the interference is markedly asymmetric (Glaser & Dungelhoff, 1984)

In each case, there exist pre-established stimulus-response (S–R) mappings between two attributes of a single stimulus and the same set of responses, one mediated by reading, the other not. For incongruent stimuli, the two S–R mappings specify different responses. As subjects can usually produce the correct name, it is clearly possible for the subject to suppress the irrelevant S–R mapping to some degree. On the other hand, the presence of interference indicates that it is impossible for the subject to suppress reading completely.

Most theorists have analysed Stroop interference in terms of interference between two responses (or response tendencies) associated with the same input. For example, when the letters RED appear, coloured green, the letters activate a well-learned association between that spelling pattern and a tendency to say "red" (or at least to retrieve that meaning or phonological form), whereas the green colour activates a learned tendency to say "green" (ditto). These response tendencies compete. Theorists have tended to focus on why this competition occurs in the first place, and its asymmetry, rather than on how it gets resolved.

One suggestion was that, because of differential practice at reading and colour naming, activation of the colour-name is intrinsically *slower* than that of the word-name, so that the name of the word tends to become available first (e.g. Morton & Chambers, 1973). This "relative speed" hypothesis seems to have been decisively disposed of by Glaser's demonstrations (Glaser & Glaser, 1982; Glaser & Dungelhoff, 1984) that the asymmetry of the interference cannot be reversed by providing several hundred msec preview of the colour—i.e. giving activation of the colour-name a head start. Others have argued that extensive practice has rendered the link between orthographic pattern and naming response *automatic* so that, unlike the link between a colour and its name, it cannot be disabled (e.g. Posner & Snyder, 1975) However, automaticity appears to be not an all-or-none matter, but one of degree. MacLeod and Dunbar (1988) taught subjects to produce colour-names in response to arbitrary shapes, and found that, early in practice, ink colour produced substantial interference with shape-naming. However, after very extensive practice at shape-naming, the interference reversed: shapes with conflicting colour names interfered with colour-naming, but not vice-versa. These findings suggest replacing the dichotomy of automatic versus controlled with a continuous variable of associative *strength*. Cohen, Dunbar, and McClelland (1990) have captured this interaction between learning and performance in a simple connectionist network model for the Stroop effect, depicted in Fig. 4.2.

The S–R mapping for the colour-naming task is modelled as feedforward connections from the colour input units, via a set of intermediate "hidden" units, to the response units. The S–R mapping for the word-naming task is modelled as feedforward connections from the word input units, via a separate set of hidden units, to the same

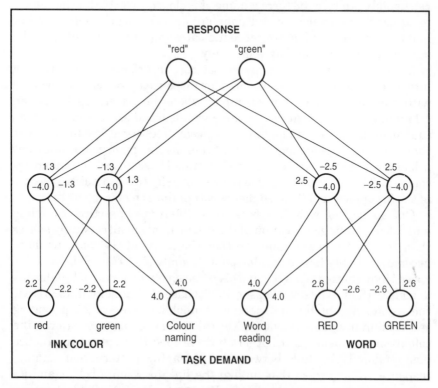

FIG. 4.2.   Cohen et al.'s network for Stroop tasks, showing the connection strengths (next to the connections) and the biases (inside the hidden units) after 10 times as much training on the word-reading task as on the colour-naming task. Reproduced from Cohen et al. (1990) by permission. © 1990, American Psychological Association.

response units. There are also task input units, connected to both sets of hidden units, and used to bias the performance of the whole network towards one S–R mapping rather than the other. A pattern of activation over the input units is propagated forwards through the network, as a function of the connection weights; a response occurs when the activation of one of the output units reaches a response threshold. The connection weights are modified as a result of practice using the backpropagation algorithm. The figure shows the weights on the connections after a training regime in which the network "experiences" 10 times as many training trials on the word-naming task than on the colour-naming task, after which the "latency" of the network was shorter for word-naming than for colour-naming, and there was marked Stroop interference, but no reverse Stroop effect.

In this simple associative model, the switching between task-sets would be modelled as pre-activation of the relevant task-node, which essentially modulates the relative gain of the two sets of S–R connections. Making the task required part of the external "input" in this simplified way is, of course, really only a placeholder for a proper account of what a task-set is and how it gets activated.

However, there are aspects of Stroop interference that are not adequately explained by competition between two S-R associations as a function of their strength. Interference with colour-naming is caused by the presence in the stimulus of not only a colour word, but any familiar word (Klein, 1964): it takes longer to name the ink colour of HAPPY, than of a visually equivalent string such as XXXXX. Now, if this is due to competition between two S–R associations as a function of their strength, we should expect to find that a word we have frequently read (MOTHER) would cause more interference than a rare word (LIMBER) and more still than a pronounceable non-word never seen before (MILBER), as the strengths of the associations should be ordered in this way. But Taylor, Murphy, and I recently found that a high-frequency word produced no more interference with colour-naming than a low-frequency word[6], and a word no more interference than a pseudoword, relative to a visually equivalent string of hieroglyphs. However, interference was greater for pronounceable nonwords than for unpronounceable letter strings (e.g. BGDXJR) than for repeated letter strings (e.g. RRRRRR) than for strings of non-alphanumeric characters (e.g. #&$£@+), matched for length. We concluded that it is not interference from the specific association between a letter string and its name/meaning that caused the effect. Rather, the rapid detection of "wordlikeness" in the stimulus automatically activates the task-set of reading, and it is the interference between whole task-sets rather than between stimulus-specific S–R mappings that causes the interference.

Of course, when the words are also colour names, additional interference may result from item-specific competition.

Thus I suggest that Stroop interference arises not merely from competition between the responses associated with a given stimulus, biased by the task-set adopted in advance (as in Cohen et al.'s model), but from competition between the *task-sets* evoked by the present and recent stimuli.

Control difficulties in dual task performance

There has been a great deal of research on the performance of simultaneous tasks. Good reviews are available from Allport (1980a), Hirst (1986), Neumann (1987), and Pashler (1993). I will touch on two strands of this research to make the point that control functions are an important limitation on our ability to combine tasks.

Complex tasks in combination

In his book *Perception and communication*, the late Donald Broadbent (1958) offered an influential account of why it is that we have difficulty comprehending, remembering, or being aware of two simultaneous verbal messages, although we can readily attend to one message and ignore the other (provided the sources are distinct in physical features such as location or voice). He proposed that various different higher-level processes—such as pattern recognition, decision-making, initiation of voluntary responses, and access to conscious awareness—all require the services of the same "central processor" (Broadbent, 1984), and that this processor can only serve only one input stream at a time. The central processor is, he and others assumed, the major bottleneck when we try to combine two tasks. The only way that two tasks requiring these high-level functions can be performed concurrently is to switch the central processor between them (much as, although much slower than, the central processor of a time-sharing computer is switched between running the programs of multiple users).

However, further research on dual task performance has made it hard to sustain this concept of a universal central bottleneck. A good example is provided by an experiment by Allport, Antonis, and Reynolds (1972), who found that undergraduate music students could, after only a few minutes of practice, sight-read piano pieces (of Grade IV standard in the Associated Boards scheme) simultaneously with shadowing (i.e. repeating) a spoken passage (from a textbook on Old Norse), with both the shadowing and the sight-reading performance no worse than when performing each task alone. Nor was there any difference in the temporal distribution of shadowing responses with and without concurrent sight-reading. Nor did a more difficult prose passage increase sight-reading errors, or a more difficult piano piece increase shadowing errors. Provided that we accept that the sight-reading task is no less demanding of "high-level" processes than the shadowing task, this result would appear incompatible with a "central processor" bottleneck[7].

Allport et al.'s conclusion was that, provided two tasks require different domain-specific modules for perceptual analysis, response output, and translation between them, and the appropriate linkages between modules are reasonably well practised, the two information streams can be routed simultaneously through the system without adverse interactions between them. It is only when the tasks compete for the same module(s) that, if the capacity limits of that module would otherwise be exceeded, switching or sharing of that module between tasks may be needed, leading to interference. The responsibility for setting up the chains of processes required for each task and keeping the two chains sufficiently insulated from each other falls to executive processes. Even when two tasks call on non-overlapping resources, executive processes may have difficulty preventing cross-talk between the streams. For example, in the early stages of practice, Allport et al. noticed a tendency for their piano-players' musical rhythm to entrain to their speech rhythm, or vice versa, as if there were leakage between timekeepers for the two tasks. Moreover, while each task was going smoothly, there was no sign of interference with the other, but if the subject made an error in one task, this tended to cause transient interference in the other. This can be attributed to executive control processes diverting resources briefly to troubleshoot the error.

For some pairs of tasks, "cross-talk"—the tendency for codes created by one task to influence the computation of output for the other—is the major problem. For example Navon and Miller (1987) found that when subjects must monitor one source for one target category (e.g. a city name), responding with the left hand, and another source for a different target category (e.g. a boy's name), responding with the right hand, there was extra interference when the "city" channel contained a girl's name, or the "boy's name" channel a state or country name: they called this "outcome conflict". I will discuss something similar later in the context of switching successively between tasks.

Hence the view advocated by theorists such as Allport (1989), McLeod, (1977, 1978) Navon, (1985), and Neumann (1987), is that the simultaneous performance of tasks is limited not by their demand on a central general-purpose processor, but by two other factors, in interaction: (i) the degree to which the two tasks compete for the same domain-specific processes, and (ii) the load on executive processes that schedule access to shared resources, maintain the connectivity between modules so as to minimise cross-talk between unshared resources, monitor and regulate progress within each task, and troubleshoot in case of task breakdown. However, it must be admitted that, although executive processes have come to play an increasingly important role in theoretical accounts of dual task interference, so far it has been largely by default: we tend to appeal rather non-specifically to executive processes to explain that component of interference for which we cannot find an account in terms of specific bottlenecks.

The psychological refractory period

A more microscopic analysis of interactions between concurrent tasks is the focus of a tradition of experimentation initiated by Welford (1952) and usually called the *psychological refractory period* (PRP) paradigm (see Pashler, 1993, for a review). The PRP procedure involves discrete trials, on each of which two stimuli are presented with their onsets separated by a short interval, the *stimulus onset asynchrony* (SOA). Each stimulus requires a rapid response. For example, one might have to press one of three buttons corresponding to the identity of a visually presented letter, followed by a vocal response ("high" or "low") to one of two tones (Pashler, 1990). The focus of this research is how the RT to each stimulus is determined by the SOA. Pashler's experiment provides a typical result. As the SOA was decreased from 700msec to 100msec, RT to the first stimulus remained roughly constant, while RT to the second stimulus increased from about 600 to about 800msec. Clearly the more the RTs overlapped, the more the second response was delayed. This suggests that there is a bottleneck in the system, and (some component of) the processing of the second stimulus had to wait until (some component of) the processing of the first was completed.

The main focus of theoretical dispute has been the locus of the bottleneck. It seems clear that the bottleneck is "central", i.e. not located in perceptual or motor processes, because the effect is not eliminated when the stimuli or responses are in different modalities, as is shown by Pashler's (1990) data. Pashler (1993), like Welford (1952) and many others in between, has argued that the bottleneck is in a process of *response selection* called on by both tasks. Once the second stimulus has been identified, it must wait until this process has been cleared by the first stimulus. This conclusion is compatible with the observation that factors believed to influence the duration of the response selection process have effects on RT for the second task roughly additive with the PRP effect. One difficulty with Pashler's theory is that other factors standardly thought to influence response selection have been shown to have effects markedly non-additive with the PRP effect. For example, most theorists would expect that increasing the number of S–R pairs for the second task would increase the duration of the response-selection process for the second task. However Hawkins, Rodriguez, and Reicher (1979) found that when the number of S–R pairings for the second task was increased from two to eight, this had a large effect at long SOAs but a smaller effect as the SOA was reduced. This suggests that the response selection process *precedes* the bottleneck, so that at short SOAs the effect of number of pairings on the time to complete response selection was absorbed in the "dead" time during which Task 2 waited for access to a subsequent bottleneck. Some have indeed argued that the bottleneck is subsequent to response selection, in a movement-initiation process (Keele & Neill, 1978). Other results are hard to reconcile with either theory.

These effects are intricate, and I do not propose to dwell on them. My main purpose is rather to draw attention to the surprising fact that, even though the PRP paradigm clearly requires the coordination close in time of two different tasks, usually accompanied by instructions to respond first to the stimulus that arrives first, much of the theoretical debate has made no reference to control processes. The implicit assumption seems to be that one can set oneself concurrently to perform two quite different tasks just as easily as one can set oneself to perform one; the only problem in that the use of Mechanism X by the first task postpones its use by the second task, and only the identity of X is disputed: is it a specific process like response selection or movement initiation, or a limited-capacity pool of processing capacity (Kahneman, 1973)? In a recent critical review, Allport (1993, p.205) makes essentially this point:

> Is the bottleneck to be thought of as a cause of attentional selectivity (as traditionally supposed) or, on the contrary, can PRP response-postponement effects be understood as the consequence of other, coordinative processes involved in maintaining the coherence of purposeful action? Control processes are of course needed to implement the organism's temporary commitment to, or "engagement" in, a particular cognitive task and to protect ongoing action choices (also ongoing endogenous memory search) from interruption or capture by potentially related, but task-irrelevant, sources of information.

Happily, this may be one of those rare moments in the history of research on a well-worked paradigm when a significant theoretical breakthrough is at hand. In recent work, Meyer and Kieras (1994a,b) have developed a production-system simulation of human information processing architecture called EPIC (for Executive Process, Interactive Control), and applied it successfully to modelling a wide range of PRP data that have hitherto appeared incompatible with any one bottleneck theory. As the name of their model implies, Meyer and Kieras have taken the bold step of explicitly modelling, in a production-system framework, executive processes as well as the perceptual, decision, and response processes required to carry out each of the two tasks. Each task is realised by creating a set of condition-action production rules, that, when specified stimuli are detected and/or identified, place symbols representing these detections or identities in working memory, and other rules that respond to the presence of such symbols by sending appropriate response features to the appropriate motor processor. In addition, there is a distinct set of executive production rules which schedule and control the operation of the task-specific rules by inserting task goals into working memory, monitoring task progress (e.g. checking for "efferent copy" signalling that one response has been initiated by a motor processor before allowing another to be sent to the same processor), shifting task priorities (e.g. by inserting symbols into working memory which specify whether, within a given task, a response symbol should be acted on immediately or when some other event has happened). When there is a change in the experimenter's instructions concerning, say, task priority, this is modelled by revising the executive rules appropriately, leaving the task-specific rules unchanged. The executive rules do not control the individual tasks directly by modifying their rules on-line, but by placing suitable symbols into working memory, and/or inducing anticipatory orienting (e.g. fixating the likely locus of a stimulus) and/or response preparation (e.g. presending features of a probable response to the motor processor). The executive processes monitor the progress of the tasks not by privileged access to their operations, but by taking note of the residual products they leave in working memory. Hence there is a substantial degree of autonomy between the task-specific production rules and the executive production rules.

Strikingly, Meyer and Kieras's model simulates a wide range of RT data from the PRP paradigm with no central-process bottleneck. There is no limit on the number of production rules that may be tested or "fired" simultaneously. Instead, the response postponement phenomena observed arise out of the coordinative measures necessary to force the task-specific processes to obey experimenter's instructions such as "Please produce your response to the visual stimulus first", and (in some cases) from peripheral perceptuo-motor constraints, such as the inability to fixate two different spatial locations simultaneously. That is, the central claim is that the major limitations on concurrent performance revealed by the PRP paradigm stem, as Allport suggested, from control processes necessary to coordinate the tasks, not from a hardware bottleneck. Moreover, these executive processes are explicitly modelled, rather than merely appealed to, as is so often the case in discussions of executive control. Meyer and Kieras's model will doubtless require amendments, but their theoretical approach is surely blazing a trail that others will follow, and extend to other domains in which control processes reveal themselves, including perhaps the following.

Experimental studies of task-switching

If we want to study the process of configuring oneself for a task, surely the most straightforward approach is to get subjects to configure themselves anew for a task, and try to measure how long this process takes, how difficult it is, and what variables influence these measures. The majority of cognitive experiments investigate a single task, like word reading or face recognition, and we usually discard data from the first few trials, during which we suppose the subject to be "settling down" to the new task; these data are assumed to be "noisy", contaminated by control processes. If we are interested in control processes, however, the first few trials are the interesting ones. Indeed, to maximise the contribution of control processes to performance, why not have the subject switch tasks on every trial?

Measuring the costs of a task switch

This idea was first realised in experiments reported in a monograph by Jersild (1927). All used the same basic design. In the Alternating condition the subject must alternate between performing two tasks (ABABABAB ...). In the Pure condition, the subject must perform just one of the tasks (sometimes AAAAAA ... , sometimes BBBBB ...). For example, in one experiment, Jersild displayed a column of 25 two-digit numbers. In the Alternating condition, the subject had to subtract 3 from the first number, add 6 to the second, subtract 3 from the third, and so on, as quickly as possible. In the Pure condition, subjects had to subtract 3 from every number (for half the lists) or add 6 to every number (for the other half). The order of pure and alternating conditions was counterbalanced. To compute the cost of switching, Jersild subtracted the average time for Pure lists from the average time for Alternating lists[8]. In this particular case, he found that the median time taken by students to work through a pure list was 85.5sec (averaged over the two tasks), whereas the median time to work through an alternating lists was 115.5sec, yielding a "switch cost" of 1.2sec per item. In another experiment in which the tasks were generating either the antonym to an adjective (e.g. COLD→"hot") or the object of an action (e.g. ANSWER→"question") the switch cost worked out at about 300msec per item. These are large values compared to many RT effects studied by cognitive psychologists! Spector and Biederman (1976) obtained results similar to Jersild's, using both card-sorting and a discrete-trials RT measure. Allport, Styles, and Hsieh (1994) obtained large switch costs when subjects had to alternate between colour naming and word naming (the stimuli were all incongruent Stroop stimuli), or between naming the number of identical digits on a display and naming the value of the digit (the number of digits and the digit value were incongruent). In each case, subjects alternated between two tasks afforded by the same stimuli.

A better measure of switch cost?

Jersild's technique of comparing alternating (ABABAB) and pure (AAAA, BBBB) blocks of trials has two disadvantages. First, the subject is placed under two extra demands in the alternating blocks: keeping two task-sets rather than one "available", and switching between them. It is not clear which is the source of the switch cost. Second, a comparison between performance in different blocks, which are evidently perceived by the subject as differing in difficulty, raises the possibility that the performance difference obtained might be contaminated by differences in effort, arousal level, or response criterion.

Robert Rogers and I therefore devised what we call the *alternating runs* paradigm, in which we measure the switch cost within blocks. Instead of alternating between a single trial on Task A and a single trial on Task B, the subjects have to alternate between runs of trials on the two tasks. In most of our experiments there are two trials in every run, so that the trial sequence is: AABBAABB ... . In order to prevent the subject losing track of which task they are supposed to be performing in response to each stimulus, we provide them with an external cue. For example, for runs of two trials, there are four possible display positions on the screen, arranged in a square, and successive stimuli are displayed in these four locations in a clockwise sequence. A subject may be told (for example) to perform Task A when the stimulus is displayed in one of the top two positions, and Task B when it is displayed in one of the other two[9]. The cost of switching tasks may be estimated simply by subtracting RT (or error rate) on the non-switch trials (A→A, B→B) from RT (or error rate) on the switch trials (B→A, A→B).

In a series of experiments reported by Rogers and Monsell (1995), the stimulus was a pair of characters, displayed close together. For the Digit task, one and only one of the characters (the subject could not anticipate which) was a digit, and the subject had to classify it as even or odd by pressing one of two keys. For the Letter task, one and only one of the characters was a letter, and the subject had to classify it as a consonant or a vowel by pressing one of (the same) two keys. (The irrelevant character could be either a member of the other stimulus set, or a neutral character, as is explained further shortly.) Here too there was a substantial cost for switching between the two tasks. Nor was it critical that the same pair of key-press responses was used for signalling the decision in each task; we have also found that when the response for the Digit task is to say "even" or "odd", and the response to the Letter task is to press one of two keys, there is still a substantial switch cost, although routing the two decisions to different response modalities does somewhat reduce the switch cost (Rogers & Monsell, submitted).

The intuitively obvious interpretation of this large RT cost of a task switch is that it measures the duration of a process of enabling and disabling connections between processing modules, and/or re-tuning the input-output mappings performed by these processes, so that the same type of input can be processed in the different way required by the new task[10]. I will call this the *task-set reconfiguration* (TSR) hypothesis. (In the case of task pairs not afforded by the same input, such as alternating between addition and antonym-generation, for which Jersild, 1927, observed no switch cost, this reconfiguration process is presumably not needed, as even if the processing chain required for adding 3 to a two-digit number is left enabled it will produce no output in response to a word.)

Anticipating a task switch

It seems intuitively obvious that when the necessity to switch tasks can be anticipated, a subject will (endogenously) initiate the TSR process prior to the arrival of the next stimulus. A number of studies have shown that, under conditions where the upcoming task is uncertain, a cue specifying the task, but not yet the stimulus, will improve performance. For example, Sudevan and Taylor (1987) found that when subjects were cued unpredictably to classify a digit as either odd or even, or as high or low, performance improved as the interval by which the cue preceded the digit increased. In the case of predictable task-switching (as in Jersild's alternation paradigm, or our alternating-runs paradigm), we might further suppose that switch costs occurred only because there was not time to complete the TSR process before the next stimulus arrived, and task-specific processing was thus delayed. Rogers and Monsell (1995) submitted this supposition to the simple test of varying the interval between each response and the next stimulus (the R–S interval) between 150msec[11] and 1.2sec, surely enough time for any anticipatory TSR process. When we first did this, we varied the R–S interval randomly from trial to trial, and were surprised to obtain no reduction in switch cost whatsoever at longer R–S intervals (Exp 2 in Fig. 4.3). We speculated that subjects might be reluctant to embark on the TSR process when they could be interrupted at any moment by the arrival of a new stimulus. In the subsequent experiments, therefore, we kept the R–S interval constant for a block of trials. Now we did observe a reliable reduction in the RT switch cost as the interval increased up to about half a second. However, only about a third of the switch cost could be eliminated by increasing the R–S interval: a substantial asymptotic switch cost was clearly present at longer R–S intervals (Exps 3 and 4 in Fig. 4.3). Allport, Styles, and Hsieh (1994, Experiment 5) report a

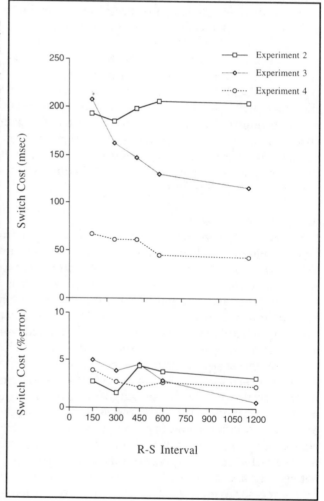

FIG. 4.3. Switch costs (mean RT and error rate for non-switch trials subtracted from mean RT and error rate for switch trials) as a function of response–stimulus interval, from Rogers and Monsell (1995). In Experiment 2 the R–S interval was randomly varied; in Experiments 3 and 4 it was constant within a block. Experiments 2 and 3 were run under the Crosstalk condition, Experiment 4 under the No-Crosstalk condition. Baseline mean RTs (error rates) on the non-switch trials were 720ms (3.4%), 628ms (3.6%), 477.2ms (4.5%) for Experiments 2, 3, and 4 respectively. Figure after Rogers and Monsell (1995), reproduced by permission. American Psychological Association.

similar finding; in their experiment, on each trial the subject was shown a pair of Stroop stimuli in sequence, and told before each trial what tasks to perform in response to each stimulus. When subjects had to switch from naming the colour of the first display to naming the word in the second display[12], there was a substantial switch cost, which diminished somewhat as the R–S interval was increased from 20msec to 550msec, but no further as the interval was increased to 1100msec[13].

Hence our intuitions were partially, but only partially, confirmed. Useful preparation for an anticipated change in task can be accomplished by a subject, given half a second or so to prepare for a predictable task switch, and this accords with the idea of a time-consuming TSR process. But there is a large and apparently irreducible component of the cost of switching tasks that even ample time for preparation does not eliminate. What causes it?

Interference from a recently activated task-set?

Allport et al. (1994, Experiment 4), using Jersild's procedure, found that switch cost depended on how *recently* the same or other tasks afforded by the same stimuli had been performed. For example, if subjects were required to switch between naming a printed word and naming the value of the repeated digit in a display for a series of eight "runs" (where each "run" was a block of seven trials alternating between the tasks and the two pure blocks of seven trials used to estimate switch cost) the initial switch cost diminished from about 70msec on the first run[14] to approximately zero on later runs. If the subject then had to switch between naming the colour of the word and reporting the number of digits, a large switch cost (about 160msec per item) occurred on the first run, and, although this cost diminished over subsequent runs, a modest switch cost remained even after eight runs. A similar pattern was observed when the two task pairs were run in the opposite order

Thus it is harder to switch to performing Task X if you have recently performed Task Y with the same type of stimulus. Although this effect "wears off" somewhat as you continue to perform Task X, the wearing-off is incomplete over several minutes of performing Task X. (We may be reminded of Reason's, 1984, observation that it is recently performed actions that tend to intrude in action errors.) Allport et al. (1994, p.436) therefore attribute the switch costs observed in their other experiments, and, one presumes, ours too, to "a kind of *proactive interference* (PI) from competing S–R mappings with the same stimuli, persisting from the instruction set on previous trials. We might call this phenomenon task set inertia (TSI)"—by analogy with proactive interference effects in memory experiments. They go on to argue:

The time costs of shifting task set that we observe in these experiments cannot be understood as the reflection of a discrete processing stage that must be completed before execution of the next S–R task can begin. Rather, like many other RT interference or conflict phenomena, they appear to represent the additional time needed for the system to settle to a unique response decision (or response retrieval) after the next imperative stimulus has arrived.

In other words, Allport et al. see a competition between S–R mappings, modulated by recency of activation, as a *sufficient* account of the switch cost observed in these experiments. The cost does not, in their view, represent the duration of a stage-like TSR process prior to task-specific processing. I have already mentioned one problematic fact for this view. The switch cost does diminish (by about a third) when the subject has adequate time to prepare, and this reduction cannot be attributed to a rapid initial decay of TSI, because it was not observed with a variable interval (Experiment 2). Our interpretation is that there is a TSR process, but our subjects were willing to embark on it in anticipation of the stimulus only if its time of arrival could be predicted. Allport et al.'s TSI account of switch cost would further appear to predict that if the subject, having performed Task A, then performs Task B for a number of trials, the TSI from Task A should interfere with performance of Task B not just on the first trial of Task B, but on a large number of subsequent trials, because TSI dissipates only gradually over a period of minutes. Rogers and I tested this with a version of the alternating runs paradigm in which the subject alternated between runs of four trials on each task, i.e. AAAABBBBBAAAA … etc. The result was very clear. Performance improved sharply from the first to the second trial of a run (as with runs of two), but there was absolutely no further improvement in performance on the third and fourth trial of a run (Rogers & Monsell, 1995, Exp. 6). Thus, although having ample time to prepare before a predictable task switch does not eliminate switch cost, performing the task just once appears to do so. We therefore conclude that the switch cost does indeed index the duration of a TSR process, but completion of the TSR process waits until triggered by a task-relevant stimulus. Indeed, we suggest that this is but another manifestation of *exogenous task-set activation*.

Exogenous task-set activation

We have already seen evidence from frontal patients and action errors that actions can be cued by stimulus contexts with which they are associated. I have argued earlier that Stroop interference must be attributed in part to activation not just of a competing response associated with the stimulus, but a whole task-set. A final piece of evidence comes from another manipulation in the experiments of Rogers and Monsell (1995). The somewhat artificial composition of the stimulus was chosen so that we could vary the relation of the irrelevant character to the response required, independently of that of the relevant character. In one condition the irrelevant character was always drawn from a "neutral" non-alphanumeric set (e.g. an @ or a #) associated with a response in neither task: the No-Crosstalk condition. In another condition (Crosstalk), the irrelevant character was, on a random two-thirds of the trials, a digit on letter-classification trials, and a letter on digit-classification trials—i.e. a character associated with a response in the now-inappropriate task—and, on the remaining third of the trials, a neutral character. As can be seen in Fig. 4.3, the switch cost was much greater in the Crosstalk condition. Moreover, in the Crosstalk condition, we could compare switch costs for trials on which the irrelevant character was associated (via the now-irrelevant S–R mapping) with the same response (congruent), the other response (incongruent), or neither (i.e. a neutral character). The switch cost was slightly smaller for congruent than for incongruent trials—a Stroop-like effect suggesting that there was some cross-talk—i.e. that the irrelevant task was not completely suppressed. However, the more striking effect was that switching was much faster with a neutral irrelevant character, than with either a congruent or an incongruent one. That is, the presence in the stimulus of a character associated with the *task* from which the subject was supposed to be switching away made switching substantially harder. We interpret both this effect, and the overall difference between No-Crosstalk and Crosstalk conditions as symptoms of exogenous control: the presence of stimulus attributes associated with a task tends to evoke that task-set and makes it harder to suppress when another task is required.

Hence, our present belief is that the process of reconfiguring task-set comprises at least two components: an endogenously initiated process which can be carried out in anticipation of the change in tasks, and may take up to half a second to complete, and an exogenously triggered component that must wait for the arrival of a task-relevant stimulus. The latter process may indeed involve a competition between active task-sets (or S–R mappings), biased by the anticipatory modulation, and influenced by their recency of activation, as Allport et al. suggest. However, there does seem to be at least some part of this post-stimulus processing that is better described as a one-off TSR process: it does not need to be done again while the same task-set remains in effect.

The agent of task-set reconfiguration

I have thus far dwelt on the *doing* of task-set reconfiguration, rather than the *doer*. As I have already noted, many authors have appeared to assume that executive processes are monolithic—for example, that the "central executive" to which Baddeley (1986) and others attribute responsibility for the maintenance of information in working memory by rehearsal, the generation of random numbers, etc., is the same "executive" as is responsible for all other control functions, including— presumably—task-set reconfiguration. However Allport and Styles (1990) have found no evidence for any interaction between, on the one hand, the task-set reconfiguration load, as indexed by increases in switch cost with the number of tasks between which the subject must switch, and, on the other hand, the concurrent maintenance of an irrelevant memory load. In a different line of research, Ward and Allport (1994) have been able to predict the time taken to initiate moves in the Tower of London task from one measure of the number of sub-goals required to solve the problem—a promising point of entry into the empirical study of planning processes—but find no evidence for an effect on this measure of the concurrent working-memory load posed by the problem. It thus appears that experimental investigations of normal control processes are, like the neuropsychological investigations reviewed earlier, beginning to yield evidence for a fractionation of "executive" function (Allport, 1993).

LAST WORDS

I started this chapter by identifying some of the control functions that have to be exercised to co-ordinate our repertoire of perceptual, cognitive, and motor processes to produce behaviour that is both goal-directed and flexible. However, as my brief exegesis of theoretical metaphors of control processes was intended to show, we still lack anything resembling a theory of control processes that does not simply consign all the tricky functions to an all-singing all-dancing "executive", or force all the competitive interactions of a parallel production system through a serial decision process.

My own bias is to suspect that a "unified" theory of control processes is an inappropriate goal. In the domain of "process control", as in domains such as "perception", "memory", and "motor control", we are dealing with irreducible complexity and heterogeneity, and the more we understand, the more we will have lots of bits of theory, rather than a single grand theory. (This is not to deny that there may be unifying theoretical principles, nor that "whole-system" modelling of the SOAR variety is valuable). It seems obvious that to gain further understanding of control functions, we must seek to exercise, manipulate, and measure them in the laboratory. Given the present lack of a theory capable of generating precise predictions, these explorations must of necessity be driven initially by theoretical hunches, some of which will be confirmed, and some unexpectedly confounded, by the data, leading to more articulated fragments of theory. I have tried to illustrate this process.

In reviewing the evidence, I began with natural history: the observation of control failures in normal and brain-damaged people. These observations demonstrate the importance of control processes in the normal brain, and provide some evidence for their heterogeneity and anatomical locus. I then looked at two established lines of experimental work—on Stroop phenomena, and on dual task interference—which, as they both concern cases where task-sets detectably compete, ought to be telling us something about control processes, but where the contribution of control processes is only now beginning to be examined seriously. I concluded with some recent attempts to measure directly the process of reconfiguring oneself for a changed task. I hope you will agree that this line of research has already yielded some surprising and illuminating findings. But clearly it also leaves very many loose ends: there is not even agreement yet about what "switch cost" measures Measuring response times in simple reactive tasks is, of course, not the only way to study control processes in the laboratory. For others, a natural approach would be to investigate planning, monitoring, and troubleshooting in complex problem-solving tasks, or the role of control processes in memory tasks, or the development of control processes in children, or animal models of control processes. In each of these domains, we have explored only the coastal fringe of the mystery: a large terra incognita remains to tempt the curious and ingenious explorer.

NOTES

1. It may instantly be objected that many cognitive psychologists have been interested in memory, or learning, over periods of days, years, lifetimes. This is true, but the analysis of memory in cognitive psychology focuses largely on what happens during the learning or acquisition episode, the episode of the retrieval attempt in question, and any intervening acquisition or retrieval episodes. Each of these episodes has a time-scale of seconds or minutes, and the basic memory tasks may be said to be "learning" and "trying to remember".

2. The American reader may need to know that a British "kettle" is (usually) a vessel that contains an electrical heating element, plugs into a wall socket, and brings two or three pints of water to the boil in a couple of

minutes. Curiously, this simple and effective device is not, in my experience, universally available in American kitchens—another mystery of mind!

3. This example is lifted shamelessly from Johnson-Laird (1983).

4. The term comes from the title of Minsky's aphoristic and thought-provoking collage of the same title (Minsky, 1985).

5. I borrow the terms *endogenous* and *exogenous* from their application to spatial orienting (e.g. Spence & Driver, 1994). The onset of a stimulus anywhere in the visual field will pull the "spotlight" of visual attention towards it: this is exogenous control. But it is also possible for the subject, given a cue such as an arrow pointing to the left, to move their spotlight voluntarily to the expected location of the stimulus in the visual field: this is endogenous control. Exogenous and endogenous control of visual orienting have different time courses and appear to be controlled by different brain mechanisms.

6. Experts may note that this results conflicts with the claims of Klein (1964) and Fox, Shor, and Steinman (1971) concerning effects of frequency. We used a discrete-trial procedure, with different types of items mixed in a block, and large item-sets carefully matched for other properties. When subjects were required to name the items themselves, there were large effects of frequency and lexical status (Monsell, Taylor, & Murphy, in prep).

7. Some authors, such as McLeod and Posner, 1984, have in fact argued that shadowing is special: "direct" links between speech perception and production processes bypass the central processor. This is quite an odd argument, as shadowing had hitherto been taken to be the paradigmatic task for "using up" the central processor! In any case, there are certainly other examples of non-interference between pairs of complex tasks, as well as other cases where manipulations of the difficulty of one of the tasks has no impact on the performance of the other, and where neither task is shadowing (see Wickens, 1984, for review).

8. One of the disadvantages of measuring the time taken to complete a whole list of trials (or card-sorts) is the problem of errors. Jersild dealt with this by the arbitrary expedient of adding to the time to complete a list a penalty equal to the average time per item for each error made. It is preferable, of course, to exploit modern technology and measure reaction time to each item, presenting the next item as soon as the response is made. As well as allowing one to exclude error RTs, this also avoids the problem of preview, which may have been responsible for Jersild's observation of a switch benefit for some pairs of tasks (see Spector & Biederman, 1976).

9. Which pair of locations is used for each task is balanced over subjects in case there are any differences in the difficulty of fixating or attending to a new location as a function of direction.

10. The increase in errors resulting from a switch may be assumed to result from trials on which the reconfiguration process is not complete before processing is attempted.

11. The shortest interval we could use while ensuring that subjects had (usually) released the key before the next stimulus appeared.

12. Allport et al. (1994) found essentially no cost for switching from word naming to colour naming, and ventured the generalisation that it is easier to switch from rather than to the dominant task of a pair; they developed a theoretical account of this generalisation. We suspected that this

observation might result from unusually slow colour-naming times in their experiment. By using easily nameable colours and distorted colour names, we were able approximately to equate colour-naming and word-naming RTs, while preserving the usual asymmetry between Stroop and reverse-Stroop effects. Under these conditions, there was no obvious asymmetry in the switch costs as a function of the direction of the switch (Monsell, Williams, Wright, & Rogers, in preparation).

13. The reduction observed by Allport et al. was not statistically reliable, which led them to discount it; however, it was of a similar order of magnitude to the statistically reliable effects observed by Rogers and Monsell (1995).

14. This observation incidentally sets a limit to the claim by Jersild (1927) and Spector and Biederman (1976) that no switch cost is observed when the stimulus clearly cues the task to be performed.

REFERENCES

Allport, A. (1980a). Attention and performance. In G. Claxton (Ed.), *Cognitive psychology: New directions*. (pp.112–153). London: Routledge & Kegan Paul.

Allport, A. (1980b). Patterns and actions: Cognitive mechanisms are content-specific. In G. Claxton (Ed.), *Cognitive psychology: New directions* (pp.26–64). London: Routledge & Kegan Paul.

Allport, D.A. (1989). Visual attention. In M.I. Posner (Ed.), *Foundations of cognitive science*. (pp.631–682). Cambridge, MA: MIT Press.

Allport, D.A. (1993). Attention and control: Have we been asking the wrong questions? A critical review of twenty-five years. In D.E. Meyer & S. Kornblum (Eds.), *Attention and performance XIV* (pp.183–218). Cambridge, MA: MIT Press.

Allport, D.A., Antonis, B., & Reynolds, P. (1972). On the division of attention: a disproof of the single-channel hypothesis. *Quarterly Journal of Experimental Psychology, 24*, 225–235.

Allport, D.A., & Styles, E.A. (1990). *Multiple executive functions, multiple resources? Experiments in shifting attentional control of tasks*. Unpublished manuscript. Oxford University.

Allport, D.A., Styles, E.A., & Hsieh, S. (1994). Shifting intentional set: exploring the dynamic control of tasks. In C. Umiltá & M. Moscovitch (Eds.), *Attention and performance XV*, (pp.421–452). Cambridge, MA: MIT Press.

Atkinson, R.C., & Shiffrin, R.M. (1968). Human memory: a proposed system and its control processes. In K.W. Spence & J.T. Spence (Eds.), *The psychology of learning and motivation* (pp.89–195). London: Academic Press.

Baars, B.J. (1980). Eliciting predictable speech errors in the laboratory. In V. Fromkin (Ed.), *Errors in linguistic performance: Slips of the tongue, ear, pen, and hand* (pp.307–318). New York: Academic Press.

Baddeley, A.D. (1986). *Working memory*. Oxford: Oxford University Press.

Bianchi, L. (1922). *The mechanism of the brain and the function of the frontal lobes*. Edinburgh: Livingstone.

Brandimonte, M., Einstein, G.O., & McDaniel, M. (Eds.) (in press). *Prospective memory: Theory and applications*. Hillsdale, NJ: Lawrence Erlbaum Associates Inc.

Broadbent, D.E. (1958). *Perception and communication*. London: Pergamon Press.

Broadbent, D.E. (1984). The Maltese Cross: A new simplistic model for memory. *The Behavioral and Brain Sciences, 7*, 55–94.

Broadbent, D.E., Broadbent, M.H.P., & Jones, J.L. (1986). Correlates of cognitive failure. *British Journal of Clinical Psychology, 25*, 285–299.

Broadbent, D.E., Cooper, P.F., Fitzgerald, P., & Parkes, K.R. (1982). The cognitive failures questionnaire (CFQ) and its correlates. *British Journal of Clinical Psychology, 19*, 177–188.

Cohen, J.D., Dunbar, K., & McClelland, J.L. (1990). On the control of automatic processes: A parallel distributed processing account of the Stroop Effect. *Psychological Review, 97*, 332–361.

Coltheart, M. (1985). Cognitive neuropsychology and the study of reading. In M.I. Posner & M. Marin (Eds.), *Attention and performance XI* (pp. 3–37). Hillsdale, NJ: Lawrence Erlbaum Associates Inc.

Damasio, A.R., & Van Hoesen, G.W. (1983). Emotional disturbances associated with focal lesions of the frontal lobe. In K. Heilman & P. Satz (Eds.), *The neuropsychology of human emotion: Recent advances.* (pp.85–110). New York: Guilford Press.

Duncan, J. (1986). Disorganisation of behaviour after frontal lobe damage. *Cognitive Neuropsychology, 3*, 271–290.

Duncan, J., Emslie, H., Williams, P., Johnson, R., & Frier, C. (in press). Intelligence and the frontal lobe: The organisation of goal-directed behaviour. *Cognitive Psychology.*.

Ellis, J. (1988). Memory for future intentions: Investigating pulses and steps. In M.M.Gruneberg, P.E.Morris, & R.N.Sykes (Eds.), *Practical aspects of memory: current research and issues*. Chichester, UK: Wiley.

Eslinger, P.J., & Damasio, A.R. (1985). Severe disturbance of higher cognition after bilateral frontal lobe ablation: Patient EVR. *Neurology, 35*, 1731–1741.

Eysenck, M. (1992). *Anxiety: The cognitive perspective*. Hove, UK: Lawrence Erlbaum Associates Ltd.

Fehrer, E., & Raab, E. (1962). Reaction time to stimuli masked by metacontrast. *Journal of Experimental Psychology, 63*, 143–147.

Fox, L.A., Shor, R.E., & Steinman, R.J. (1971). Semantic gradients and interference in naming colour, spatial direction, and numerosity. *Journal of Experimental Psychology, 91*, 59–65.

Freud, S. (1901). *Psychopathology of everyday life* [J. Strachey, Trans.]. London: Ernest Benn, reprinted 1966.

Frith, C.D. (1992). *The cognitive neuropsychology of schizophrenia*. Hove, UK: Lawrence Erlbaum Associates Ltd.

Galwey, W.T. (1976) *Inner tennis: Playing the game*. New York: Random House.

Glaser, M.D., & Glaser, W.R. (1982). Time course analysis of the Stroop phenomenon. *Journal of Experimental Psychology: Human Perception and Performance, 8*, 875–894.

Glaser, W.R., & Dungelhoff, F.-J. (1984). The time course of picture–word interference. *Journal of Experimental Psychology: Human Perception and Performance, 10*, 640–654.

Goldberg, E. & Tucker, D. (1979). Motor perseveration and long–term memory for visual forms. *Journal of Clinical Neuropsychology, 1*, 273–288.

Goldberg, G., Mayer, N.H., & Toglia, J.U. (1981). Medial frontal cortex and the alien hand sign. *Archives of Neurology, 38*, 683–686.

Hawkins, H.L., Rodriguez, E., & Reicher, G.M. (1979). *Is time sharing a general ability?* ONR Technical Report No. 3, University of Oregon, Eugene, OR.
Hebb, D.O., & Penfield, W. (1940). Human behavior after extensive removal from the frontal lobes. *Archives of Neurology and Psychiatry, 44,* 421–438.
Henderson, L. (1994). Signs of madness: Towards a cognitive account of the clinical features of schizophrenia. *Quarterly Journal of Experimental Psychology, 47A,* 497–516.
Hirst, W. (1986). The psychology of attention. In J.E. Ledoux & W. Hirst (Eds.), *Mind and brain: Dialogues in cognitive neuroscience* Cambridge: Cambridge University Press.
Humphrey, N. (1992). *A history of the mind.* London: Chatto & Windus
James, W. (1890). *Principles of psychology.* New York: Holt.
Jersild, A.T. (1927). Mental set and shift. *Archives of Psychology,* Whole No. 89.
Johnson-Laird, P.N. (1983). *Mental models.* Cambridge: Cambridge University Press.
Kahneman, D. (1973). *Attention and effort.* Englewood Cliffs, NJ: Prentice Hall.
Keele, S.W., & Neill, W.T. (1978). Mechanisms of attention. In E.C. Carterette & M.P. Friedman (Eds.), *Handbook of perception, Vol IX: Perceptual processing* (pp.3–47). London: Academic Press
Klein, G.S. (1964). Semantic power measured through the interference of words with colour-naming. *American Journal of Psychology, 77,* 576–588.
Knight, R.T., Hillyard, S.A., Woods, D.L., & Neville, H.J. (1981). The effects of frontal cortical lesions on event-related potentials during auditory selective attention. *Electroencephalography and Clinical Neurology, 52,* 571–582.
Kvavilashvili, L. (1992). Remembering intentions: A review of existing experimental paradigms. *Applied Cognitive Psychology, 6,* 507–524.
Lhermitte, F. (1983). 'Utilization behaviour' and its relation to lesions of the frontal lobes. *Brain, 106,* 237–255.
Logan, G.D. (1985). Executive control of thought and action. *Acta Psychologica, 60,* 193–210.
Luria, A.R. (1966). *Higher cortical functions in man.* New York: Basic Books.
Luria, A.R., Pribram, K.H., & Homskaya, E.D. (1964). An experimental analysis of the behavioural disturbance produced by a left arachnoidal endothelioma. *Neuropsychologia, 2,* 257–280.
MacLeod, C.M. (1991). Half a century of research on the Stroop effect: An integrative review. *Psychological Bulletin, 109,* 163–203.
MacLeod, C.M., & Dunbar, K. (1988). Training and Stroop-like interference: Evidence for a continuum of automaticity. *Journal of Experimental Psychology: Learning Memory and Cognition, 14,* 126–135.
Mathews, A. (1988). Anxiety and the processing of threatening information. In V. Hamilton, G.H. Bower, & N.H. Frijda (Eds.), *Cognitive perspectives on emotion and motivation.* Dordrecht, Netherlands: Kluwer Academic Publishers.
McLeod, P. (1977). A dual task response modality effect: support for multiprocessor models of attention. *Quarterly Journal of Experimental Psychology, 29,* 651–667.
McLeod, P. (1978). Does probe RT measure central processing demand? *Quarterly Journal of Experimental Psychology, 30,* 83–89.
McLeod, P., & Posner, M.I. (1984). Privileged loops form percept to act. In H. Bouma & D.G. Bouwhuis (Eds.), *Attention and performance X.* London: Lawrence Erlbaum Associates Ltd.

Meyer, D.E. & Kieras D.E. (1994a). *EPIC Computational models of psychological refractory-period effects in human multiple-task performance.* ONR-EPIC Technical Report No.2, University of Michigan.

Meyer, D.E. & Kieras D.E. (1994b). *A computational theory of human multiple-task performance: The EPIC architecture and strategic response-deferment model.* Submitted manuscript.

Milner, B. (1963). Some effects of different brain lesions on card sorting: the role of the frontal lobes. *Archives of Neurology, 9,* 90–100.

Minsky, M. (1985). *The society of mind.* New York: Simon & Schuster.

Monsell, S., Doyle, M.C., & Haggard, P.N. (1989). Effects of frequency on visual word recognition tasks: Where are they? *Journal of Experimental Psychology, 118*(1), 43–71.

Monsell, S., Taylor, T., & Murphy, K. (in preparation). *Effects of lexicality and frequency on Stroop colour-naming: A task-set activation account.*

Monsell, S., Williams, N., Wright, I., & Rogers, R. (in preparation). *Costs of switching between colour-naming and word-naming tasks need not be asymmetrical.*

Morton, J. (1969). Categories of interference. *British Journal of Psychology, 60,* 329–346.

Morton, J., & Chambers, S.M. (1973). Selective attention to words and colours. *Quarterly Journal of Experimental Psychology, 25,* 387–397.

Navon, D. (1985). Attention division or attention sharing? In M.I. Posner & O.S.M. Marin (Eds.), *Attention and Performance, XI.* Hillsdale, NJ: Lawrence Erlbaum Associates Inc.

Navon, D., & Miller, J. (1987). Role of outcome conflict in dual-task interference. *Journal of Experimental Psychology: Human Perception and Performance, 13,* 435–448.

Neumann, O. (1987). Beyond capacity: A functional view of attention. In H. Heuer & A.F. Sanders (Eds.), *Perspectives on perception and action* (pp.361–394). Hillsdale, NJ: Lawrence Erlbaum Associates Inc.

Neumann, O., & Klotz, W. (1994). Motor responses to non-reportable, masked stimuli: Where is the limit of direct parameter specification? In C. Umiltà & M. Moscovich (Eds.), *Attention and performance XV* (pp.123–150). Cambridge, MA: MIT Press.

Newell, A. (1973). Production systems: models of control structures. In W.C. Chase (Ed.), *Visual information processing.* New York: Academic Press.

Newell, A. (1980). Reasoning, problem-solving and decision processes. In R. Nickerson (Ed.), *Attention and Performance VIII* (pp.693–718). Hillsdale, NJ: Lawrence Erlbaum Associates Inc.

Newell, A. (1990). *Unified theories of cognition.* Cambridge, MA: Harvard University Press.

Newell, A., Rosenbloom, P.S., & Laird, J.E. (1989). Symbolic architectures for cognition. In M.I. Posner (Ed.), *Foundations of cognitive science* (pp.93–131). Cambridge, MA: MIT Press.

Newell, A., & Simon, H.A. (1972). *Human problem solving.* Englewood Cliffs, NJ: Prentice-Hall.

Norman, D.A. (1981). Categorization of action slips. *Psychological Review, 88,* 1–15.

Norman, D.A., & Shallice, T. (1986). Attention to action: Willed and automatic control of behaviour. In R.J. Davidson, G.E. Schwartz, & D. Shapiro (Eds.), *Consciousness and self-regulation* (pp.1–18). New York: Plenum.

Owen, A.M., James, M., Leigh, P.N., Summers, B A., Marsden, C.D., Quinn, N.P., Lange, K.W., & Robbins, T.W. (1992). Fronto-striatal cognitive deficits at different stages of Parkinson's Disease. *Brain, 115,* 1727–1751.

Owen, A.M., Roberts, A.C., Polkey, C.E., Sahakian, B.J., & Robbins, T.W. (1991). Extra-dimensional versus intra-dimensional shifting performance following frontal lobe excisions, temporal lobe excisions or amygdalo-hippocampectomy in man. *Neuropsychologia, 29,* 993–1006.

Pashler, H. (1990). Do response modality effects support multiprocessor models of divided attention? *Journal of Experimental Psychology: Human Perception and Performance, 16,* 826–842.

Pashler, H. (1993). Dual-task interference and elementary mental mechanisms. In D.E. Meyer & S. Kornblum (Eds.), *Attention and performance XIV.* Cambridge, MA: MIT Press.

Posner, M.I., & Snyder, C.R.R. (1975). Attention and cognitive control. In R.L. Solso (Ed.), *Information processing and cognition: The Loyola symposium* (pp.55–85). Hillsdale, NJ: Lawrence Erlbaum Associates Inc.

Reason, J.T. (1979). Actions not as planned: The price of automatization. In G. Underwood & R. Stevens (Eds.), *Aspects of consciousness.* London: Academic Press.

Reason, J.T. (1984). Lapses of attention in everyday life. In R. Parasuraman & R.D. Davies (Eds.), *Varieties of attention.* Orlando, FL: Academic Press.

Reason, J.T. (1990). *Human error.* Cambridge: Cambridge University Press.

Rogers, R., & Monsell, S. (1995). The costs of a predictable switch between simple cognitive tasks. *Journal of Experimental Psychology: General, 124,* 207–231.

Rogers, R., & Monsell, S. (submitted). *The effect of response modality on the costs of switching between tasks.*

Schwartz, M.F., Reed, E.S., Montgomery, M., Palmer, C., & Mayer, N.H. (1991). The quantitative description of action disorganisation after brain damage: A case study. *Cognitive Neuropsychology, 8,* 381–414.

Shallice, T. (1982). Specific impairments of planning. *Philosophical Transactions of the Royal Society, B298,* 199–209.

Shallice, T. (1988). *From neuropsychology to mental structure.* Cambridge: Cambridge University Press.

Shallice, T. (1994). Multiple levels of control processes. In C. Umiltà & M. Moscovitch (Eds.), *Attention and Performance XV.* Cambridge, MA: MIT Press.

Shallice, T. & Burgess, P. (1991). Higher-order cognitive impairments and frontal lobe lesions in man. In H.S. Levin, H.M. Eisenberg, & A.J. Benton (Eds.), *Frontal lobe function and dysfunction* (pp.125–138). New York: Oxford University Press.

Shallice, T., & Burgess, P. (1993). Supervisory control of action and thought selection. In A. Baddeley & L. Weiskrantz (Eds.), *Attention: Selection, awareness, and control* (pp.171–187). Oxford: Oxford University Press.

Shallice, T., Burgess, P.W., Schon, F., & Baxter, D.M. (1989). The origins of utilization behaviour. *Brain, 112,* 1587–1598.

Shiffrin, R.M., & Schneider, W. (1977). Controlled and automatic human information processing II. Perceptual learning, automatic attending, and a general theory. *Psychological Review, 84,* 127–190.

Spector, A., & Biederman, I. (1976). Mental set and mental shift revisited. *American Journal of Psychology, 89,* 669–679.

Spence, C. & Driver, J. (1994). Covert spatial orienting in audition: Exogenous and endogenous mechanisms. *Journal of Experimental Psychology: Human Perception and Performance, 20,* 555–574.

Stroop, J.R. (1935). Studies of interference in serial verbal reactions. *Journal of Experimental Psychology, 18,* 643–662.

Sudevan, P., & Taylor, D.A. (1987). The cuing and priming of cognitive operations. *Journal of Experimental Psychology: Human Perception and Performance, 13,* 89–103.

Treisman, A.M., & Gelade, G. (1980). A feature integration theory of attention. *Cognitive Psychology, 12,* 97–136.

Ward, G., & Allport, A. (1994). *Working memory and the construction of plans of action: An experimental study.* Submitted manuscript.

Welford, A.T. (1952). The "psychological refractory period" and the timing of high–speed performance—A review and a theory. *British Journal of Psychology, 43,* 2–19.

Wickens, C.D. (1984). Processing resources in attention. In R. Parasuraman & D.R. Davies (Eds.), *Varieties of attention* (pp.63–102). Orlando, FL: Academic Press.

CHAPTER FIVE

Consciousness

Andrew W. Young MRC Applied Psychology Unit, Cambridge

Ned Block Massachusetts Institute of Technology

Consciousness remains the greatest unsolved mystery of the mind. At present, we have no idea how to get a fully satisfying account. None the less, some modest progress has been made in identifying different aspects of the problem, marshalling pertinent data, and exploring the feasibility of different types of solution. So all is not hopeless. In fact, many contemporary discussions in philosophy, psychology, and neuroscience share a widespread perception that we are at last starting to get somewhere with this very difficult topic.

THE EXPLANATORY GAP

> How it is that anything so remarkable as a state of consciousness comes about as a result of irritating nervous tissue, is just as unaccountable as the appearance of Djin when Aladdin rubbed his lamp.

So said T.H. Huxley in 1866. This explanatory gap (Levine, 1983) is still with us. Advances in neuroscience have not given us an account of subjective experience; what it is like to see red, have a pain, or just to be awake.

For example, it has been known for many years that wakefulness and arousal are influenced by the brain stem reticular formation, and especially noradrenergic neurons in the locus coeruleus. These and many other facts about sleep and wakefulness are presented in textbooks of physiological psychology (Carlson, 1991). In essence, we know that when we are awake, it is because neurotransmitters are sprinkled into the synapses of huge numbers of neurons in the cerebral cortex by ascending pathways with very widespread projections. Similarly, doctors are able to distinguish different levels of perturbation of consciousness, ranging from delirium through stupor and coma to brain death, and they know many of the neuroanatomical correlates of such states (Bates & Cartlidge, 1994). These facts certainly point us to the view that consciousness is a product of brain activity, because it is clear that it is intimately linked to the underlying anatomy and biochemistry. For this reason, we can reject the Cartesian view that consciousness does not have a physical basis; instead, it is undoubtedly a product of what our brains are doing at the time. However, the explanatory gap remains; the anatomical and biochemical facts seem to tell us nothing about what it *feels* like to be conscious. Worse, it is hard to even imagine future work in neuroscience that would close this gap.

What we would like is a theory that links the activity of cortical neurons to consciousness, or at least to some aspect of consciousness. Then we could understand what it feels like to be us in terms of a combination of our understanding of the functions of cortical neurons and the modulatory influences of neurotransmitters.

Many philosophers and neuroscientists believe that the explanatory gap will close and then disappear as our knowledge of brain function increases (Flanagan, 1992). However, at present the gap remains dauntingly large.

A NEUROBIOLOGICAL THEORY

To take a closer look into this chasm, let's buy the story that what we must do is to marry our knowledge of the modulatory properties of neurotransmitter systems to an account of how cortical neurons mediate at least one aspect of consciousness. For this purpose, we can select visual awareness as the aspect of consciousness we will explore, because the anatomy of the visual system has been extensively studied and a detailed account of visual awareness has been offered by Crick and Koch (1990).

Crick and Koch (1990) are quite clear in their enterprise; they recognise that our awareness of the things we see forms an important aspect of consciousness, they claim that it requires a scientific explanation, and they consider that the problem can only be solved by an explanation at the neural level. To this end, they seek to define what unusual features might be characteristic of the activity of neurons in the cerebral cortex concerned with vision when we are conscious of seeing something.

This seems like a reasonable start. We know that consciousness is not simply a consequence of *any* neuronal activity because there are plenty of things the neurons in our central nervous systems do that seem to be independent of consciousness, like adjusting the size of the eye's pupil to the prevailing illumination, or which carry on automatically but can be subject to occasional conscious intervention, like breathing. In general, these automatic activities do not require the activity of neurons in the cerebral cortex. Even for the cerebral cortex, though, neuronal activity is not in itself sufficient to produce consciousness; for example, many neurophysiological studies of the responses of neurons in the visual system have been conducted on anaesthetised, unconscious animals. Further, studies of the brain's electrical activity show that when we are in deep sleep, cortical neurons still do *something*, but that something is different from how they function when we are awake (Carlson, 1991). Conversely, we know that when cortical neurons are damaged, loss of sensation can result. In the case of vision, damage to the visual cortex creates a region of apparent blindness which can be mapped and related precisely to the area of damaged cortical tissue (Kolb & Whishaw, 1990).

Putting these facts together it is clear that intact visual cortex is necessary for normal visual experience, but that normal visual experience only happens when cortical neurons are working in a certain way.

Anatomical studies of the visual system have revealed a startlingly intricate arrangement, involving distinct areas in the cerebral cortex and several parallel cortical and subcortical visual pathways (Weiskrantz, 1990; Zeki, 1993). In general, it seems that the task of seeing is devolved to separate processing streams containing components that have become specialised for particular purposes, responding selectively to wavelength (needed for colour perception), orientation (for perception of form and space), temporal change (movement), and so on. This holds not only for basic aspects of vision, such as the perception of lightness and orientation, but also for higher-order visual abilities involved in the perception and recognition of complex shapes, such as faces (Perrett, Hietanen, Oram, & Benson, 1992).

These specialist areas in the brain have been shaped by evolution, and during evolution specialisation can carry costs as well as benefits. Hence, the optimal balance of costs and benefits is likely to allow scope for some cross-talk between specialist areas, and we would not expect the kind of discrete components found in a human-engineered product like a radio.

The presence of functional specialisation has led neurophysiologists to propose that the brain must somehow co-ordinate activity within and between these different specialist regions to achieve an integrated percept; this is known as the binding problem. Crick and Koch (1990, p.269) put it like this:

> If you are currently paying attention to a friend discussing some point with you, neurons in area MT that respond to the motion of his face, neurons in area V4 that respond to its hue, neurons in auditory cortex that respond to the words coming from his face and possibly the memory traces associated with recognition of the face all have to be 'bound' together, to carry a common label identifying them as neurons that jointly generate the perception of that specific face.

The solution proposed by Crick and Koch is that binding is achieved through a degree of synchronisation of the firing of the neurons involved, so that "neurons in different parts of cortex responding to the currently perceived object fire action potentials at about the same time" (Crick & Koch, 1990, p.270). In particular, they note evidence of synchronous firing of some neurons in the cat's cerebral cortex, with frequencies in the 40–70Hz range. This synchronised activity is, in Crick and Koch's view (1990, p.272), how binding takes place:

> We suggest that one of the functions of consciousness is to present the result of various underlying computations and that this involves an attentional mechanism that temporarily binds the relevant neurons together by synchronizing their spikes in 40Hz oscillations. These oscillations do not themselves encode additional information, except in so far as they join together some of the existing information into a coherent percept. We shall call this form of awareness 'working awareness'.

Although it is obviously speculative, this is an ambitious attempt to tie visual awareness to a particular feature of cortical activity. Right or wrong, it therefore has much to commend it, because it is detailed, clear, and potentially falsifiable. Moreover, the same general approach has been adopted in other cases where there is an apparent need to bind together different parts of the visual scene that belong with each other, as in shape recognition (Hummel & Biederman, 1992), and it has even been suggested that synchronised oscillations can usefully be incorporated into models of language understanding and human reasoning (Shastri & Ajjanagadde, 1993). This wide applicability of the idea of dynamic binding through synchronised oscillation is consistent with Crick and Koch's view that it may prove to be a quite general feature of consciousness. But how much can this approach explain?

Crick and Koch's claim is that a solution to the binding problem will provide a basis for understanding visual awareness. There is some plausibility to the idea that binding and consciousness might be intimately related, because the binding problem gains its force from the discrepancy between the subjective unity of visual experience (on which, more later) and the apparently fragmented nature of visual processing pathways in the brain. For example, when we see a moving blue square, the movement, colour, and shape are represented in different cortical areas and pathways, yet we experience them as attributes of a single object. However, we have a suspicion that looking for a direct solution to this neat trick in the form of a binding agent may prove as misleading as searching the brain for the little screen on which the visual picture is assembled and displayed.

For the sake of the argument, though, we will set aside the insidious possibility that there is actually no distinguishable binding mechanism. This allows us to focus on the hypothesis that the neural basis of binding is to be found in phase-locked 40Hz neural oscillations. Let us suppose that this is indeed true. But how does a 40Hz neural oscillation explain, as Nagel (1974) puts it, what it is like to be us? What is so special about a 40Hz oscillation as opposed to some other physical state?

To see the force of this point, one needs only to consider the implications of the fact that binding through synchronised activity is already being incorporated into some computer simulations (Hummel & Biederman, 1992; Shastri & Ajjanagadde, 1993). Does this mean that building some form of binding machinery into its program makes the computer conscious? We suspect not, but in the absence of any convincing reason to settle the argument either way, it has to be conceded that binding in itself offers an incomplete account.

Because of this incompleteness, one can ask why couldn't there be weird green space creatures with brains just like ours in their physical and functional properties, including their 40Hz oscillation patterns, whose owners' experiences were very unlike ours, or who were zombies with no subjective experiences at all? We don't have to suppose that there really could be creatures with brains just like ours who have different experiences or no experiences to ask for an account of why not. But no one has a clue about how to answer these questions.

To be fair to Crick and Koch, they did not set out to solve this particular problem. Instead, they argue that several topics are best set aside at the moment, and they include among these the problem of qualia (whether my experience of red is the same as yours, what it feels like to be me, etc). But unless this problem is addressed, the explanatory gap remains. Even though we might reasonably feel that Crick and Koch's hypothesis has the potential to reduce the gap a little bit, we have not been given compelling reasons to expect that in future a large number of similar small reductions will suffice to eliminate it.

PERSPECTIVES FROM PHILOSOPHY

We gain some perspective on the explanatory gap if we contrast the issue of the physical and functional basis of consciousness with the issue of the physical and functional basis of thought. In the case of thought, we do have theoretical proposals about what thought is, or at least what human thought might be, in scientific terms. Cognitive scientists have had some success in explaining some features of thought processes in terms of the notions of representation and computation. There are many disagreements among cognitive scientists; especially notable is the disagreement between connectionists and classical 'language of thought' theorists (Ramsey, Stich, & Rumelhart, 1991). However, the notable fact is that in the case of thought, we actually have more than one substantive research program and their proponents are busy fighting it out, comparing which research program handles which phenomena best.

It is true that some philosophers have expressed concern that an approach that views the mind as the embodiment of a computer program instead of grounding its explanations securely in biology, is at best incomplete and quite possibly doomed to failure (Searle, 1984). We share some of these concerns, but remain impressed by the achievements of the segment of cognitive science that is oriented around the computer model of the mind (Johnson-Laird, 1988). Cognitive science can provide a platform from which to work towards a neurobiology of thought. But in the case of consciousness, we have nothing worthy of being called an equivalent research programme. Researchers are stumped.

Needless to say, philosophers have taken many different attitudes towards this problem, but four of them stand out. First, there is *eliminativism*, the view that consciousness as it is commonly understood involves a set of conceptual confusions in our everyday beliefs, and hence simply does not exist (Dennett, 1988). So there is nothing for there to be an explanatory gap about. Second, we have various forms of *reductionism*, notably functionalism and physicalism. According to these views, there is such a thing as consciousness, but there is no singular explanatory gap; that is, there are no mysteries concerning the physical basis of consciousness that differ in kind from run of the mill unsolved scientific problems about the physical and functional basis of liquidity, inheritance, or computation. On this view, there is an explanatory gap, but it is unremarkable. A third view is what Flanagan (1992) calls the new mysterianism. Its most extreme form is *transcendentalism* (White, 1991), the view that consciousness is simply not a natural phenomenon and is not explainable in terms of science at all. A less extreme form of new mysterianism is that of McGinn (1991), which concedes that consciousness is a natural phenomenon but emphasises *our* problem in understanding the physical basis of consciousness. McGinn argues that there are physical properties of our brains that do in fact explain consciousness, but although this explanation might be available to some other type of being, it is cognitively closed off to us; just as we can understand the motor system of a cockroach even though the cockroach cannot, so a superior being might be able to understand the physical explanation of human consciousness, but humans cannot. A fourth view that has no well-known name (Flanagan, 1992; Nagel, 1974; Searle, 1992), holds that although there may be important differences between a naturalistic explanation of consciousness and naturalistic explanations of other phenomena, there is no convincing reason to regard consciousness as non-natural or unexplainable in naturalistic terms. This view is suggested by Nagel's remark that we are like the person ignorant of relativity theory who is told that matter is a form of energy but who does not have the concepts necessary to appreciate how. The explanatory gap exists because we lack the scientific concepts. But future theory may provide those concepts.

FORMS OF CONSCIOUSNESS

The wide range of opinions held by those who have written about consciousness reflect the difficulty of the topic and our current scientific ignorance. However, we also think that they represent a degree of confusion, best epitomised by the widely adopted assumption that there is a single phenomenon denoted by 'consciousness' that requires a unitary explanation. This assumption allows discussions of consciousness to proceed as if everyone is talking about the same thing. This has rightly been considered unwise (Allport, 1988), and our view is that, like many complex phenomena, consciousness involves different aspects which will need to be accounted for in different ways. We thus reject the idea that one should seek *the* solution to *the* problem of consciousness; instead, it is essential to be clear about which aspect of consciousness each putative solution is meant to cover.

As a start, we will distinguish some different phenomena that terms like 'consciousness' and 'awareness' (we regard these as approximate synonyms) are used to designate:

1. *Phenomenal consciousness:* the experience of seeing, hearing, feeling pain, etc.
2. *Access consciousness:* a mental state is access conscious if you can think about it, report its content, and use it to guide action. Access consciousness applies most directly to occurrent states, but we can extend the notion to memories. In this extended sense, we are access conscious when recognising an object or a face or remembering a past event.
3. *Monitoring and self consciousness:* this would include thinking about one's own actions and their effects, and monitoring perceptual information for discrepancies with current plans and hypotheses. Self consciousness also involves the possession of a concept of the self and the ability to use this concept in thinking about oneself. It is possible to distinguish monitoring from self consciousness (for example, not all monitoring seems to involve consciousness of self), but we have kept them together here because much of self consciousness involves monitoring what one is doing.

This list is grounded in the distinctions made by Block (1991). Of course, we recognise that there are also different forms of consciousness *within* each of these different categories. It seems obvious enough that the phenomenal awareness involved in seeing something is not like phenomenal awareness of hearing or touch, and even within vision the phenomenal 'feel' of colour, shape, and other visual attributes can be quite different. Similarly, remembering what you did on your holidays last year is a different experience to recognising that an object is a table, even though both are considered forms of access consciousness because they involve bringing stored knowledge to mind, and access to the content of one's thought is different from access to the content of one's pain. Likewise, monitoring the process of stopping your car at a red traffic light need not involve the same skills as monitoring the course of a conversation.

So any complete explanation is going to need to be able both to account for different forms of consciousness and to account for each of the variants within each form. Clearly, it is going to look quite complicated, but we should not be deterred by complications if they are needed to establish the true state of affairs.

So far, we have mainly been talking about phenomenal consciousness. But the other concepts of consciousness, access consciousness, monitoring consciousness, and self consciousness bear a special relationship to phenomenal consciousness. One could imagine phenomenal consciousness (e.g. the sensation of seeing red) without access consciousness, monitoring or self consciousness For example, many people have had the experience of noticing a loud noise and *at the same time* realising that the noise has been going on for some time and that one had been hearing it for some time. So the experience of a loud noise took place for a time without the reasoning system having access to the content of that experience, and without any thought to the effect that one was having that experience. But it is harder to imagine any of these without some form of phenomenal consciousness. Perhaps we can imagine a zombie who has access consciousness without phenomenal consciousness. But it is hard to imagine how we non-zombies could be in such a situation. This makes it easy for eliminativists or reductionists about phenomenal consciousness to tacitly slide from phenomenal consciousness to one or another of these other concepts, which are more clearly functional in nature.

We have said that access consciousness and monitoring consciousness are more clearly functional in nature. That is to say they are constituted by information-processing relations and so are obviously in the domain of current cognitive theories. Phenomenal consciousness, by contrast, is not self-evidently a cognitive phenomenon at all.

There are important differences between access consciousness and phenomenal consciousness that must be acknowledged. The type of consciousness depends on the type of content; a phenomenally conscious state must have phenomenal content, and an access-conscious state must have representational content. Access consciousness is therefore a functional notion, but phenomenal consciousness is not. Whereas access consciousness applies to state tokens, or rather tokens at times, phenomenal consciousness is best thought of as a feature of state types. Let us explain. The following inscription, 'teeth', which you have just read, contains five letter tokens, but of only three letter types. There is a token of the type bath in many houses, but the type bath itself is an abstract object that doesn't exist anywhere in space-time. Here is why access is a matter of tokens at times: a single token state might be access conscious at one time but not another, because of changes in information flow in the system, just as your keys are accessible at some times but not others (e.g. when you lose them). The type is neither access conscious or not; access consciousness is a feature of tokens. By contrast, there is such a thing as a phenomenally conscious type or kind of state. For example, the feel of pain is a phenomenally conscious type or kind of state. Every pain must have that feel.

In distinguishing a number of different concepts of consciousness, we are claiming that for serious thinking we need this kind of conceptual clarification. There are two notable sorts of trouble that writers get into by not making these distinctions; both involve conflating different forms of consciousness. One is to be found in Jaynes (1976) and Dennett (1991), who allege that consciousness is a cultural construction; Jaynes even gives its invention a date between the events reported in the *Odyssey* and the *Iliad*. Of course, certain aspects of consciousness do indeed show clear evidence of being culturally constructed; especially some features of self consciousness (Neisser, 1988). However, Jaynes (1976) and Dennett (1991) seem to be talking about phenomenal consciousness; but, with no disrespect to the ancient Greeks, if one accepts the distinctions we have described, consciousness could not have been *invented* by anyone. If there is such a thing as phenomenal consciousness, it has been around for a very long time as a basic biological feature of us. What Jaynes and Dennett ought to be saying is that there is no such thing as phenomenal consciousness as distinct from the other consciousnesses. They ought to be reductionists or eliminativists about consciousness. The conflation is especially apparent in Jaynes (1976), where 'consciousness' in the sense in which it is supposed to have been invented by the Greeks is something like a *theory* of consciousness in roughly the phenomenal sense.

A second type of problem of conflation has nothing to do with reductionism or eliminativism. Consider, for example, Searle's (1992) reasoning about a function of consciousness. Searle mentions Penfield's description of epilepsy patients suffering absence (petit mal) seizures who are apparently 'totally unconscious', but nonetheless continue their activities of walking or driving home or playing a piano piece, but in an inflexible and uncreative way. Searle says that the lack of consciousness explains the lack of flexibility and creativity, and so one of the functions of consciousness is to add powers of flexibility and creativity. Searle is talking about the function of *phenomenal consciousness*, but he gives no reason to think that people suffering absence seizures lack *that* kind of consciousness. For example, Searle describes the epileptic walker as threading his way through the crowd. Isn't there something it is like for him to see, say, a red sign, at which he knows to turn right? What is most obviously deficient in these patients is not phenomenal consciousness, but monitoring and self consciousness. When Penfield said that the patients are totally unconscious, he appears to have had some sort of monitoring consciousness in mind, not phenomenal consciousness.

SELECTIVE IMPAIRMENTS OF CONSCIOUSNESS

We have shown that distinguishing different types of consciousness can help in discussing theoretical issues. However, we also claim that these distinctions have direct empirical importance. Specifically, different types of brain injury can lead to impairments that affect one or other of the forms of consciousness we have outlined, often in highly selective ways. The existence of these selective impairments of consciousness suggests that they are implemented by different neural mechanisms, and strongly supports the utility of the underlying distinctions.

A wide range of neuropsychological impairments can be considered relevant (Milner & Rugg, 1992; Schacter, McAndrews, & Moscovitch, 1988; Young & de Haan, 1990). Here, we will look at some examples of problems affecting phenomenal consciousness, access consciousness, and monitoring and self consciousness.

Phenomenal consciousness

A consequence of brain injury involving the primary visual cortex, area V1, can be a loss of vision for part of the visual field, known as a scotoma. To test for a visual field defect the person is usually asked to report what he or she sees when stimuli are presented at different locations in the visual field. Notice that vision is tested by asking about phenomenal consciousness, and that this is lost for stimuli presented within the scotoma. Such work has shown that there is an orderly mapping of the area of lost vision onto the damaged region of visual cortex.

The fact that the loss of phenomenal visual consciousness can be restricted to an area corresponding to the damaged region of visual cortex is in itself of considerable interest, as it so clearly highlights the role of visual cortex in the creation of phenomenal visual experience. However, what has really captured the attention of neuroscientists and philosophers has been the demonstration of accurate responses to visual stimuli presented within the scotoma (Pöppel, Held, & Frost, 1973; Weiskrantz, 1986, 1990; Weiskrantz, Warrington, Sanders, & Marshall, 1974). These accurate responses are usually elicited with tasks in which the patient is encouraged to 'guess' what has been presented. Weiskrantz's term 'blindsight' neatly sums up the paradoxical result of accurate responses to stimuli that people insist they do not 'see', and for which there is no phenomenal visual experience.

Weiskrantz et al. (1974) showed that their patient, DB, could point to where he guessed a flash of light had been presented, and that he could discriminate the orientation of stimuli presented within his scotoma. By asking DB to guess whether a presented stimulus was a sine-wave grating of vertical dark and light bars they were able to determine his visual acuity (in terms of the narrowest grating that could be detected). Gratings with bar widths of 1.5′ could be detected in the sighted part of his field of vision, and a rather less fine but still impressive 1.9′ in the 'blind' field.

Later studies have confirmed and extended the original findings. In particular, DB could detect the presence or absence of a light stimulus even when it was introduced or extinguished quite slowly; he could readily distinguish static from moving stimuli; and more detailed testing of acuity in the scotoma showed that (unlike normal vision) it increased as the stimuli were moved to positions further away from fixation.

As well as using forced-choice guessing, blindsight phenomena can be demonstrated by very different methods; Weiskrantz (1986; 1990) gives authoritative reviews. For example, it is possible to demonstrate automatic reactions in the form of skin conductance changes (Zihl, Tretter, & Singer, 1980) or altered pupil diameter (Weiskrantz, 1990). Several studies have also demonstrated interactions between stimuli presented in the blind and sighted parts of the visual field. Pizzamiglio, Antonucci, and Francia (1984) noted that a full-field rotating disk produced a larger subjective tilt than did stimulation of one visual hemifield alone, for both normal and hemianopic subjects. Marzi, Tassinari, Agliotti, and Lutzemberger (1986) found that bilateral light flashes produced faster reaction times to detect a flash than did a single unilateral stimulus, even when one of the bilateral flashes fell in a hemianopic area of the visual field, from which a single flash would not have been detected.

Some of the most tantalising findings were noted by Torjussen (1976; 1978), who found that patients with right hemianopias reported seeing a circle when it was presented so as to fall half in the blind and half in the sighted region, but they reported seeing a semicircle if this was presented in the sighted region, and nothing if a semicircle was presented in the blind right visual field. Torjussen's findings are particularly significant because they show that the interaction between the stimuli in the blind and sighted parts of the visual field can affect what people report that they see in the blind region. Notice that presenting a semicircle in the blind field alone was insufficient for it to be perceived, but essentially the same stimulus was reported as having been seen when it formed part of a complete figure that extended into the sighted field.

Studies of blindsight, then, strongly suggest that the processing of visual stimuli can take place even when there is no phenomenal awareness of seeing them. Although accurate visual processing is involved, the pathways mediating these effects do not have the same sensitivity as normal vision. It has been widely speculated that the non-conscious visual processing found in blindsight is mediated subcortically, but detailed study of the visual pathways underlying these effects has shown clear involvement of cerebral cortex outside the primary visual area V1 (Cowey & Stoerig, 1991, 1992). This can happen because the primary visual pathway through area V1 is not the only visual pathway with cortical projections; there are other pathways that bypass V1. Hence, visual areas outside V1 can be involved in visual functions without corresponding visual experience.

These facts might lead one to suppose that the primary visual cortex, area V1, is the unique source of phenomenal visual experience, but this does not seem to be correct; the full picture is going to be more complicated, and more interesting.

Important findings come from cases in which one particular aspect of phenomenal visual experience is preserved or lost. We will consider recent reports involving preserved perception of movement (Barbur, Watson, Frackowiak, & Zeki, 1993) and loss of colour vision (Heywood, Cowey, & Newcombe, 1991).

Barbur et al. (1993) investigated case GY, a man who had sustained injuries in a road accident when a child; these included total destruction of primary visual cortex, area V1, in the left cerebral hemisphere. GY had been investigated in previous work on blindsight (Barbur, Ruddock, & Waterfield, 1980), when it was noted that flashed or rapidly moving targets presented to his 'blind' hemifield did elicit a form of visual sensation, whereas static or slowly moving targets were reported as unseen. Whereas the blindsight work had concentrated on these unseen stimuli, Barbur et al. (1993) turned their attention to GY's relatively preserved (though by no means perfect) perception of movement. Using a measure of cerebral blood flow when GY was asked to judge the direction of a rapidly moving stimulus, they found increased activity in visual areas in the left hemisphere beyond the destroyed V1. This demonstration of a form of conscious perception of movement without area V1 shows that V1 is not essential to *all* visual experience. It appears more likely that visual experience is associated with activity of the cortical areas that are particularly specialised for that type of activity (in this case, an area specialised for the perception of movement). However, there is a clear contrast with the evidence of involvement of visual areas other than V1 in blindsight (Cowey & Stoerig, 1991, 1992), which only serves to emphasise the mystery of why some types of cortical activity seem to generate a conscious visual experience and some don't.

Work on achromatopsia is also relevant. Achromatopsic patients experience the world in shades of grey, or in less severe cases colours can look very washed out (Meadows, 1974b). This is quite different to the forms of colour-blindness produced by deficiencies in one of the three types of cone receptor in the retina, for which there is still experience of colour but certain colours are not discriminated from each other. Instead, severe achromatopsias produced by cortical injury are described by the patients themselves in terms that suggest they are experienced as more like watching black and white television. Hence, achromatopsia provides an interesting example of loss of one aspect of visual experience; colour.

The full details of the mechanisms underlying human colour vision are not known, but some of their essential features have been established. The retina contains three types of cone, each of which is maximally sensitive to light of a different wavelength. Outputs from these three types of cone are converted into colour-opponent signals for red–green and blue–yellow dimensions, and a separate luminance (brightness) response.

This arrangement means that we are more sensitive to light of certain wavelengths than others, and the shape of the function relating light sensitivity to wavelength across the colour spectrum for normal daytime vision has distinct peaks which, because of the opponent cone mechanisms, do not correspond to the sensitivity peaks of the cones themselves. Heywood et al. (1991) therefore measured this spectral sensitivity function for an achromatopsic patient who has no experience of colour, MS. Their study followed up previous observations of preserved behavioural responses to wavelength for this patient (Mollon, Newcombe, Polden, & Ratcliff, 1980). In Heywood et al.'s (1991) test, MS described all the stimuli he saw as "dim white" or "grey", despite the differences in wavelength. Similarly, other work established that MS could not match or name colours, and performed at random when asked to arrange colour patches by hue. However, although MS showed a general overall loss of sensitivity, Heywood et al. (1991) found that he showed maximal sensitivity to the same wavelengths as a normal observer. This demonstrates the presence of opponent cone mechanisms despite the complete loss of colour experience.

There is a striking difference between the absence of colour experience for MS and the preservation of opponent cone mechanisms shown in his spectral sensitivity function. This difference is highlighted by the fact that MS was also able to detect boundaries defined by a change in wavelength, which would look like a change in colour to a normal observer. MS could do this even when the colours on each side of the boundary were of matched brightness (Heywood et al., 1991). Thus, he was able to distinguish whether or not a series of hues was in the correct chromatic order as long as the adjacent colour patches abutted one another. If a small (5mm) gap was introduced between each colour patch, his performance deteriorated to chance level. Heywood et al. (1991) account for this by suggesting that the salience of any chromatic border will depend on the contrast between the hues on each side of the border; a random series of adjacent colour patches will have some very sharp borders (where very different hues abut each other) and some that are less sharp, whereas for an ordered series there should be no variation in the salience of each border.

In cases of achromatopsia, then, there is evidence that some aspects of colour processing mechanisms continue to function. However, although some of the cortical mechanisms that show sensitivity to different wavelengths still operate, there is no subjective experience of colour.

Memory and recognition without access consciousness

Access consciousness is involved when we remember something that happened in the past, or recognise a familiar object or face. Amnesic patients, who often cannot remember what they were doing a few hours ago, are therefore experiencing a dense impairment of access consciousness. In such cases, performance in direct tests of memory can be at chance. Direct tests would include recalling the items from a list learned earlier, picking them out from a list of previously learned items and new distractors, and so on. Following Warrington and Weiskrantz (1968, 1970), however, many studies have documented preserved memory in amnesia if memory is tested indirectly, through priming effects.

Warrington and Weiskrantz (1968, 1970) asked amnesic patients to identify fragmented pictures or words, and showed that subsequent identification of the same stimuli was facilitated. In other words, it becomes easier to recognise a fragmented picture of an object if you have already had to recognise the same object before. This type of finding holds as much for amnesics as for normal people, and it can be obtained for amnesic patients even when they fail to remember having taken part in any previous testing sessions. Such findings seem to arise when amnesics' memories are tested indirectly, in terms of the facilitation of subsequent recognition of the same stimuli (Schacter, 1987). As we have noted, direct tests, such as asking whether or not items were among those previously shown, lead to very poor performance. Hence amnesics show a form of memory without access consciousness, in which their performance can be affected by previous experiences they completely fail to remember overtly. Access consciousness of a content, you will recall, is a matter of a representation of its content being 'inferentially promiscuous', i.e. freely available as a premise in reasoning, and in the consequent utility of these contents in guiding action and speech. The amnesic patients just mentioned have memory representations that affect their responses when they encounter the fragmented stimuli again, but not so as to produce access consciousness.

The key point here is that in amnesia the central difficulty need not be with memory per se, as priming effects clearly involve a form of remembering. Rather, the problem lies in being able to deploy the remembered information in reasoning, guiding action, and reporting; in other words, it does look like a failure of access consciousness. Of course, there is also a failure of monitoring consciousness, because the patient does not know he or she has any memory of the event, but the failures of access and monitoring are distinct. What is not clear, though, is whether access consciousness, which is so conspicuously lacking in amnesia, depends on a different memory system to that involved in priming effects on indirect tests, or whether it involves adding something to what are essentially the same memory traces.

An even more circumscribed deficit of access consciousness can be found in prosopagnosia, an uncommon neurological deficit affecting the recognition of familiar faces. Prosopagnosic patients usually fail all tests of overt recognition of familiar faces (Hécaen & Angelergues, 1962; Meadows, 1974a). They cannot name the face, give the person's occupation or other biographical details, or even state whether or not a face is that of a familiar person (all faces seem unfamiliar). Even the most well-known faces may not be recognised, including famous people, friends, family, and the patient's own face when looking in a mirror. In contrast, recognition from non-facial cues (such as voice, name, and sometimes even clothing or gait) is usually successful.

Although prosopagnosic patients no longer recognise familiar faces overtly, there is substantial evidence of covert recognition from physiological and behavioural measures (Bruyer, 1991; Young & de Haan, 1992).

Bauer (1984) measured skin conductance while a prosopagnosic patient, LF, viewed a familiar face and listened to a list of five names. When the name belonged to the face LF was looking at, there was a greater skin conductance change than when someone else's name was read out. However, if LF was asked to choose which name in the list was correct for the face, his performance was at chance level. The same effect was found for personally known faces (LF's family) and famous faces he would only have encountered in the mass media.

Bauer's (1984) study showed compellingly a difference between overt recognition, which was at chance level for LF, and some form of preserved covert recognition, as evidenced by his skin conductance responses. Comparable findings were reported by Tranel and Damasio (1985, 1988), using a different technique in which the patients simply looked at a series of familiar and unfamiliar faces. Skin conductance changes were greater to familiar than unfamiliar faces, showing that it is possible to demonstrate a preserved electrophysiological response to the familiarity of the face alone.

A number of behavioural indices of covert recognition in prosopagnosia have also been developed, including priming and interference techniques. Consider, for example, what happens if you are asked to classify a printed name as belonging to a politician or a non-politician, and the name is presented together with an irrelevant face which you are asked to ignore. You find that you cannot successfully ignore the distractor face, and if it belongs to the wrong category it will interfere with the speed of your response to the target name. This happens because recognition operates automatically; you cannot simply switch the recognition mechanism off by deciding not to recognise the distractor face. The same pattern of interference of distractor faces on the classification of name targets is found in some prosopagnosic patients, even though they do not recognise the distractor faces overtly (de Haan, Bauer, & Greve, 1992; de Haan, Young, & Newcombe, 1987; Sergent & Signoret, 1992).

In a typical priming experiment, subjects are asked to classify a target name as familiar or unfamiliar, but the target name is immediately preceded by a prime which may itself be a face or a name. On each trial in the experiment, then, a prime is presented and then a target name; subjects have to classify the target name as quickly as possible. Studies of this type have demonstrated that responses to the target name are facilitated if the prime is the same person as the target (e.g. if Ronald Reagan's face is used as the prime preceding the name 'Ronald Reagan') or a close associate (e.g. if Nancy Reagan's face is used as the prime preceding the name 'Ronald Reagan'). This holds for prosopagnosic patients even though they do not recognise the face primes overtly (de Haan et al., 1992; Young, Hellawell, & de Haan, 1988). Moreover, it is possible to compare the size of the priming effect across face primes (which the patients mostly do not recognise overtly) and printed name primes (which they can recognise). These have been found to be exactly equivalent; the possibility of overt recognition of name primes makes no additional contribution to the priming effects observed.

Findings of covert recognition in prosopagnosia show responses based on the unique identities of familiar faces, even though overt recognition of these faces is not achieved. Prosopagnosia can thus be considered a selective deficit of access consciousness, in which access to information about the identities of familiar faces is lost. The phenomenal experience of familiarity is also lost, though the phenomenal experience of seeing a face remains, and there may even be relatively good preservation of other aspects of face perception, such as the perception of sex or emotional expression (Bruyer et al., 1983). However, recognition of identity only seems to take place at a non-conscious level.

There has been some progress in understanding what may be involved. One clue is that the techniques used to demonstrate covert recognition in prosopagnosia have often been used with normal subjects as tools for investigating relatively automatic aspects of recognition which do not need mediation that is conscious in any sense (Young, 1994; Young & Bruce, 1991). Even skin conductance changes to stimuli that were masked to prevent overt recognition can be found in normal people (Ellis, Young, & Koenken, 1993). A second clue is that the loss of overt recognition of familiar faces found in prosopagnosia need not be absolute. This was discovered by Sergent and Poncet (1990), who observed that their patient, PV, could achieve overt recognition of some faces if several members of the same semantic category were presented together. This only happened when PV could determine the category herself. For the categories PV could not determine, she continued to fail to recognise the faces overtly even when the occupational category was pointed out to her. This phenomenon of overt recognition provoked by multiple exemplars of a semantic category has been replicated with case PH by de Haan, Young, and Newcombe (1991) and with case PC by Sergent and Signoret (1992). PV, PH, and PC were all noted to be very surprised at being able to recognise faces overtly.

These observations fit naturally into a model in which activation must cross some form of threshold before it can result in access consciousness. This can be simulated quite simply with an interactive activation model in which excitation can be continuously passed from one functional unit to another, but a separate threshold is set to determine any explicit output. As a minimum, access consciousness requires an explicit representation.

Burton, Bruce, and Johnston (1990) had proposed a simulation of this type that could encompass several findings related to normal face recognition. It was then easy to demonstrate that the prosopagnosic pattern of preserved priming effects without explicit classification of face inputs could be simulated with this model by halving the connection strengths between two of its pools of functional units (Burton et al., 1991). This makes the finding of this pattern in some cases of prosopagnosia much less mysterious.

We can thus understand one way in which covert responses can be preserved when there is no overt discrimination, and this seems highly relevant to understanding access consciousness. However, although it represents a step forward, this type of simulation should not be mistaken for a full solution to the problem of understanding access consciousness. What has actually been established so far is only that this is one form of possible mechanism, not that it is the only or the correct answer. Further, explaining access consciousness is not the same as explaining phenomenal consciousness. As we noted earlier, zombies aside, it is hard to imagine access consciousness without phenomenal consciousness. But what reason do we have to think that the units in a computer program become phenomenally conscious when their activation passes whatever threshold is necessary for access? Maybe they do, but the fact that we do not know whether they do or not shows that an understanding of access consciousness does not necessarily involve an understanding of phenomenal consciousness.

Monitoring and self consciousness

Problems in self consciousness seem to arise after frontal lobe lesions, when patients may engage in socially inappropriate behaviours without apparent concern or embarrassment (Damasio, Tranel, & Damasio, 1990; Stuss, 1991), but these are poorly understood. Rather more progress has been made in understanding monitoring problems that lead to unawareness of impairment (anosognosia).

The classic observations of unawareness of impairment were made by Von Monakow (1885) and Anton (1899), whose patients denied their own blindness or deafness. Subsequent reports have mostly concentrated on denial of blindness, now known as Anton's syndrome. Most emphasise that the patients are unaware of their blindness, behave as if they can see, and may even confabulate visual experiences (Raney & Nielsen, 1942; Redlich & Dorsey, 1945). There are, however, some cases in which insight is achieved. Raney and Nielsen (1942) described a woman who, after a year of apparent lack of insight into her problems, exclaimed "My God, I am blind! Just to think, I have lost my eyesight!".

As well as blindness and deafness, a wide range of types of impairment can be subject to anosognosia (McGlynn & Schacter, 1989). An important observation is that patients with more than one deficit may be unaware of one impairment but perfectly well aware of others. Von Monakow (1885) had noted that his patient complained of other problems, even though he was not aware of his visual impairment. Anton (1899) made similar observations, and suggested that unawareness of impairment of a particular function is caused by a disorder at the highest levels of organisation of *that* function.

This position has been further developed by Bisiach et al. (1986), who demonstrated dissociations between anosognosia for hemiplegia and anosognosia for hemianopia. Paralysis to one side of the body (hemiplegia) and blindness for half the field of vision (hemianopia) are relatively common consequences of brain injury. The fact that patients can show awareness of their hemiplegias but not their hemianopias, and vice versa, shows that anosognosia does not result from a general change in the patient's monitoring abilities or of access consciousness of perceptual states, but can be specific to particular disabilities. Bisiach et al. (1986, p. 480) concluded that "monitoring of the internal working is not secured in the nervous system by a general, superordinate organ, but is decentralized and apportioned to the different functional blocks to which it refers".

Note that monitoring problems need not be restricted to deficits of phenomenal consciousness; for example, unawareness of visual recognition impairments has also been noted. A detailed description of a case involving unawareness of impaired face recognition, SP, is given by Young, de Haan, and Newcombe (1990).

Unawareness of impairment, then, does not result from any overall change in the patient's ability to monitor or access. Like other impairments of consciousness, monitoring problems can be highly selective.

UNITY OR DISUNITY OF CONSCIOUS EXPERIENCE

The neuropsychological impairments we have discussed fit neatly against our distinctions between phenomenal consciousness, access consciousness, and monitoring and self consciousness. In blindsight, there is no phenomenal consciousness of stimuli projected to the blind field; there is also no access to those perceptual contents and no monitoring of the contents (until the patient hears his or her own guesses). The same is true for achromatopsia, showing that defects of consciousness can exist in very restricted aspects of experience. Prosopagnosia is primarily a defect of access consciousness, but the phenomenal feel of familiarity is also missing. Nonetheless, prosopagnosics often show information about the faces they have seen when tested indirectly. In amnesia, there is impaired access to memories of things that happened in the past, but the influence of representations of these events is evident in indirect measures. Anosognosia can also be a highly selective defect confined to monitoring a particular form of access or phenomenal consciousness.

The main point, then, is that these defects of consciousness are highly selective. Phenomenal, access, and monitoring consciousness function well in one domain, but can be defective in another domain.

One thrust of such findings is to highlight the danger of thinking that the subjective unity of conscious experience implies that a unitary brain system is involved. Many discussions of conscious experience begin by emphasising its subjective unity and continuity (James, 1890), and some have argued that materialist theories cannot account for this unity (Tallis, 1991). The hidden agenda is that subjective unity is then taken to imply that there is a place in the brain where everything is put together; Dennett and Kinsbourne (1992) label this the Cartesian Theatre, because Descartes had proposed that integration requires a single interface between mind and brain. This conception lurks behind many contemporary accounts of consciousness, although few neuroscientists now accept Descartes' proposed locus for the interface of the pineal gland.

The Cartesian Theatre fits with what is for many people a compelling intuition. At present, we do not know that it is definitely wrong, and it remains possible to argue that the types of neuropsychological dissociation we have described reflect disconnection of different functional modules from a single, central conscious mechanism (Schacter, 1987; Young & de Haan, 1990). However, the weight of evidence now makes this look unlikely. So many different types of dissociation are being revealed that one has to wonder whether it isn't the subjective unity of conscious phenomena that is illusory. Even if there were multiple conscious mechanisms, why shouldn't they have a subjective 'feel' of being unified in their operation?

Another hypothesis is that the contents of consciousness correspond to the information that is made available to executive mechanisms to co-ordinate and integrate what would otherwise be independent processing streams (Baars, 1988; Morris & Hampson, 1983). This could include the feedback of information that these executive mechanisms need to continue to make available to themselves, as well as information from perceptual, memory, and monitoring systems. From this perspective, the different types of loss of conscious awareness caused by brain injuries are much less of a surprise (Morris, 1992). However, the principal assumption of a single locus for consciousness remains; both Baars (1988) and Morris and Hampson (1983) think that there is only a single executive system.

A major problem is that these approaches tend to drop the issue of explaining phenomenal consciousness. Even if there is a single executive system, which if true would certainly be pertinent to understanding access consciousness, what exactly does it have to do with *phenomenal* consciousness? These theorists start out trying to explain phenomenal consciousness, but they run the risk of ending up with no place for it.

A related argument to the approach linking consciousness to executive mechanisms is used by Damasio (1992, p.208), who points out that "the rejection of *one* biologically impossible Cartesian Theater does not amount to rejecting the sense of *one* self doing the experiencing", and argues that a satisfactory model of consciousness "should indicate how the dis-integrated fragments operate to produce the integrated self". Again, there is an attempt to account for subjective unity by arguing that there is indeed a high degree of unity, but it is imposed late in the system.

Marcel (1993) offers reasons to doubt even this. He draws attention to dissociative phenomena in anosognosia which have potentially important implications. First, as has been noted by Bisiach and Geminiani (1991), there can be inconsistencies between denial as evidenced in actions and verbal reports. For example, a patient with left-sided paralysis following a right hemisphere stroke may bemoan his or her paralysis but keep trying to get out of bed and walk, whereas another patient denies having any deficit on verbal interrogation but makes no attempt to get out of bed. In the one case, a verbally acknowledged deficit does not seem to constrain behaviour, whereas in the other behaviour is constrained even though there is no verbal acknowledgement. Which are we to take as reflecting the patient's 'real' insight, when words and actions are inconsistent with each other?

A second type of dissociation noted by Marcel (1993) reflects the use of a first-person or third-person perspective. It is standard practice in investigations of anosognosia to ask the patient directly about his or her disabilities; "Can you walk?", "Can you tie your shoes?", etc. But Marcel (1993) reports that when he and Tegnér asked anosognosic patients with paralysis affecting one side of the body to rate how well the examiner could perform each activity—"if I [the questioner] were in your [the patient's] current condition"—much better insight into the implications of the paralysis could be obtained.

Marcel (1993) points out that such phenomena are reminiscent of hypnosis and other dissociative states; part of the patient's mind seems to know the relevant facts, but another part doesn't. However, it is unlikely that they arise after brain injury for purely psychodynamic reasons. For example, denial of paralysis is more common after brain injury affecting the right cerebral hemisphere, which creates paralysis of the left side of the body, than after brain injury affecting the left cerebral hemisphere and consequent right-sided paralysis (Bisiach & Geminiani, 1991). So it is unlikely that denial of paralysis only reflects an emotional reaction, as for a right-handed person paralysis of the right hand is potentially much more upsetting, but it is left-sided paralysis that is usually denied. Even more strikingly, it is known that failure to acknowledge left-sided paralysis (anosognosia for hemiplegia) is often associated with a more general failure to respond to the left side of space (known as unilateral neglect), and that temporary remission of both problems can be obtained after stimulation of the vestibular system through irrigation of the canals of the left outer ear with cold water

(Cappa, Sterzi, Vallar, & Bisiach, 1987). This procedure generates a reflex response which involves eye and head turning in the direction of the stimulated ear, but the exact mechanism by which it leads to remission of unilateral neglect and anosognosia is not understood in detail. However, such findings again point one away from psychodynamic interpretations.

Dissociative phenomena in neuropsychology need not be restricted to anosognosia; they may also be fairly common for delusions caused by brain injury. Consider, for example, the Capgras delusion, which involves the bizarre conviction that one's relatives have been replaced by impostors (Ellis & de Pauw, 1994). This delusion can arise in a variety of pathological settings, which include damage to temporo-parietal and frontal areas of the right cerebral hemisphere (Alexander, Stuss, & Benson, 1979; Lewis, 1987; Spier, 1992). Although violence against the impostors is noted in some Capgras patients (Silva, Leong, & Weinstock, 1992), this is much less frequent when the delusions have a clear organic basis (Malloy, Cimino, & Westlake, 1992). In fact, while Capgras patients complain that their relatives have been replaced, a number do not otherwise act in accordance with this belief, showing neither violence nor aggression to the impostors, and failing to report the matter to the police or to initiate any search for their 'original' relatives. Notice that this is not just a motor versus verbal dissociation; telephoning the police station would be just as much a verbal action as stating that your husband is an impostor.

The thrust of such examples is to undermine the idea of a unified self overseeing what we do. If different aspects of our behaviour can be so inconsistent, we can infer that our sense of self is built on a coalescence that can be disrupted under unusual or pathological circumstances. The intuition of a unified consciousness is so directly tied to a first-person perspective that, without a unified self, the case for unified consciousness collapses.

CONSCIOUSNESS AND EVOLUTION

The fact that consciousness is so intimately related to what our nervous systems are doing has led many people to conclude that a biologically-based account will be needed. Searle (1992, p.90) has made the point eloquently:

> Consciousness, in short, is a biological feature of human and certain animal brains. It is caused by neurobiological processes and is as much a part of the natural world order

as any other biological features such as photosynthesis, digestion, or mitosis.

This line of reasoning leads naturally to questions about the evolutionary background to consciousness, but these are not easy to answer. Not every behaviour is affected directly by natural selection, and there are many possibilities for emergent properties or unintended consequences of behaviours whose utility or survival value was initially related to quite different purposes. To illustrate this, Searle (1992, p.106) uses the example of alpine skiing:

> The spread of skiing has been simply phenomenal; and the sacrifices that people are willing to make in money, comfort, and time for the sake of a few hours on a ski slope is at least pretty good evidence that they derive satisfactions from it that are inherent to their biological nature. But it's simply not the case that we were selected by evolution for our predilection for alpine skiing.

Despite these difficulties, Searle (1992) argues that there are evolutionary advantages to consciousness. We have already discussed his argument that consciousness gives us flexibility and creativity, based on the lack of these during attacks of absence (petit mal) epilepsy. However, we noted that this line of reasoning seems to work better for monitoring and access consciousnesses than for phenomenal consciousness.

In general, it seems to us that different forms of consciousness serve different purposes. Phenomenal consciousness and access consciousness are likely to be intimately linked to intentional actions; patients who show blindsight in laboratory tasks don't respond to objects located in their blind field in everyday life, and prosopagnosic patients who show covert recognition effects in the laboratory do not act as if they recognise people from their faces.

To see why certain types of consciousness have become linked to intentional actions, one needs to consider the delicate balance between speed of response and flexibility of response. Perceptual systems have evolved to create representations of external events that can permit effective action in the world that an organism inhabits. Fast responses are best made by dedicated, relatively inflexible systems. Flexibility of response requires more sophisticated representations of events, which take longer to compute. These costs of flexibility become especially marked when time is spent not only in constructing an adequate representation, but also in weighing up possible alternative actions. An obvious way to balance the competing demands of flexibility and speed is therefore to allow many actions to run off under automatic control, and to involve conscious mechanisms which can allow greater choice only when these are needed. This is a particularly convenient solution for the nervous system, in which many actions (like breathing) can be safely left under automatic pilot much of the time, and only require occasional conscious intervention (if you are about to stick your head underwater, etc).

A compelling demonstration of this comes from the dissociation of action and conscious perception found in the elegant work of Milner, Goodale and their colleagues (Goodale & Milner, 1992; Goodale, Milner, Jakobson, & Carey, 1991; Milner et al., 1991). They have made a very thorough investigation of a neuropsychological case, DF, with severely impaired shape perception. When DF was asked to make judgements about the orientation or size of an object, she performed very poorly. However, when DF was asked to put her hand into a slot she immediately oriented it correctly, and she shaped her fingers appropriately for the size of an object she was about to pick up (Goodale & Milner, 1992; Goodale et al., 1991). In general, DF could make accurate responses in tasks that involved a well-practised everyday movement that can be run off without conscious control (putting your hand into something, or picking something up), whereas inaccurate responses arose in tasks that need continual conscious intervention.

Other forms of consciousness, such as monitoring and self-consciousness, may well be more intimately linked to different purposes, including trouble-shooting and the prediction of the social behaviour of others. In discussing possible functions of consciousness, we therefore need to keep clear which form of consciousness might have which type of function.

To many people, it seems acceptable to assign functional roles to cognitive types of consciousness, but less clear in the case of phenomenal consciousness. Velmans (1991) spells out this position, arguing for an epiphenomenalist stance in which phenomenal consciousness *results* from human information processing but does not *enter into it* in any causal way. He supports this stance by demonstrating that phenomenal consciousness is not essential to information processing, in the sense that it would not in principle be impossible for any of the things we do to be undertaken without it. This argument fails to see the point that evolution can often adopt any one of many different options. The issue of epiphenomenalism is not whether consciousness is essential to information processing, but rather whether it plays an actual role, even if something else could substitute for it (Block, 1991). For example, the heart does not have the essential function (in Velmans' sense) of pumping blood, if blood vessels could be constructed that squeeze the blood along on their own. But in the human body, the heart does have the actual function of pumping blood.

Although we therefore do not agree with Velmans' (1991) position, we recognise that phenomenal consciousness presents special difficulties of explanation. Indeed, we have emphasised repeatedly the problem of explaining what it feels like to be us.

One way forward may be to adopt an evolutionary approach, the most detailed of which has been offered by Humphrey (1992, 1994). Humphrey (1992) argues that, in evolutionary terms, the first function of sensations was to mediate affective responses to stimulation occurring at the body surface, because an animal "that had the means to sort out the good from the bad—approaching or letting in the good, avoiding or blocking the bad—would have been at a biological advantage" (Humphrey, 1992, p.142). He says, then, that sensation evolved to allow something to be done about the stimulus, and that this was originally done at the point of stimulation; the animal both detected and responded to the stimulus with the same bit of its skin, much as we still do if we wiggle a toe when it itches. Humphrey (1992) claims that this fundamental coupling of sensation, affect, and action plans is maintained even for more highly developed senses, like vision, which seem subjectively to carry information about the world beyond the body. According to Humphrey, this is achieved through the construction of internal feedback loops to substitute for overt actions; in his view, feeling a particular sensation corresponds to issuing whatever instructions are required to create the appropriate outgoing signal from the brain.

At present, we find it easier to imagine how this idea can fit bodily sensations than external senses like hearing or vision. However, it has to be remembered that eyes evolved by grouping together light sensitive receptor cells which were originally at the body surface (Gregory, 1972), and that the advantage of hearing or vision is simply that they extend one's capacity to respond outwards, to encompass stimuli beyond those that are in direct contact with the surface of the body. So Humphrey's (1992) claim that a general solution to the problems of phenomenal consciousness is possible should not be lightly dismissed. Moreover, even if his approach does prove only to work for bodily sensations (pain, itching, and so on), accounting successfully for how these feel would in itself be a major step forward, justifying Humphrey's (1992, p.219) optimistic conclusion:

> A seeming miracle? No, as close to a real miracle as anything that ever happened. The twist may be that it takes only a relatively simple scientific theory to explain it.

REFERENCES

Alexander, M.P., Stuss, D.T., & Benson, D.F. (1979). Capgras syndrome: a reduplicative phenomenon. *Neurology, 29*, 334–339.

Allport, A. (1988). What concept of consciousness? In A.J. Marcel & E. Bisiach (Eds.), *Consciousness in contemporary science* (pp.159–182). Oxford: Oxford University Press.

Anton, G. (1899). Ueber die Selbstwahrnemung der Herderkrankungen des Gehirns durch den Kranken bei Rindenblindheit und Rindentaubheit. *Archiv für Psychiatrie und Nervenkrankheiten, 32*, 86–127.

Baars, B.J. (1988). *A cognitive theory of consciousness*. Cambridge: Cambridge University Press.

Barbur, J.L., Ruddock, K.H., & Waterfield, V.A. (1980). Human visual responses in the absence of the geniculo-calcarine projection. *Brain, 103*, 905–928.

Barbur, J.L., Watson, J.D.G., Frackowiak, R.S.J., & Zeki, S. (1993). Conscious visual perception without V1. *Brain, 116*, 1293–1302.

Bates, D. & Cartlidge, N. (1994). Disorders of consciousness. In E.M.R. Critchley (Ed.), *The neurological boundaries of reality* (pp. 383–399). London: Farrand.

Bauer, R.M. (1984). Autonomic recognition of names and faces in prosopagnosia: a neuropsychological application of the guilty knowledge test. *Neuropsychologia, 22*, 457–469.

Bisiach, E. & Geminiani, G. (1991). Anosognosia related to hemiplegia and hemianopia. In G.P. Prigatano & D.L. Schacter (Eds.), *Awareness of deficit after brain injury: clinical and theoretical issues* (pp.17–39). Oxford: Oxford University Press.

Bisiach, E., Vallar, G., Perani, D., Papagno, C., & Berti, A. (1986). Unawareness of disease following lesions of the right hemisphere: anosognosia for hemiplegia and anosognosia for hemianopia. *Neuropsychologia, 24*, 471–482.

Block, N. (1991). Evidence against epiphenomenalism. *Behavioral and Brain Sciences, 14*, 670–672.

Bruyer, R. (1991). Covert face recognition in prosopagnosia: a review. *Brain and Cognition, 15*, 223–235.

Bruyer, R., Laterre, C., Seron, X., Feyereisen, P., Strypstein, E., Pierrard, E., & Rectem, D. (1983). A case of prosopagnosia with some preserved covert remembrance of familiar faces. *Brain and Cognition, 2*, 257–284.

Burton, A.M., Bruce, V., & Johnston, R.A. (1990). Understanding face recognition with an interactive activation model. *British Journal of Psychology, 81*, 361–380.

Burton, A.M., Young, A.W., Bruce, V., Johnston, R., & Ellis, A.W. (1991). Understanding covert recognition. *Cognition, 39*, 129–166.

Cappa, S.F., Sterzi, R., Vallar, G., & Bisiach, E. (1987). Remission of hemineglect and anosognosia after vestibular stimulation. *Neuropsychologia, 25*, 775–782.

Carlson, N.R. (1991). *Physiology of behavior* (4th edn.). Boston: Allyn & Bacon.

Cowey, A. & Stoerig, P. (1991). The neurobiology of blindsight. *Trends in Neurosciences, 14*, 140–145.

Cowey, A.& Stoerig, P. (1992). Reflections on blindsight. In A.D. Milner & M.D. Rugg (Eds.), *The neuropsychology of consciousness* (pp.11–37). London: Academic Press.

Crick, F. & Koch, C. (1990). Towards a neurobiological theory of consciousness. *Seminars in The Neurosciences, 2*, 263–275.

Damasio, A.R. (1992). The selfless consciousness. *Behavioral and Brain Sciences, 15*, 208–209.

Damasio, A.R., Tranel, D., & Damasio, H. (1990). Individuals with sociopathic behavior caused by frontal damage fail to respond autonomically to social stimuli. *Behavioural Brain Research, 41*, 81–94.

de Haan, E.H.F., Bauer, R.M., & Greve, K.W. (1992). Behavioural and physiological evidence for covert face recognition in a prosopagnosic patient. *Cortex, 28*, 77–95.

de Haan, E.H.F., Young, A., & Newcombe, F. (1987). Face recognition without awareness. *Cognitive Neuropsychology, 4*, 385–415.

de Haan, E.H.F., Young, A.W., & Newcombe, F. (1991). Covert and overt recognition in prosopagnosia. *Brain, 114*, 2575–2591.

Dennett, D.C. (1988). Quining qualia. In A.J. Marcel & E. Bisiach (Eds.), *Consciousness in contemporary science* (pp.42–77). Oxford: Oxford University Press.

Dennett, D.C. (1991). *Consciousness explained*. Harmondsworth: Allen Lane; The Penguin Press.

Dennett, D.C. & Kinsbourne, M. (1992). Time and the observer: the where and when of consciousness in the brain. *Behavioral and Brain Sciences, 15*, 183–201.

Ellis, H.D. & de Pauw, K.W. (1994). The cognitive neuropsychiatric origins of the Capgras delusion. In A.S. David & J.C. Cutting (Eds.), *The neuropsychology of schizophrenia* (pp.317–335). Hove, UK: Lawrence Erlbaum Associates Ltd.

Ellis, H.D., Young, A.W., & Koenken, G. (1993). Covert face recognition without prosopagnosia. *Behavioural Neurology, 6*, 27–32.

Flanagan, O. (1992). *Consciousness reconsidered*. Cambridge, MA: MIT Press.

Goodale, M.A. & Milner, A.D. (1992). Separate visual pathways for perception and action. *Trends in Neurosciences, 15*, 20–25.

Goodale, M.A., Milner, A.D., Jakobson, L.S., & Carey, D.P. (1991). A neurological dissociation between perceiving objects and grasping them. *Nature, 349*, 154–156.

Gregory, R.L. (1972). *Eye and brain: the psychology of seeing* (2nd edn.). London: World University Library.

Hécaen, H. & Angelergues, R. (1962). Agnosia for faces (prosopagnosia). *Archives of Neurology, 7*, 92–100.

Heywood, C.A., Cowey, A., & Newcombe, F. (1991). Chromatic discrimination in a cortically colour blind observer. *European Journal of Neuroscience, 3*, 802–812.

Hummel, J.E. & Biederman, I. (1992). Dynamic binding in a neural network for shape recognition. *Psychological Review, 99*, 480–517.

Humphrey, N. (1992). *A history of the mind*. London: Chatto & Windus.

Humphrey, N. (1994). The private world of consciousness. *New Scientist, 8* January, 23–25.

James, W. (1890). *The principles of psychology, Vol. 1*. New York: Dover. [1950 reprint of original edition published by Henry Holt & Co.]

Jaynes, J. (1976). *The origin of consciousness in the breakdown of the bicameral mind*. Boston: Houghton–Mifflin.

Johnson-Laird, P.N. (1988). *The computer and the mind: an introduction to cognitive science*. London: Fontana.

Kolb, B. & Whishaw, I.Q. (1990). *Fundamentals of human neuropsychology* (3rd edn.). New York: W.H. Freeman.

Levine, J. (1983). Materialism and qualia: the explanatory gap. *Pacific Philosophical Quarterly, 64,* 354–361.

Lewis, S.W. (1987). Brain imaging in a case of Capgras' syndrome. *British Journal of Psychiatry, 150,* 117–121.

Malloy, P., Cimino, C., & Westlake, R. (1992). Differential diagnosis of primary and secondary Capgras delusions. *Neuropsychiatry, Neuropsychology, and Behavioral Neurology, 5,* 83–96.

Marcel, A.J. (1993). Slippage in the unity of consciousness. In Ciba Foundation Symposium No. 174, *Experimental and theoretical studies of consciousness.* Chichester, UK: Wiley.

Marzi, C.A., Tassinari, G., Agliotti, S., & Lutzemberger, L. (1986). Spatial summation across the vertical meridian in hemianopics: a test of blindsight. *Neuropsychologia, 24,* 749–758.

McGinn, C. (1991). *The problem of consciousness.* Oxford: Blackwell.

McGlynn, S. & Schacter, D.L. (1989). Unawareness of deficits in neuropsychological syndromes. *Journal of Clinical and Experimental Neuropsychology, 11,* 143–205.

Meadows, J.C. (1974a). The anatomical basis of prosopagnosia. *Journal of Neurology, Neurosurgery, and Psychiatry, 37,* 489–501.

Meadows, J.C. (1974b). Disturbed perception of colours associated with localized cerebral lesions. *Brain, 97,* 615–632.

Milner, A.D., Perrett, D.I., Johnston, R.S., Benson, P.J., Jordan, T.R., Heeley, D.W., Bettucci, D., Mortara, F., Mutani, R., Terazzi, E., & Davidson, D.L.W. (1991). Perception and action in 'visual form agnosia'. *Brain, 114,* 405–428.

Milner, A.D. & Rugg, M.D. (Eds.) (1992). *The neuropsychology of consciousness.* London: Academic Press.

Mollon, J.D., Newcombe, F., Polden, P.G., & Ratcliff, G. (1980). On the presence of three cone mechanisms in a case of total achromatopsia. In G. Verriest (Ed.), *Colour vision deficiencies, V* (pp.130–135). Bristol, UK: Hilger.

Morris, P.E. (1992). Cognition and consciousness. *The Psychologist: Bulletin of the British Psychological Society, 5,* 3–8.

Morris, P.E. & Hampson, P.J. (1983). *Imagery and consciousness.* London: Academic Press.

Nagel, T. (1974). What is it like to be a bat? *Philosophical Review, 83,* 435–450.

Neisser, U. (1988). Five kinds of self-knowledge. *Philosophical Psychology, 1,* 35–59.

Perrett, D.I., Hietanen, J.K., Oram, M.W., & Benson, P.J. (1992). Organization and functions of cells responsive to faces in the temporal cortex. *Philosophical Transactions of the Royal Society, London, B335,* 23–30.

Pizzamiglio, L., Antonucci, G., & Francia, A. (1984). Response of the cortically blind hemifields to a moving visual scene. *Cortex, 20,* 89–99.

Pöppel, E., Held, R., & Frost, D. (1973). Residual visual function after brain wounds involving the central visual pathways in man. *Nature, 243,* 295–296.

Ramsey, W., Stich, S., & Rumelhart, D. (Eds.) (1991). *Philosophy and connectionist theory.* Hillsdale, NJ: Lawrence Erlbaum Associates Inc.

Raney, A.A. & Nielsen, J.M. (1942). Denial of blindness (Anton's symptom). *Bulletin of Los Angeles Neurological Society, 7,* 150–151.

Redlich, F.C. & Dorsey, J.F. (1945). Denial of blindness by patients with cerebral disease. *Archives of Neurology and Psychiatry, 53,* 407–417.

Schacter, D.L. (1987). Implicit memory: history and current status. *Journal of Experimental Psychology: Learning, Memory, and Cognition, 13,* 501–518.

Schacter, D.L., McAndrews, M.P., & Moscovitch, M. (1988). Access to consciousness: dissociations between implicit and explicit knowledge in neuropsychological syndromes. In L. Weiskrantz (Ed.), *Thought without language* (pp. 242–278). Oxford: Oxford University Press.

Searle, J. (1984). *Minds, brains and science: The 1984 Reith lectures.* London: British Broadcasting Corporation.

Searle, J.R. (1992). *The rediscovery of the mind.* Cambridge, MA: MIT Press.

Sergent, J. & Poncet, M. (1990). From covert to overt recognition of faces in a prosopagnosic patient. *Brain, 113,* 989–1004.

Sergent, J. & Signoret, J.-L. (1992). Implicit access to knowledge derived from unrecognized faces in prosopagnosia. *Cerebral Cortex, 2,* 389–400.

Shastri, L. & Ajjanagadde, V. (1993). From simple associations to systematic reasoning: a connectionist representation of rules, variables and dynamic bindings using temporal synchrony. *Behavioral and Brain Sciences, 16,* 417–451.

Silva, J.A., Leong, G.B., & Weinstock, R. (1992). The dangerousness of persons with misidentification syndromes. *Bulletin of the American Academy of Psychiatry Law, 20,* 77–86.

Spier, S.A. (1992). Capgras' syndrome and the delusions of misidentification. *Psychiatric Annals, 22,* 279–285.

Stuss, D.T. (1991). Disturbance of self-awareness after frontal system damage. In G.P. Prigatano & D.L. Schacter (Eds.), *Awareness of deficit after brain injury: Clinical and theoretical issues* (pp 63–83). Oxford: Oxford University Press.

Tallis, R. (1991). A critique of neuromythology. In R. Tallis & H. Robinson (Eds.), *The pursuit of mind* (pp.86–109). Manchester, UK: Carcanet.

Torjussen, T. (1976). Residual function in cortically blind hemifields. *Scandinavian Journal of Psychology, 17,* 320–322.

Torjussen, T. (1978). Visual processing in cortically blind hemifields. *Neuropsychologia, 16,* 15–21.

Tranel, D. & Damasio, A.R. (1985). Knowledge without awareness: an autonomic index of facial recognition by prosopagnosics. *Science, 228,* 1453–1454.

Tranel, D. & Damasio, A.R. (1988). Non-conscious face recognition in patients with face agnosia. *Behavioural Brain Research, 30,* 235–249.

Velmans, M. (1991). Is human information processing conscious? *Behavioral and Brain Sciences, 14,* 651–726.

Von Monakow, C. (1885). Experimentelle und pathologisch-anatomische Untersuchungen Über die Beziehungen der sogenannten Sehsphäre zu den infracorticalen Opticuscentren und zum N. opticus. *Archiv für Psychiatrie und Nervenkrankheiten, 16,* 151–199.

Warrington, E.K. & Weiskrantz, L. (1968). New method of testing long–term retention with special reference to amnesic patients. *Nature, 217,* 972–974.

Warrington, E.K. & Weiskrantz, L. (1970). Amnesia: consolidation or retrieval? *Nature, 228,* 628–630.

Weiskrantz, L. (1986). *Blindsight: a case study and implications.* Oxford: Oxford University Press.

Weiskrantz, L. (1990). The Ferrier Lecture, 1989. Outlooks for blindsight: explicit methodologies for implicit processes. *Proceedings of the Royal Society, London, B239*, 247–278.

Weiskrantz, L., Warrington, E.K., Sanders, M.D., & Marshall, J. (1974). Visual capacity in the hemianopic field following a restricted occipital ablation. *Brain, 97*, 709–728.

White, S. (1991). *The unity of the self*. Cambridge, MA: MIT Press.

Young, A.W. (1994). Conscious and nonconscious recognition of familiar faces. In C. Umiltà & M. Moscovitch (Eds.), *Attention and Performance, XV: conscious and nonconscious information processing* (pp.153–178). Cambridge, MA: MIT Press/Bradford Books.

Young, A.W. & Bruce, V. (1991). Perceptual categories and the computation of 'grandmother'. *European Journal of Cognitive Psychology, 3*, 5–49.

Young, A.W. & de Haan, E.H.F. (1990). Impairments of visual awareness. *Mind & Language, 5*, 29–48.

Young, A.W. & de Haan, E.H.F. (1992). Face recognition and awareness after brain injury. In A.D. Milner & M.D. Rugg (Eds.), *The neuropsychology of consciousness* (pp.69–90). London: Academic Press.

Young, A.W., de Haan, E.H.F., & Newcombe, F. (1990). Unawareness of impaired face recognition. *Brain and Cognition, 14*, 1–18.

Young, A.W., Hellawell, D., & de Haan, E.H.F. (1988). Cross-domain semantic priming in normal subjects and a prosopagnosic patient. *Quarterly Journal of Experimental Psychology, 40A*, 561–580.

Zeki, S. (1993). *A vision of the brain*. Oxford: Blackwell.

Zihl, J., Tretter, F., & Singer, W. (1980). Phasic electrodermal responses after visual stimulation in the cortically blind hemifield. *Behavioural Brain Research, 1*, 197–203.

CHAPTER SIX

Why do we need emotions?

Philip T. Smith and Susan M. Kemp-Wheeler
University of Reading

The merely descriptive literature of the emotions is one of
the most tedious parts of psychology. *William James.*

INTRODUCTION

We are entering an era in which machines display a variety of
sophisticated skills (play chess, pilot aeroplanes, do household chores).
But machines are not embarrassed if they lose to a human chess novice,
they do not feel remorse if they crash an aeroplane, and they do not get
bored with housework. In this respect they are crucially non-human.
Machine cognition is 'cold': tasks are carried out with varying degrees
of success, but the machine displays no associated states that in humans
we might call arousal or emotion. In contrast, human cognition is 'hot':
seemingly, even the most trivial events elicit from us an emotional
response. An undone shoelace irritates us, a next-door neighbour's smile
pleases us, if England win a cricket match we are amazed.

If computers flourish without emotions, why do we need them? There
are several types of answer, not all mutually exclusive. First, computers
and humans are built from different material, and it could be that
emotions are needed only for the efficient running of carbon-based
systems (living organisms); in contrast, silicon-based systems
(computers) can get on perfectly well without emotions.

A second type of answer is that we have emotions because we have bodily feelings, particularly those controlled by the autonomic nervous system. The advantage of emotions, according to this view, derives not from anything intrinsic to the emotional experience itself, but from the concomitant changes in the body (e.g. a pounding heart pumps more blood around the body, in preparation for fight or flight). Thus, computers do not need emotions because they do not need to prepare themselves in this way.

A third view is that emotions are crucially associated with *appraisal* (Lazarus & Folkman, 1984). Appraisal is an evaluation of the significance of the current situation for the individual. In adult humans, 'significance' extends beyond direct bodily experiences (hunger, pain) to the web of cognitions that we call the self. Emotions like embarrassment or remorse are experienced as such because of our perceptions about how current events are affecting our self-esteem or our status as a pillar of the community. This then offers us a third reason why machines do not experience emotions: they have no fully developed concept of 'self' and thus cannot carry out the appraisal necessary for all but the most rudimentary emotions. (We can imagine a robot bumping into objects in a vain attempt to find its way out of a cul-de-sac, and even suppose that it might move into an internal state we could label 'frustration', because its goal, to move out of the cul-de-sac, has not been achieved, but no current robot would have thoughts such as 'I'm making a right fool of myself in front of all these people', and so no current robot could be embarrassed.)

When described in this simple fashion, appraisal seems to downplay the bodily sensation aspects of emotion in favour of quite elaborate cognitions. The trouble with this view is that it seems in danger of making emotion too cognitive. The twin hallmarks of cognitions are that they take time (they are not reflex responses to a situation) and that they are largely under control (you may choose to carry on reading this chapter or choose to slam the book shut and throw it across the room). But emotions are often 'immediate' (a door opening when you are alone in an empty house ...) and difficult to control, both in terms of persistence of an underlying mood (the difficulty of 'snapping out of' a depressed state) and in terms of the outward manifestations of emotions (trying to stop giggling in a seminar, trying to stop crying in the cinema). Viewed in this way, emotions differ from cognitions in being *automatic*, in the sense used by cognitive psychologists, such as Shiffrin (1988). (Automatic processes are said to be initiated without significant delay, and to lack susceptibility to conscious control.) From this perspective, emotional responses are able to act quickly to interrupt ongoing cognitive activity (fear of a charging bull interrupts your musings on a country walk) and are not readily turned off and ignored (so anxiety at the possibility of missing an appointment keeps you checking your watch). These are both examples of emotions being used to change or maintain priorities in a complex system, and, as such, they are already present in modern computer systems, which have elaborate ways, for example, of assigning priorities to competing multiple users.

An assigning priorities view glosses over why emotions are associated with particular patterns of bodily sensations. Any signal could be used to change or maintain a computer's priorities, so why do emotions have the phenomenal qualities we experience? One possible reason for emotions having particular phenomenal qualities is that such sensations are intrinsically rewarding or aversive: *feeling* happy is pleasurable in its own right, independent of the cause of the happiness. Such a state of affairs removes a cognitive burden from an organism: it does not need to evaluate exhaustively its progress towards its complex goals, all it needs to do is check whether it is happy or not. The pot-holer, the stamp collector, and the sado-masochist are divided in their goals, but united in their pursuit of happiness.

Emotions may have a role in assigning priorities within the self, but also between groups of individuals, possibly inter-species as well as intra-species. The mood of the meeting may swing in our favour, the crowd could grow ugly. On this view, it is the external *expression* of emotion that is crucial. We expect people with whom we interact to display emotion: the emotions they display may not always please us, but we would find them disconcertingly non-human if they showed no emotion at all. (One way of creating the impression of non-human aliens in science fiction is to reduce their display of emotions, via expressionless faces and monotone voices.) What is the functional significance of these displays? Partly, emotions can affect crowds in the same way as they affect individuals (to prepare for flight or fight), but, perhaps more important, they can promote social bonds between individuals (the most obvious and important example being between parent and child). This view of emotions requires that the basic emotions be culture-free, so mother and infant can recognise each other's emotions before the infant has been exposed to any given culture, and their expression shall similarly be universal. Such an approach puts great emphasis on non-verbal behaviour, particularly facial expression, as the key to emotion.

In summary, computers lack emotions because they are made out of non-organic material, do not have bodily sensations, do not have a concept of self, and do not participate in subtle non-verbal social interactions. In the next section we sketch the history of these ideas, and then go on to see how they have developed in modern psychology.

HISTORICAL BACKGROUND

It is inappropriate to attempt a comprehensive historical survey of different views of the emotions. We select five authors born before 1900 whose views are still well-represented in current debates, by way of introducing the central issues we wish to discuss.

We start, of course, with Aristotle. Aristotle's most extensive discussion of emotion appears in his *Rhetorica* (English translation, 1924). Aristotle treats emotion in this context (essentially a treatise on public speaking) because he believes an orator needs to get an audience into 'the right frame of mind' in order to influence them: "The Emotions are all those feelings that so change men as to affect their judgements, and that are also attended by pain or pleasure." (*Rhetorica*, Book II.1). This single sentence is sufficient to direct us to several of the major issues discussed by modern psychologists which we shall address later: do emotions influence the way people think; are emotions crucially involved in *change* of activity; and is there a primary categorisation of emotions (positive vs negative) linked to whether they are associated with pleasure or pain? Although Aristotle classifies many of the emotions in opposing pairs (Anger vs Calmness; Friendship vs Hatred; Fear vs Confidence; Shame vs Shamelessness; Kindness vs Unkindness; Pity vs Indignation) he does not use pain and pleasure as a systematic means of discriminating them. He notes, for example that Anger is accompanied both by pain ("for a conspicuous slight") and by pleasure ("because the thoughts dwell upon the act of vengeance, and the images then called up cause pleasure"), and Pity and Indignation are both accompanied by pain (at unmerited bad fortune and unmerited good fortune, respectively). Translation is a particularly acute problem for us when we attempt to understand Aristotle, but it is present whenever we encounter someone with a different linguistic or cultural background to ours (perhaps only Athenians of the 4th century BC could fully understand what Aristotle meant by particular emotions). This raises another question we need to address later, namely to what extent emotions can be accurately recognised cross-culturally.

Spinoza discussed the emotions in his *Ethica* (1677, English translation 1910). For Spinoza, the link between emotion and ethics was that emotions may lead people to behave unethically ("... a man who is submissive to his emotions is not in power over himself, but in the hands of fortune to such an extent that he is often constrained, although he may see what is better for him, to follow what is worse", 1910, p.141). Emotion is defined as "... the modifications of the body by which the power of action in the body is increased or diminished, aided or restrained, and at the same time the ideas of these modifications" (pp.84–85). These quotations raise two issues that we discuss later: the first is why emotions are difficult to control; the second is whether emotions are associated with characteristic patterns of action. When it comes to listing the emotions, Spinoza outstrips Aristotle, defining 48, as diverse as Modesty (no.43) and Drunkenness (no.46). The modern reader would probably prefer to interpret these as states that are often accompanied by emotions. The three basic emotions, for Spinoza, are Desire, Pleasure, and Pain. The remaining 45 are defined largely with reference to these three, for example, Hatred "... is pain accompanied by the idea of an external cause" (p.130) and Anger "... is the desire whereby through hatred we are incited to work evil to him we hate" (p.137). Note that in Spinoza's system, Anger is a complex emotion, derived from several more basic ones, whereas Aristotle and many modern theorists see Anger as basic. Thus a major question that we need to discuss is whether there are such things as basic emotions, and how we can identify them. Note also the prominence of Desire in Spinoza's system, drawing our attention to the idea that emotions can be present only in organisms with goals.

No brief historical survey is complete without mention of William James. The James-Lange theory of emotions has achieved considerable prominence (Lange was a Danish physiologist and contemporary of William James). James's thesis, as propounded in his 1890 book, is that "Emotion follows upon the bodily expression in the coarser emotions at least" (p.449). (For James, the coarser emotions are Grief, Fear, Rage, and Love). "... [W]e feel sorry because we cry, angry because we strike, afraid because we tremble ..." (p.450). Although the James-Lange theory finds little support nowadays, James's vivid writing directs our attention to an aspect of emotion underplayed by Aristotle and Spinoza, namely that having an emotion involves bodily feelings, sometimes of a very intense nature (James, 1890, p.452):

> Can one fancy the state of rage and picture no ebullition in the chest, no flushing of the face, no dilation of the nostrils, no clenching of the teeth, no impulse to vigorous action, but in their stead limp muscles, calm breathing, and a placid face? The present writer, for one, certainly cannot. The rage is as completely evaporated as the sensation of its so-called manifestations, and the only thing that can possibly be supposed to take its place is some cold-blooded and dispassionate judicial sentence, confined entirely to the intellectual realm, to the effect that a certain person or persons merit chastisement for their sins ... A purely disembodied human emotion is a nonentity.

This takes us back to the central question of this chapter: why do we need emotions? Why cannot we make do with 'some cold-blooded and dispassionate judicial sentence'? In James's treatment, the emotions are epiphenomenal, the consequence, not the instigator of some action. One might speculate that the emotions might serve some function in aiding a state to persist (remaining fearful and hence cautious even after the predator has vanished from view, for example), but James plays down the persistence of emotions ("Refuse to express a passion, and it dies. Count ten before venting your anger, and its occasion seems ridiculous." ibid, p.463).

When it comes to the expression of emotions, Darwin is the most influential 19th-century writer. In 1872 he published *The expression of the emotions in man and animals* (our quotations are taken from the 'popular' edition of 1904). This book is quoted approvingly by James and Freud, and forms the basis for important modern work on emotional expression, especially facial expression. One of Darwin's central ideas, encapsulated in his 'Principle of Serviceable Associated Habits', is that every expression of emotion has or had functional significance in some (possibly limited) circumstances, but the expression itself can also appear in related circumstances, where its functional significance is slight. Some of these expressions Darwin appears to believe are learned (weeping derives from a chain of events whereby the infant learns to protect its eyes when screaming), but are more commonly innate, where the action may have been 'serviceable' to an ancestor, sometimes a remote one, but now has no direct function (Darwin, 1904, pp.262-3):

> [The expression of sneering] is one of the most curious which
> occurs in man. It reveals his animal descent: for no one, even
> if rolling on the ground in a deadly grapple with an enemy,
> and attempting to bite him, would try to use his canine teeth
> more than his other teeth.

Observations like this point the way to modern debates about how far emotional expression and the emotions themselves are innate and thus identical across cultures.

In another principle, that of the 'direct action of the nervous system', Darwin recognised that certain expressions of emotion may be involuntary, occurring when 'the nerve-force is generated in excess'. This finds echoes in the work of Freud, where emotional expression is sometimes seen as the dissipation of energy generated by internal conflicts. Freud's views on emotions are complex, and he changed his views in the course of his career. The emotion that received most attention from Freud is Anxiety. In early Freud, Anxiety is transformed libido (frustrated sex is expressed as Anxiety) and indeed he claims (1929, p.337). that any unconscious emotional excitation can be so transformed: "Anxiety is … general current coin for which all affects are exchanged … when the corresponding ideational content is under repression." In later Freud, Anxiety is a reaction to danger. In neither case does the emotion appear to be of direct functional significance, and Freud follows Darwin in seeing the expression of Anxiety as a reaction to earlier circumstances: in early Freud, Anxiety shares symptoms with copulation (breathlessness, etc); in late Freud, Anxiety is related to birth trauma. Freud's work again raises questions about the control of emotions and whether we 'need' to express them: do we count 10 with William James to dissipate our rage, or, following Freud, repress our rage thereby transmuting it into Anxiety?

CRITERIA FOR RECOGNISING AND CLASSIFYING EMOTIONS

What is an emotion? Is there such a thing as a basic emotion? If there are basic emotions, how many are there?
One view, which we cannot find anyone in the literature actually proposing, but which will serve as a useful straw person, is that emotions are merely states of an organism, not different in kind to what are usually referred to as non-emotional states, such as being tired, being drunk, or being underwater. That particular states influence cognition is well established: the classic demonstration is that of Godden and Baddeley (1975) who showed that divers asked to learn material underwater or on land performed better if the circumstances in which they learned the material were reinstated at the time of recall (recalling underwater if they had learned underwater, recalling on land if they had learned on land). Such state-dependent memory effects have also been demonstrated with moods (e.g. Bower, 1981), and sometimes these effects can be very large (in one of Bower's experiments where subjects learned material in a happy or sad mood and recalled material in a happy or sad mood, subjects recalling in a mood congruent with their learning mood recalled nearly twice as much as subjects recalling in an incongruent mood). Bower's work has stimulated a substantial amount of work in the last 10 years, and it appears the effects he reported vary somewhat with the population of subjects being studied and/or the ways mood is manipulated (e.g. see Blaney, 1986; Matt, Vàzquez, & Campbell, 1992; Singer & Salovey, 1988). Nonetheless a consensus remains that mood affects memory.

However, we find it difficult to accept that the primary value of an emotion is as a memory aid, a means of reinstating for the organism a previous context in which material was learned. Suppose fear helps us remember what we last did when we were fearful: there may be some survival value in such a mechanism for organisms that live in simple environments (fear makes them freeze, pull in their horns, close their shells), but in complex environments fearful situations can require a diversity of responses. In different situations fear might lead us to jump out of the way, hide, call the police, turn the gas off, or pretend to be a Chelsea supporter: a stereotyped fear response for all situations is unlikely to be appropriate.

So we must find a set of criteria for identifying an emotion that go beyond it being a mere state of the organism. There have been various attempts to achieve this by examining our use of language. One such attempt is Ortony's (1987) feel-be test. This derives from the observation that statements involving feeling or being are virtually synonymous if the state is an emotional one (*I feel angry* = *I am angry*) but not synonymous if the state is not necessarily emotional (*I feel abandoned* ≠ *I am abandoned*). This distinction helps us disentangle some complex emotions; for example, as *being guilty* does not necessarily equal *feeling guilty*, we might want to define guilt as a state often accompanied by emotions such as remorse and anxiety, but not the basis of a distinct emotion. The trouble with Ortony's criterion is that it makes a major philosophical claim: that emotions are unique among our mental states in being ones about which we cannot be mistaken. If we report that we are hot or not tired, objective measurements can prove we are wrong (we may *feel* hot, but the thermometer contradicts us), but Ortony claims there is no possibility of our being mistaken if we report that we are or are not anxious. We doubt that this statement is strictly true: for example, we can conceive of a situation where a person honestly denies that they are anxious, but their anxiety is betrayed by non-verbal cues such as frowning, restlessness, etc. Nonetheless Ortony's claim is surely right almost all the time, which points to emotions being associated with peculiarly distinctive and unambiguous sensations, but it does not help us to define an emotion.

Another attempt to distinguish emotions by linguistic means is provided by Johnson-Laird and Oatley (1989). The roots of their work are to be found in Miller and Johnson-Laird (1976), who demonstrated that words in a particular semantic field (e.g. verbs of motion) were not homogeneous but differed to the extent that relations, causes, or intentions were implicated: compare, for example, *The ball fell* (which tells us simply about direction of motion) with *John dropped the ball* (which tells us what caused the ball to fall, but not whether John did it intentionally) and *John chased the ball* (which tells us John had an intention to retrieve the ball). Applying such criteria to emotions, Johnson-Laird and Oatley came up with seven levels, shown in Table 6.1. A key point to pull out of this analysis is that only basic emotions exist without being implicated directly in relations with other people, events or goals: higher-level emotions need objects (to love *someone*, to please *someone*), events (to be glad *about something*) or goals (to desire *something*).

According to Johnson-Laird and Oatley's analysis, there are five emotion *modes*: Happiness, Sadness, Fear, Anger, and Disgust. *Basic* emotions are situated in one of these modes, and cannot be analysed further. Thus the following are illustrations of the mode of Happiness, differing only in intensity: Languorous, Peaceful, Serene, Cheerful, Happy, Jolly, Gay, Merry, Euphoric, Exuberant, Elated, Ecstatic. Other emotional levels are built on the basic emotion level (see Table 6.1).

If emotion modes defy further componential analysis, how can we tell whether two emotional labels refer to the same or to different emotion modes? One of Johnson-Laird and Oatley's suggestions is the *but* test. Consider two adjectives X and Y. We can form four statements linking X and Y with *but* and *not*:

She was X but Y ... (1)
She was X but not Y ... (2)
She was Y but X ... (3)
She was Y but not X ... (4)

TABLE 6.1
Johnson-Laird and Oatley's Seven Categories for Emotion Words

Level	Label	Examples	Analysis
0	Generic emotions	Feeling	
1	Basic emotions	Happiness	
2	Emotional relations	Love	To experience intense happiness in relation to object or person, who may also be object of sexual desire
3	Caused emotions	Gladness	Happiness for a known reason
4	Causatives	Please	To cause happiness
5	Emotional Goals	Desire	To have a goal, which may be sexual, and which if attained causes happiness
6	Complex emotions	Complacent	Happiness from evaluation of one's current state, and, from speaker's point of view, ignoring dangers or difficulties

If X and Y are near synonyms, like *Jolly* and *Merry*, then none of the four statements is possible ((2) and (4) are not true, and (1) and (3) sound odd). If X and Y refer to the same emotion mode, but differ in intensity, then only one of the four statements is possible, either (2) or (4) (try X=*happy* and Y=*ecstatic*). Finally, if X and Y are associated with different emotion modes and are of similar intensity, or only one of them has emotional content, then all the statements are possible (try X=*distraught* and Y=*angry*, or X=*happy* and Y=*underwater*). Johnson-Laird and Oatley remark that the *but* test should be used with caution, as well they might, as it can be used to undermine their claim that there are five unanalyseable emotion modes. Critics, such as Frijda (1987), have argued for two basic emotions, based on pleasure and pain, and the *but* test seems to bolster Frijda's position. We are quite unable to accept *but* sentences involving *happy* and any of the negative emotions, *sad* being the clearest case, suggesting that Happy and Sad have something in common, namely presence or absence of pleasure or of pain.

For Johnson-Laird and Oatley (1989), a further criterion for a basic emotion is that it does not require further componential analysis to be understood. This can be examined via an extension of the *but* test, which we might call the *but I'm ignorant* test. For each level in Table 1 beyond the basic level (level 1), sentences expressing ignorance about an emotion seem odd. Consider the following sentences:

I am in love but I don't know with whom. (Level 2)
I am glad, but I don't know why. (Level 3)
Something pleases me, but I don't know what. (Level 4)
I desire something, but I don't know what. (Level 5)
He is complacent, but I don't know about what. (Level 6)

All these sentences sound odd, because the emotional term requires some additional information to be fully understood (with whom you are in love, what event has made you glad, etc). In contrast, claim Johnson-Laird and Oatley, basic emotions can be felt in the absence of knowledge of their causes: *I feel happy, but I don't know why* is acceptable. Although we accept that this test is effective for establishing the status of words in levels 2 to 6, we doubt its value in establishing basic emotions. First, intensity seems to play a role in this test: *I feel ecstatic but I don't know why* is more difficult to accept than *I feel cheerful but I don't know why*. Second, 'rapid onset' emotions (emotions that develop quickly, usually in response to a specific event) fail the *but I don't know why* test: *I am disgusted but I don't know why* sounds distinctly odd. Third, the test fails to distinguish between emotional and non-emotional terms: *I feel hot but I don't know why* is acceptable.

To summarise this section, purely linguistic analysis has thrown up many interesting features of how we use emotional words, but has not resolved the issue of what a basic emotion is. Perhaps it is a mistake to regard emotions as static entities that can be studied in snapshots to which linguistic labels are attached. Emotions extend and change in time, and it is to these changes that we next turn.

How long do emotions last?

Some understanding of what emotions are can be gained from examining how long they last. An *emotional reaction* can be fleeting (the joy we might feel in scoring a goal is immediately dissipated when the goal is disallowed). On other occasions the emotion can persist for hours or more, and would be described as a *mood*. On the longer term, we refer to someone who is often in a happy mood as having a happy *predisposition*. Finally, we might distinguish *underlying emotional states*, which reflect a person's relationship to their long-term goals, and which might rarely if ever be explicitly expressed. The friend you have not seen for years, who asks "Are you happy?" is not asking about mood or predisposition, but about whether you are satisfied with your life.

How theorists handle these temporal distinctions interacts with their views about basic emotions. Ortony and Clore (1989), for example, do not believe there are any basic emotions, and that what Johnson-Laird and Oatley (1989) construe as basic are simply those emotions that can persist long enough to be labelled as moods. Ortony and Clore point out that it is easier to say "I feel X but I don't know why" when X is a mood than when X is an emotional reaction. If the goal I thought I had scored is disallowed, my emotional reaction may be quite complex (anger, embarrassment, surprise, frustration) and quite difficult to analyse, but there is no doubt what its cause is. In contrast a sad mood may be provoked by several incidents, spread out in time, none of which is particularly memorable: in such a case it might be difficult to pinpoint a cause of my sadness.

There are two aspects of the temporal course of emotional responses that require special comment. One is that the bodily feelings associated with an emotion and our appraisal of them may not always be in synchrony. For example, our heart may still pound for many minutes after a potentially dangerous situation, which frightened us, has been averted. It is tempting to see this as an inevitable design fault of the system: cognitions can change very rapidly, but bodily changes are slower (heart rate cannot change instantaneously, for example). Another way of looking at this, however, would be to suppose that it is one of the functions of emotions to persist, to act as reminders that conflicts need to be resolved or actions may be needed (the anxious person is constantly alerted to the possibility of threat, the angry person is on guard against the possibility of further insults).

A second observation about the temporal course of emotional response is that the emotional trajectory itself, its rises and falls, may have functional significance and repay further study. Frijda, Mesquita, Sonneman, and van Goozen (1991) asked subjects to estimate how long various emotions persisted, and to indicate how their intensity varied over time. Subjects reported some emotions persisting for hours or even days. Frijda et al. draw attention to the complexity of the emotional responses (anger, sadness, shame, contempt, and disgust all elicited in one episode, for example).

A concept to borrow from the cognitive science literature here is that of *problem space*. This is a specification of the possible states of the world and of the paths connecting such states: for example, positions in a game of chess could be possible states of the world, and various chess moves would be the paths linking these states. Typically there are goal states in problem space (in chess, those positions in which the opponent's king is checkmated). Finding paths through problem space to goal states can be a tricky business for any problem of significant complexity. Among the algorithms that have been developed for finding goal states are *hill-climbing* procedures: a goal state is characterised as the highest point in a terrain, and the hill-climbing procedure looks for the path with the steepest gradient leading away from the current state. If the problem space is simple, following the path with the steepest gradient will get us to the top of the hill as quickly as possible, and hence attain our goal state (see Fig. 6.1). The trouble with the hill-climbing procedure is that it can become trapped at *local maxima*, that is, it can take us to the top of a hill that is locally the highest point in the terrain, but which is lower than the global maximum, the highest hill, which is our goal (again, see Fig. 6.1). There are various ways to try to avoid local maxima, the most obvious being to start from several different points in the problem space and see which starting point leads to the highest final state.

The relevance of this digression for emotion is as follows. In order to get a hill-climbing procedure to work, we need a measure of height (to be able to label states according to whether they are better or worse than our current state), a set of procedures for moving around problem space (a sort of cognitive mountain bike that enables us to move up the hill), and a stopping rule (deciding when further exploration is unlikely to lead to significant improvement). Emotions could be seen as ways of embodying all these abstract properties: height corresponding to positive affect or lack of negative affect, and how vigorously we move around problem space and how persistently we search for global maxima

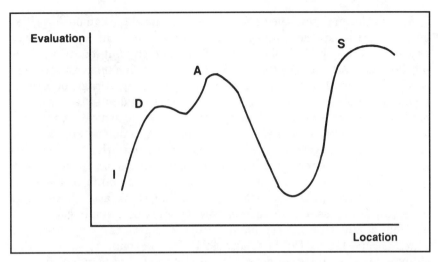

FIG. 6.1.   An emotional landscape. I is initial position, D and A are local maxima, S is the global maximum. The figure illustrates the problem for a hill-climbing algorithm, which cannot reach the global maximum, S, from the initial position, I, without going downhill for part of the route.

corresponding to emotional arousal. Consider a report of an emotion episode in Frijda et al. (1991, p.200):

> One night I walked home from making a call in a phone booth. Two boys were leaning against a car, and one said to the other about me: 'tasty piece, that, I would like to get on top of her'. The remark almost made me vomit ... After coming home I became very, very angry ... I threw something across my room. [This mood persisted until the next morning, then] after an hour or so my mood changed, ... I thought the boy who had made the remark just ridiculous, it made me laugh, and I felt above it.

The sequence of emotions here—initial disgust, then persistent anger, finally dissipating in laughter—can be seen as an attempt to move around the problem space depicted in Fig. 6.1: the narrator, placed in an unacceptable position (I), tries to make her way back to a level of satisfaction, initially by ascending a peak marked 'disgust' (D); this route leads on to a substantial peak, marked 'anger' (A). 'Anger', however, is a local minimum: the narrator searches persistently around this peak for higher ground, in vain. Finally, by descending to a lower level or perhaps restarting the search process from a different location, the narrator is able to reach the high ground of satisfaction (S).

The reader may find the notion that our mental life can be described as if we were exploring an emotional landscape as fanciful, without explanatory power. Undoubtedly the idea is sketchy, but it does have the merit of characterising emotional processes as dynamic rather than static. On a small scale, the ideas in the preceding paragraph can be given more substance, using that branch of artificial intelligence called *neural networks* (systems of interconnected units, whose patterns of activations might correspond to positions in problem space). One technique used in this area is *simulated annealing*, where the system initially explores energetically many different areas of problem space, but gradually 'cools' into a more stable state, which often turns out to be a desired goal state. The schedule of cooling (how fast, whether any reheating is necessary, etc) affects how quickly and reliably goal states are found and bears resemblances to the emotional trajectories in humans reported by Frijda et al. (1991). It is beyond the scope of this chapter to develop these ideas, but the interested reader will find an example of a problem solver using simulated annealing in Smolensky (1986) and can explore its properties on a PC or a Macintosh with the help of the McClelland and Rumelhart (1988) package.

THE FUNCTIONS OF EMOTIONS

The position that we have developed so far is that emotions are a set of dynamic processes that help us to achieve various goals (self-preservation in the face of danger, enhancement of self-esteem, etc). Some emotional episodes may persist for a sufficient length of time and be accompanied by sufficiently stereotypical changes in neurophysiology for our culture to give them a label (anger and fear are good examples). But if we are to answer the central question of this chapter, why we need emotions, we have to show that emotions are not merely epiphenomenal concomitants of goal-seeking, but have genuine functional significance in helping people achieve their goals.

Do emotions change the way we think?
The bulk of studies reviewed in this section show that people in different moods exhibit different cognitive biases. The puzzle is to explain in what way, if any, these biases have functional significance, i.e. enable people to operate more effectively.

Studies that have investigated this fall into two types. First, there are laboratory studies where subjects undergo a mood induction procedure (MIP) to put them into the emotional state the researcher wishes to study. At least 16 techniques can be identified and these include watching films, reading self-referent statements, listening to music, hypnosis, recalling personal memories, and false feedback after a cognitive task (Martin, 1990).

The procedure developed by Velten (1968), in which subjects read statements such as "I'm discouraged and unhappy about myself" to induce depression, is probably the most widely used technique, at least until recently, although considerable concern has been expressed about its effectiveness (Kenealy, 1986). One major concern is that apparent changes in mood may reflect only the influence of demand characteristics.

A second method used to study the role of emotion in cognition is to compare people in in two or more naturally occurring mood states. This has been done using clinical samples and in analogue research with people scoring highly on anxiety and depression rating scales without meeting the criteria for clinical disorder. One concern about these studies is that they equate depression with sadness. In fact, depression can be diagnosed without sadness (DSM III-R: American Psychiatric Association, 1987), and the clinical syndrome is more than a mood disorder and generally includes a disruption in eating, sleeping, motivation, etc. Emotions such as anger, fear, disgust, etc may also be aroused (Polivy, 1981). Indeed, the psychoanalytic view of depression is that it is primarily associated with anger. Therefore, differences between depressed and non-depressed people may reflect something other than a difference in their mood states.

In spite of our concerns with the methodology of research in this area, there is a consensus view that emotions do affect the way we think. In particular, emotions have been found to affect the way we evaluate ourselves and others (see Clark & Williamson, 1989, for a review). For example, Coyle and Uretsky (1987) found that in comparison to students watching positive film clips, those who had watched negative clips rated themselves less healthy. Forgas, Bower, and Krantz (1984) found that subjects in a good mood after recalling happy memories judged themselves to be more socially adept than those in a relatively bad mood after recalling depressing memories. After manipulating mood by having subjects read a story with either a positive or negative ending, Diener and Iran-Nejad (1986) found that positive mood was associated with subjects' ratings of themselves as more ambitious and less lonely.

Other studies that show that when we feel happy we make more positive judgements about ourselves and our lives include that by Schwarz and Clore (1983) who found that subjects who described a recent happy event, and then rated how satisfied they were with their current life circumstances, produced higher satisfaction scores than subjects who had not been previously asked to describe a happy event. Using a similar mood manipulation procedure, subjects asked to recall a previous romantic success rated themselves more able, not only in the romantic domain, but also in interpersonal and athletic achievements than those previously asked to recall a neutral situation (Kavanagh & Bower, 1985). Furthermore, Forgas and Moylan (1988) found that subjects who had watched a happy film were more optimistic about their future personal wealth than subjects who had not seen the film.

This positive bias extends beyond evaluations of the self to judgements made about others and the environment. For example, subjects made to feel elated after reading positive self statements rated others as more honest, sociable, creative, tolerant, altruistic, and conscious of the environment than subjects who did not read these statements, and shoppers given free gifts considered their cars and televisions performed better and needed less servicing than those not given gifts (Isen, Shalker, Clark, & Karp, 1978).

The general finding from these studies is that positive mood is associated with more positive judgements, although this is not universally true. White, Fishbein, and Rutstein (1981, Study 2) reported that a happy MIP resulted in men rating an attractive woman more romantically appealing than men who were in a neutral mood, but they also rated an unattractive woman as *less* appealing than did the control group. Moreover, it is noteworthy that positive feelings do not extend to recommending more lenient prison sentences for drink drivers or heroin trafficking (Forgas & Moylan, 1988).

Studies that led psychologists to believe that negative mood is associated with negative evaluations include that by Kavanagh and Bower (1985) who showed that subjects' ratings of self efficacy were decreased after recalling a romantic failure in comparison to people who had previously imagined a neutral situation. Vestre and Caulfield (1986) gave mildly depressed and non-depressed students neutral personality feedback and found that depressed students were more accurate in their perceptions but perceived it to be less favourable than the non-depressed group. Griffitt (1970) had subjects work in either an uncomfortably hot and humid room, or a normal working environment. As expected, the environmental conditions led subjects who were hot and sticky to rate their mood more negatively and they subsequently rated a stranger less attractive than those who worked in the comfortable setting. However, Forgas and Moylan (1988) found that watching a sad or aggressive film did not lead to a decrease in ratings of life satisfaction in comparison to subjects who had yet to see a film.

Cognitive bias

One difficulty in interpreting all the studies that compare judgements of people in a positive mood with those in a negative mood is that it is impossible to know where the bias lies. Differences could arise because negative mood is associated with bias, because positive mood is associated with bias, or because bias occurs in both positive and negative moods. Obviously the way to get round this problem is to compare all moods with a neutral (control) condition and studies that do this reveal the very interesting—and somewhat surprising—finding that when biases arise they seem to be associated with positive rather than negative moods and emotions. We think the even-handedness shown by people who are depressed especially surprising as traditionally the beliefs and judgements of the mentally ill have been assessed against the (presumed) accuracy of the cognitions of the healthy.[1]

The majority of studies that compare the perceptions and judgements of people in a negative mood with those in a neutral mood show that negative mood is generally associated with more accurate perceptions and more negative evaluations. There are exceptions however, and it may be that these findings only arise in very specific circumstances. For example, Alloy and Abramson (1988) suggest that "depressive realism" may occur only when judgements are made about the self rather than other people, when judgements are made in public rather than private and especially when they are made on the basis of ambiguous information, and when there is a delay before the inference is made.

Some studies that investigate the effect emotion has on judgement compare performance with an objective reality. Studies that ask subjects to make predictions or judge contingency fall into this category. For example, Golin, Terrell, and Johnson (1977) asked students to predict how successful they would be at throwing dice. Success was previously defined as dice rolls of 2, 3, 4, 9, 10, 11, and 12 and the objective, chance-determined probability was 44%. Depressed students' expectancies of success were accurate reflections of the objective probability of success, whereas non-depressed students had expectations that were inappropriately high. The accuracy of judgements made by depressed subjects was also seen in a study by Alloy and Abramson (1979). Here the experimenters manipulated the relationship between a response subjects made and the onset of a light. Contrary to the expectations of the experimenters at the time, depressed subjects judged their degree of control accurately whereas non-depressed subjects demonstrated various illusions of control, depending on the exact nature of the task.

It is clear from these studies that emotion does affect the way we think. We need to ask how emotion leads to these ways of thinking and what function these biases serve. One mechanism proposed to account for the effect of mood on judgements is the mood congruency hypothesis. This explanation rests on the notion that mood states facilitate the recall of mood-congruent memories. One assumes that we store in memory positive, negative, and neutral thoughts about ourselves, other people, and our environment. When we want to make a judgement about these things, we generally do not have the time or inclination to try to recall everything that is relevant, so we base our judgement on the recollection of just a few thoughts. If mood enhances the likelihood of recalling mood-congruent memories, then negative moods are likely to facilitate the recall of negative memories and predispose to negative judgements. Likewise, positive moods will increase the likelihood of positive evaluations because positive memories will be those most likely to come to mind. The notion that memories can be influenced by mood congruency is a particular manifestation of the state dependent memory phenomena we discussed earlier. As we remarked then, it is difficult to see that the primary function of emotions is to promote these effects, as mood-congruent memories do not have a sufficiently high probability of being relevant to the situation in which we find ourselves.

Research has yet to investigate whether it is mood congruency that underpins the influence of mood on judgement, but there is now a substantial body of evidence for this phenomenon (see Blaney, 1986; Matt et al., 1992) in the mood and memory literature. Of course, more than one mechanism may be involved. Another possible candidate is that mood itself may be used as a piece of information when making judgements. For example, I may rate my liking for my tutor highly when I am happy, because if I liked her less I would expect to feel less happy when thinking about her. There is some evidence that this phenomenon does occur (Schwarz & Clore, 1983). Another mechanism that might underpin these findings is self schema processing. Schemas are stored bodies of knowledge built partly of memories but also containing beliefs, attitudes, and assumptions. We have a schema for every facet of our lives. For example, "sitting in warm water without one's clothes" is part of our "bath schema". Schemas act as conceptual filters and lead us to interpret and remember information that is consistent with them. A number of studies have shown that non-depressed people possess strong positive self schemas, whereas the schemas of mildly or moderately depressed people are more balanced with both positive and negative elements (Greenberg, Vàzquez, & Alloy, 1988). This could account for the evenhandedness of depressed subjects and overly positive self-view of non-depressed people, although Dykman, Abramson, Alloy, and

Hartlage (1987) have found both depressed and non-depressed subjects show positive biases, negative biases, and accurate recall of ambiguous feedback depending on the match between each group's self schema and the valence of feedback.

There are other cognitive biases associated with mood which go beyond mood congruency, and again it is people in a positive mood who appear to perform worse. Several studies of persuasion have shown that subjects in a happy mood pay less attention than subjects in a sad mood to the quality of the arguments presented to them (Bless, Bohner, Schwarz, & Strack, 1990; Worth & Mackie, 1987). Perhaps a better way of describing these results is that one of the functions of negative moods is to make us more critical (if things are not going right, it pays to check the environment more carefully).

What is the function of cognitive bias?
What function do the optimistic and self-enhancing biases and illusions of non-depressed people fulfil? One possibility is that they enhance and maintain self-esteem. Low levels of self-esteem are maladaptive because the individual cares so little for the self that basic needs may not be met. A person with a low level of self-esteem may not care what they eat and in an extreme state may not eat at all, and may take active steps towards suicide. One would expect people with high levels of self-esteem to care about themselves to the degree that they take advice about diet, exercise, alcohol intake, etc and thus increase the likelihood of their survival. Furthermore, optimism may enhance successful coping with events that are life-threatening (e.g. Silver & Wortman, 1980) and decrease susceptibility to physical symptoms that are stress related (e.g. Scheier & Carver, 1985).

A second motivational theory to account for positive allusions and optimistic biases of those in a good mood concerns impression management. Several social psychologists (e.g. Arkin, Appelman, & Burger, 1980) have suggested that they occur in order to increase or maintain the esteem of others rather than self-esteem, although of course some people derive their esteem from the view others take of them. In this light, depression is seen to result from a breakdown in the mechanisms that ensure the approval of others, and helps to explain the success of inter-personal psychotherapy as an effective treatment (Elkin et al., 1989).

A final point is that it might be naive to believe that findings from the laboratory generalise to real life, and until more ecologically valid research is done interpretations should be made with caution. It is entirely possible, for example, that the optimism of non-depressed subjects accurately reflects their everyday experiences in which they are often praised and often successful. We know that our judgements are based on recollections of similar circumstances (known as the availability heuristic, Tversky & Kahneman, 1973), so if non-depressed people usually get positive feedback that is what they would always anticipate. In comparison to the artificially evenhanded feedback in the laboratory environment, their expectations will then seem overly optimistic and illusory. One further perspective in this field should also be mentioned and that is the self-fulfilling prophecy. A number of studies show that inaccurate beliefs about the environment lead people to behave in ways consistent with these beliefs. Someone optimistic about their chances of success may try harder and as a result experience more success which strengthens their belief in their own competence, etc. (Scheier, Weintraub, & Carver, 1986). Hence, biases that are initially erroneous may in the end turn out to be accurate. This perspective does not try to account for initial biases but offers another reason for the adaptiveness of optimism.

ABNORMAL PSYCHOLOGY AND THE EMOTIONS

We would all be happier if we did not have emotions

This oxymoron suggests itself when we consider the millions of people in the world who suffer some emotional disorder, such as depression, phobias, and post-traumatic stress disorder. How can we regard emotions as functional, when plainly they are dysfunctional for so many people? In this section we follow Öhman (1993) quite closely, to whom the interested reader is referred for more details. Öhman's thesis is close to Darwin's: emotions have their origins in the evolutionary history of the species. In the case of fear, which functions to alert the organism to danger, the organism must be innately provided with specifications of what stimuli signal danger or else be able to learn the class of dangerous stimuli very quickly. This means that humans are predisposed to learn fear responses to 'biologically significant' stimuli such as snakes and spiders, because these were most threatening for our ancestors. A further feature of the fear response is that to be functional it must have a low threshold (better to suffer many false alarms, 'detecting' a predator that is absent, than make one fatal mistake, missing the predator that is present). It follows that as a species we run the risk of there being individuals with fear thresholds even lower than the trigger in 'normal' people who are likely to produce dysfunctionally excessive numbers of fear responses, and these responses may well be attached to the snakes and spiders that threatened our ancestors. This sort of argument Öhman is able to repeat successfully for other common phobias, such as blood phobia.

Social phobias (avoidance of social situations, through fear of appearing foolish) are treated by Öhman in a similar fashion, being the result of hypersensitivity to a set of biologically grounded social fears. According to Öhman (1993, p.518), these social fears "… resulted from a dominance–submissiveness system, the adaptive function of which was to promote social order by means of facilitating the establishment of dominance hierarchies." How far modern human society is regulated by dominance hierarchies is debatable, but there is no mistaking them in other social primates, which is relevant evidence from an evolutionary perspective. We discuss other social aspects of emotions in a later section.

Another theme found in the work of several clinical psychologists and psychotherapists, and which Öhman endorses, is that we may not always be aware of our emotions. This is a matter of some dispute: Ortony (1987, p.295) states categorically that "… it is not normally possible for a person who is in an emotional state to be unaware of it", citing no less a person than Freud in his support. However, it is crucial for Öhman's views on the functions of emotions that we sometimes be unaware of our own emotions, or at least of the reasons for changes in our bodies' arousal. This is because emotions such as fear need an automatic hotline to warn the organism of danger, and automatic processes (like breathing, for example) do not require attention or awareness. But this functional aspect of the system (registering danger automatically and therefore, sometimes, without awareness) has a dysfunctional feature—that we may find our nervous system becoming increasingly aroused without knowing the cause of the arousal. This can lead to catastrophic misinterpetation which is the central feature of a panic attack: the sufferer believes something dreadful is happening to them, e.g. they are having a heart attack, and this sets in train a vicious circle of fear responses and further misinterpretations.

The tangled web of dysfunctional emotions that can be set up as a result of inappropriate adjustments in the information-processing system is what psychotherapists routinely face. Greenberg (1993) classifies emotional expression into four types. (1) Biologically adaptive primary affective responses, which are 'normal', but the client may not be aware of them; (2) secondary reactive emotional responses, which represent the client's attempt to cope with the emotions generated by (1), for example crying in frustration when angry; (3) instrumental emotional responses, for example, crying to attract sympathy; (4) learned maladaptive primary responses, such as the phobias we have already discussed. All of these emotional expressions can be seen to emanate from an adaptive information-processing system, but all can lead to inappropriate behaviour. An appropriate emotional response of anger in a situation where one has been wronged can lead to an inappropriate response (punching someone who is bigger than you); secondary reactive emotional responses have the effect, in our hill-climbing analogy, of sending the client off in a non-optimal direction; instrumental emotional responses preserve the client at a local maximum, where a short-term sacrifice of easily won sympathy may be necessary to make long-term gains; and learned maladaptive responses are the price exacted by a hypersensitive alarm system.

Why are emotions difficult to control?

The previous section has already provided some reasons for emotions being difficult to control. First and foremost, as part of a system that receives signals via automatic pathways about dangers in the environment, emotions often function well because of their lack of susceptibility to control: it does not pay to ignore a potentially threatening stimulus.

This automaticity of emotional response may apply to emotional expression too. Part of the functional value of emotional expression is that, for most of us most of the time, it is an accurate reflection of our internal states and thus can be trusted by an observer. Socialisation trains us to attempt to hide our emotions if the context demands it, but the success is often limited: we can train a child to thank uncle politely for the disappointing present, but it is less easy to get the child to keep the tone of disappointment out of their voice. The price we pay for a hot line direct from our internal states to their bodily expression is limited control.

This poor control of physiological responses can lead to persistence of emotion for unreasonable lengths of time. A woman who feels angry that her smoked salmon has been stolen from a communal fridge may find it a few hours later hidden by other food, but remain angry for days. When she says she continues to feel angry, she is almost certainly reporting an awareness of bodily changes that only days later return to normal. In fact, there are many techniques that give us control over the physical changes associated with emotion, for example, relaxation techniques, hypnosis, and meditation, but few people are taught such techniques in the Western world. Indeed, the number of prescriptions for anxiolytic drugs and beta blockers per head of population attests to the fact that most people believe that bodily responses, such as the fight/flight response, can be controlled only by external means.

The difficulty in controlling emotional expression is associated by many theorists with the need to dissipate arousal via some form of expression, 'appropriate' or not. Freud's (1929) view of anxiety as the expression of other, repressed, emotions, and Tinbergen's (1940) description of displacement activity in animals who are reining in their aggressive displays, can both be characterised in this way. At a more mundane level, painfully ineffectual attempts to stop giggling in some inappropriate situation, such as a seminar, probably also fit into this category.

Not all failures to control emotions stem from the automatic nature of the input and output mechanisms associated with emotions. Failures at a cognitive level to recognise all the schemas being activated by an emotional episode may prolong emotional responses. For example, a young man may be devastated by a girlfriend wanting to end a relationship that has lasted only a few weeks. His strength of feeling may arise, not because this is the end of a brief affair, but because it awakens in him fundamental beliefs about being unloveable and therefore destined for a life of loneliness and isolation. This man's attempts to control his feelings by attention to, and analysis of, his relationship with this particular woman will, therefore, be in vain.

A final reason why emotions may be difficult to control is that once they arise they may influence information processing in ways that further enhance that emotional state. Hence a vicious circle ensues in which the emotion is maintained through processes that are not under conscious control. For example, many studies now exist that suggest that depressed mood enhances the likelihood of recalling unhappy memories (Matt et al., 1992). One characteristic of depression is rumination, and rumination on unhappy memories is likely to enhance the feelings of sadness (Teasdale, 1983). Recent research has suggested that perhaps a vicious circle of a similar nature maintains or exacerbates anxiety. MacLeod and Mathews (1988) have found that, in situations where there is stimulus competition, anxious subjects preferentially attend to threatening rather than neutral words, whereas the opposite effect is seen in the non-anxious. If this is a phenomenon that occurs outside the laboratory and is preconsciously determined as MacLeod and Mathews believe, we may have a better understanding of why anxiety is difficult to control. Anxiety may lead people to focus on further threatening stimuli which may enhance their feelings of anxiety and so on in a vicious circle that is obviously not under their control.

To summarise this section, dysfunctional emotional reactions are like pain. Pain is unpleasant and there are occasions (at the dentist's) when most of us profit from temporary analgesia. But pain is part of a functional system, warning us of tissue damage and the like, and to be permanently insensitive to pain is a serious incapacity. To be permanently emotionally insensitive would be a similar misfortune.

THE SOCIAL AND DEVELOPMENTAL PSYCHOLOGY
OF EMOTIONS

The development of emotions

From an evolutionary perspective, emotions probably first developed as part of responses by the individual to threats in the environment. However they have come to have substantial significance at a social level. In line with our general strategy of questioning the need for emotions, we can ask whether a social organism without emotions could exist. There is no evidence of the existence of such a creature among the higher animals; indeed, it could be argued, the more advanced the organism the greater the need for emotions. This is because emotional expression is such an effective communicator: as we have already remarked, emotional expression is a reliable indicator of emotional states, the system for learning to encode and decode messages about emotional states is quickly learned, and once learned is used automatically and effortlessly. The language of emotion lacks the subtleties of human language, but is superior in its immediacy, both to learn and to use.

There are disputes about how universal and/or innate emotions are. On the one hand there is the influential work of Ekman (e.g. Ekman, 1984) which claims that facial expression of the basic emotions is recognisable cross-culturally. Here the emphasis must be on *expression*, rather than underlying emotional state: there is no doubt that most of us can recognise a face that is crying or about to cry, but it may not be clear from the face alone whether this is the face of someone who has just experienced a serious disappointment, won an Olympic gold medal, or been peeling onions. Advocates of the cultural specificity of emotional expression cite systems for communicating emotion that can be acquired only from a close acquaintance with a particular culture, the most exotic example being the Kaluli's use of fragments of bird song to characterise different emotions (Feld, 1982).

However the universal vs culture-specific dispute is resolved, there is no doubt that young children learn to use and perceive emotions very quickly. A study by Stenberg and Campos (1990), where infants are restrained against their will by an experimenter, suggests displays of anger by infants appear as young as 4 months, and by 7 months infants direct their anger towards their mothers (who are not the immediate cause of the restraint they are experiencing), suggesting an understanding of the social role of emotional display. Lewis's (1993) model of emotional development has all the basic emotions appearing within the first six months of life, and by 3 years of age the child's range of emotions falls not far short of an adult's. In contrast, acquisition of speech proceeds at a slower rate. The 2-year-old child has a much greater range of emotional expression than linguistic expression.

The young child also is sensitive to the emotional expressions of others, reacting negatively, for example, to "background anger" (anger not directed at the child) from 12 months old (see Lemerise & Dodge, 1993, for a review).

The social psychology of emotions

Consider a case study:

> L. is an adult male. Ph. is a rather precocious five-year-old. Initially L.'s relations with Ph. were very positive: she seemed quicker and more flexible than her peers. But gradually things turned sour. It seemed to L. that Ph. was becoming deliberately uncooperative. She often gave repetitive and unhelpful responses. L. began losing his temper with her: on one shameful occasion he swore at her and kicked her. The worst thing was she kept running out of toner on Sunday mornings, when there was nobody around to help.

Of course, L. is a lecturer and Ph. is a photocopier. The 'case study' illustrates humans' strong bias to personify their environment, and the amount of emotion that can be invested in our social relations even with inanimate but personified objects.

It can be argued forcefully that social relationships are crucial to our understanding of all the emotions. First, because many emotions require another person, in addition to the self, for the emotion to make sense: if one is in love, one is in love with someone; if one is embarrassed, it is because someone is witness to one's actions. Second, even if an emotion does not ostensibly refer to others (happiness, sadness) it needs to be understood with respect to concepts such as self-esteem, and our self-esteem is constructed very much in relation to how others see us. Advocates of the self as a social construct (e.g. Mead, 1964; Oatley, 1988) would endorse this position.

Merely to associate emotions with a socially constructed self probably does not go far enough in explaining why humans invest so much emotional energy in social interactions and why emotional status can be such a strong predictor of the course of social relationships. Nowhere is this clearer than in marital relationships: the break up of a marriage (or other significant relationship) is so often a stormy affair. Why do humans behave this way; why cannot rational beings make a Jamesian 'cold-blooded and dispassionate judicial sentence' about ending a relationship, without all the heartbreak? The strength of emotion is not merely anecdotal: in a study looking at the predictors of subsequent marital separation, Gottman and Levenson (1992) found that one of the best predictors was the wife's facial expression: if she registered disgust on her face more than once per minute, the relationship was not likely to last! We do not expect the reader to be surprised by this statistic, but we may be saddened by the emotional pain this tip of the iceberg represents.

There have been a number of attempts to give social relationships a central role in defining emotions. For example, Kemper (1978) characterises emotions with respect to the key social concepts of power and status: decrease in one's power leads to anxiety, increase in one's status leads to pride, etc. A more functional approach, more in line with the tenor of this chapter, sees emotion as part of a cohesive device that keeps social groups together. Collins (1990), following the seminal work of Durkheim (1915) and Goffman (1967), sees group cohesion as being promoted by the emotional energy generated at 'ritual interactions' (social occasions of significance for group members, such as a religious service or a football match). The famous Bateman cartoons, where an individual is seen innocently ignoring a convention at some social gathering much to the indignation of all the onlookers, is eloquent testimony to the emotional investment of group members .

CONCLUSIONS

We return to the question that started this survey: if machines get by without emotions, why do we humans need them? One answer we gave in our Introduction, but did not explore, was that machines and humans are built out of different material—silicon-based materials for computers, carbon-based for humans. Some philosophers believe this difference is crucial (Searle, 1980, p.424): "intentionality [possessing internal states such as beliefs and hopes, which are essential for a fully fledged emotional system] ... is a biological phenomenon, and it is as likely to be as causally dependent on the specific biochemistry of its origins as lactation, photosynthesis, or any other biological phenomena." We do not need to adopt such a mystical line. The position we have adopted in this chapter is that current machines do not think, have states of consciousness, or have emotions because they do not have to interact with a complex and unpredictable environment in the way that we do.

The other day one of us placed a floppy disk that contained a virus into a PC, and asked the computer to read the disk. The machine emitted a high-pitched noise and produced a flashing message asking us to remove the disk. It then closed down and refused to operate until the danger was removed. It does not require too vivid an anthropomorphising imagination to recognise this as a fear response. Computers will develop emotions when they are embedded in a sufficiently rich environment for emotions to be useful. The virus anecdote illustrates that some very simple environments already exist where the computer can profit from an 'emotional' display. Of course differences between the way computers work and the way bodies work mean that machines and people may not display the same range of emotions: for example the arousing or energising aspects of emotions may be more important for a sluggish biological system than for a more responsive computer system. But this should not distract us from the essential insight that complex systems need global states to set and monitor priorities, to react to an uncooperative environment, and to interact with other members of our species.

Yes, we would be much happier if we did not have emotions, but we would not survive.

NOTES

1. Accuracy often has to be defined as that of the majority view. It may be that someone diagnosed as suffering from schizophrenia does communicate with God via energy emitted from light bulbs, but a consensus view would consider these to be psychotic delusions.
2. As we have already noted, anger against the self may present as depression.

REFERENCES

Alloy, L.B. & Abramson, L.Y. (1979). Judgement of contingency in depressed and nondepressed students: Sadder but wiser? *Journal of Experimental Psychology: General, 108*, 441–485.

Alloy, L.B. & Abramson, L.Y. (1988). Depressive realism: Four theoretical perspectives. In L.B.Alloy (Ed) *Cognitive Processes in Depression*. New York: Guilford Press.

American Psychiatric Association (1987). *Diagnostic and statistical manual of mental disorders*. (3rd edition, revised). Washington, DC: American Psychiatric Association.

Aristotle (1924). *Rhetorica* [translated by W. Rhys Roberts]. In W.D. Ross (Ed.), *The Works of Aristotle, Volume XI*. Oxford: Clarendon Press.

Arkin, R.M., Appelman, A.J., & Burger, J.M. (1980). Social anxiety, self-presentation, and the self-serving bias in causal attribution. *Journal of Personality and Social Psychology, 38*, 23–35.

Blaney, P. (1986). Affect and memory: a review. *Psychological Bulletin, 99*, 229–246.

Bless, H., Bohner, G., Schwarz, N., & Strack, F. (1990). Mood and persuasion: a cognitive response analysis. *Personality and Social Psychology Bulletin, 16,* 331–345.
Bower, G. (1981). Mood and memory. *American Psychologist, 36,* 129–148.
Clark, M.S. & Williamson, G.M. (1989). Moods and social judgements. In H.L. Wagner & A.S.R. Manstead (Eds.), *Handbook of social psychophysiology.* New York: Wiley.
Collins, R. (1990). Stratification, emotional energy, and the transient emotions. In T.D. Kemper (Ed.), *Research agendas in the sociology of emotions.* Albany: State University of New York Press.
Coyle, R.T. & Uretsky, M.B. (1987). Effects of mood on the self-appraisal of health status. *Health Psychology, 6,* 239–253.
Darwin, C. (1904). *The expression of the emotions in man and animals.* [Popular edition]. London: John Murray.
Diener, E. & Iran-Nejad, A. (1986). The relationship in experience between various types of affect. *Journal of Personality and Social Psychology, 50,* 1031–1038.
Durkheim, E. (1915). *The elementary forms of religious life. A study in religious sociology* [translated J.W.Swain]. London: George Allen & Unwin.
Dykman, B.M., Abramson, L.Y., Alloy, L.B., & Hartlage, S. (1987). Processing of ambiguous and unambiguous feedback by depressed and nondepressed college students: schematic biases and their implications for depressive realism. *Journal of Personality and Social Psychology, 56,* 431–445.
Ekman, P. (1984). Expression and the nature of emotion. In K.P. Scherer & P. Ekman (Eds.), *Approaches to emotion.* Hillsdale, NJ: Lawrence Erlbaum Associates Inc.
Elkin, I., Shea, M.T., Watkins, J.T., Imber, S.D., Scotsky, S.M., Collins, J.F., Glass, D.R., Pilkonis, P.A., Leber, W.R., Docherty, J.P., Fiester, S.J., & Parloff, M.B. (1989). National Institute of Mental Health Treatment of Depression Collaborative Research Program. *Archives of General Psychiatry, 46,* 971–982.
Feld, S. (1982). *Sound and sentiment: Birds, weeping, poetics and song in Kaluli expression.* Philadelphia: University of Pennsylvania Press.
Forgas, J.O., Bower, G.H., & Krantz, S.E. (1984). The influence of mood on perceptions of social interactions. *Journal of Experimental Social Psychology, 20,* 497–513.
Forgas, J.P. & Moylan, S. (1988). After the movies: transient mood and social judgements. *Personality and Social Psychology Bulletin, 4,* 478–489.
Freud, S. (1929). *Introductory lectures in psycho-analysis* (2nd edn.). London: George Allen & Unwin.
Frijda, N. (1987). Comment on Oatley and Johnson-Laird's "Towards a cognitive theory of emotions". *Cognition and Emotion, 1,* 51–58.
Frijda, N.H., Mesquita, B., Sonneman, J., & van Goozen, S. (1991). The duration of affective phenomena or emotions, sentiments and passions. In K.T. Strongman (Ed.), *International review of studies on emotion.* (Vol. 1., pp.187–225). New York: John Wiley.
Godden, D.R. & Baddeley, A.D. (1975). Context-dependent memory in two natural environments: on land and under water. *British Journal of Psychology, 66,* 325–331.
Goffman, E. (1967). *Interaction ritual.* Garden City, NY: Doubleday/Anchor.
Golin, S., Terrell, F. & Johnson, B. (1977). Depression and the illusion of control. *Journal of Abnormal Psychology, 86,* 440–442.

Gottman, J.M. & Levenson, R.W. (1992). Marital processes predictive of later dissolution: behavior, physiology and health. *Journal of Personality and Social Psychology, 63*, 221–233.

Greenberg, L.S. (1993). Emotion and change processes in psychotherapy. In M. Lewis & J.M. Haviland (Eds.), *Handbook of emotions*. New York: The Guilford Press.

Greenberg, M.S., Vàzquez, C.V. & Alloy, L.B. (1988) Depression versus anxiety: Differences in self—and other—schemata. In L.B. Alloy (Ed.), *Cognitive processes in depression*, New York: Guilford Press.

Griffitt, W. (1970). Environmental effects on interpersonal affective behavior: ambient effective temperature and attraction. *Journal of Personality and Social Psychology, 15*, 240–4.

Isen, A.M., Shalker, T.E., Clark, M. & Karp, C. (1978). Affect, accessibility of material in memory and behavior: a cognitive loop. *Journal of Personality and Social Psychology, 36*, 1–12.

James, W. (1890). *The principles of psychology*, (Vol. 2). New York: Henry Holt.

Johnson-Laird, P.N. & Oatley, K. (1989). The language of emotions: An analysis of a semantic field. *Cognition and Emotion, 3*, 81–123.

Kavanagh, D.J. & Bower, G.H. (1985) Mood and self-efficacy: impact of joy and sadness on perceived capabilities. *Cognitive Therapy and Research, 9*, 507–525.

Kemper, T.D. (1978). *A social interactional theory of emotions*. New York: Wiley.

Kenealy, P.M. (1986). The Velten Mood Induction Procedure: A methodological review. *Motivation and Emotion, 10*, (4), 315–335.

Lazarus, R.S. & Folkman, S. (1984). *Stress, appraisal, and coping*. New York: Springer.

Lemerise, E.A. & Dodge, K.A. (1993). The development of anger and hostile interactions. In M. Lewis & J.M. Haviland (Eds.), *Handbook of emotions*. New York: Guilford Press.

Lewis, M. (1993). The emergence of human emotions. In M. Lewis & J.M. Haviland (Eds.), *Handbook of emotions*. New York: Guilford Press.

MacLeod, C. & Mathews, A. (1988). Anxiety and the allocation of attention to threat. *Quarterly Journal of Experimental Psychology, 40A* (4), 653–670.

Martin, M. (1990). On the induction of mood. *Clinical Psychology Review, 10*, 669–697.

Matt, G.E., Vàzquez, C., & Campbell, W.K. (1992). Mood-congruent recall of affectively toned stimuli: a meta-analytic review. *Clinical Psychology Review, 12*, 227–255.

McClelland, J.L. & Rumelhart, D.E. (1988). *Explorations in parallel distributed processing*. Cambridge, MA: MIT Press.

Mead, G.H. (1964). The social self. In A.J. Reck (Ed.), *Selected writings of George Herbert Mead*. Indianapolis IN: Bobbs-Merrill.

Miller, G.A. & Johnson-Laird, P.N. (1976). *Language and perception*. Cambridge: Cambridge University Press.

Oatley, K. (1988). On changing one's mind. In A.J. Marcel & E. Bisiach (Eds.), *Consciousness in contemporary science*. Oxford: Clarendon Press.

Öhman, A. (1993). Fear and anxiety as emotional phenomena: clinical phenomenology, evolutionary perspectives, and information-processing mechanisms. In M. Lewis & J.M. Haviland (Eds.,) *Handbook of emotions*. New York: Guilford Press.

Ortony, A. (1987). Is guilt an emotion? *Cognition & Emotion, 1*, 283–298.

Ortony, A. & Clore, G.L. (1989). Emotions, moods, and conscious awareness. *Cognition and Emotion, 3*, 125–137.

Polivy, J. (1981). On the induction of mood in the laboratory: discrete moods or multiple affect states? *Journal of Personality and Social Psychology, 41*, 803–817.

Scheier, M.F. & Carver, C.S. (1985). Optimism, coping and health: Assessment and implications of generalized outcome expectancies. *Health Psychology, 4*, 219–247.

Scheier, M.F., Weintraub, J.K., & Carver, C.S. (1986). Coping with stress: Divergent strategies of optimists and pessimists. *Journal of Personality and Social Psychology, 51*, 1257–1264.

Schwarz, N. & Clore, G.L. (1983). Mood, misattribution, and judgments of wellbeing: informative and directive functions of affective states. *Journal of Personality and Social Psychology, 45*, 513–523.

Searle, J.R. (1980). Minds, brains and computers. *The Behavioral and Brain Sciences, 3*, 417–424.

Shiffrin, R.M. (1988). Attention. In R.C. Atkinson, R.J. Herrnstein, G. Lindzey & R.D. Luce (Eds.), *Stevens' handbook of experimental psychology,*(2nd edn., Vol. 2). New York: Wiley.

Silver, R.C. & Wortman, C.B. (1980). Coping with undesirable life events. In J. Garber & M.E.P. Seligman (Eds.), *Human helplessness: Theory and applications*. New York: Academic Press.

Singer, J.A. & Salovey, P. (1988). Mood and memory: evaluating the network theory of affect. *Clinical Psychology Review, 8*, 211–251.

Smolensky, P. (1986). Information processing in dynamical systems: foundations of harmony theory. In D.E. Rumelhart & J.L. McClelland (Eds.), *Parallel distributed processing*, Vol.1. Cambridge, MA: MIT Press.

Spinoza, B. (1910). *Ethics* [translated by A.Boyle]. London: J.M.Dent & Sons.

Stenberg, C.R. & Campos, J.J. (1990). The development of anger expressions in infancy. In N.L. Stein, B. Leventhal, & T. Trabasso (Eds.), *Psychological and biological approaches to emotion*. Hillsdale, NJ: Lawrence Erlbaum Associates Inc.

Teasdale, J.D. (1983). Negative thinking in depression: cause, effect or reciprocal relationship? *Advances in Behaviour Research and Therapy, 5*, 3–25.

Tinbergen, N. (1940) Die Uebersprungbewegung. *Zeitschrift für Tierpsychologie, 4*, 1–40.

Tversky, A. & Kahneman, D. (1973). Availability: A heuristic for judging frequency and probability. *Cognitive Psychology, 4*, 207–232.

Velten, E. (1986) A laboratory task for induction of mood states. *Behavior Research and Therapy, 6*, 473–482.

Vestre, N.D. & Caulfield, B.P. (1986). Perception of neutral personality descriptions by depressed and nondepressed subjects. *Cognitive Therapy and Research, 10*, 31–36.

White, G.L., Fishbein, S., & Rutstein, J. (1981) Passionate love and misattribution of arousal. *Journal of Personality and Social Psychology, 41*, 56–62.

Worth, L.T. & Mackie, D.M. (1987). Cognitive mediation of positive affect in persuasion. *Social Cognition, 5*, 76–94

CHAPTER SEVEN

Can animals think?

Stephen E.G. Lea and Marthe Kiley-Worthington
University of Exeter

INTRODUCTION

Both to psychologists and to non-psychologists, it may seem surprising that the question "Can animals think?" should figure as one of the Unsolved Mysteries of the Mind. Most non-psychologists who have any dealings with animals, or at least with mammals and birds, assume quite naturally that they can and do think, and furthermore that their thought is not unlike ours. "He understands every word I say" may be a clichéd caricature of the way dog-lovers approach their pets, but most dog owners would probably accept it as an exaggeration, not an error. Kemp and Strongman (1994) have recently shown that 40% of a general population sample unhesitatingly attribute consciousness to animals, barely fewer than would do the same for very young children or severely mentally handicapped adults.

On the other hand, the majority of psychologists, whether they work with humans or with other animals, would find it surprising that anyone could seriously suppose that animals might be able to think. From the time of C. Lloyd Morgan (1894) and J. B. Watson (1913) onwards, most work on animal psychology has been under the influence of behaviourism. Not all those commonly regarded as behaviourists would deny the possibility of animal thought: to give only the most obvious example, Tolman (1932) went to great lengths to define thought (he called it "ideation") in such a way that it could properly be attributed to an animal such as a rat. But the radical behaviourism of Skinner (e.g. 1950), which was the dominant influence in animal psychology up to about 1970, effectively ruled such questions out of the field of scientific enquiry, even if it did not in fact deny the existence or even the significance of private events (Skinner, 1969, Ch. 9). Psychologists working on human cognition have been strong in their rejection of behaviourism, but they have been no more sympathetic to the idea of animal thought. On the contrary, they have emphasised the huge gulf separating human beings from other animals, so that the idea of animal cognitive processes in any way resembling human ones has been virtually taboo.

This divergence between lay and technical views of the world should alert us to a potential problem. Is there indeed something there, which the everyday dog owner takes for granted, but the psychologist, whether working with animal subjects or human participants, refuses to see? We should not be too hasty, in an excess of academic humility, to discard the specialist point of view. Both the behaviourist and the human cognitive psychologist are responding to real problems. Lloyd Morgan's objective analyses, for example of his dog's acquisition of the habit of opening a gate (Morgan, 1894, p.289) cast into very real doubt the naive mentalism of many anecdotal accounts of "animal intelligence", such as Romanes (1886) had collected. From the other direction, early cognitive psychologists from Bartlett (1932, pp.214–5) onwards had to emphasise that human cognition involved processes that were never going to be touched by the dominant behaviourist approach to learning (see also Bruner, 1990, pp.2–4). Given the long association of behaviourism with experiments on animal learning, and the all-pervading influence of human language on human cognition, it is hardly surprising that cognitive psychology perceived a gulf between human and animal cognitive processes so deep as to override the basic Darwinian continuity between humans and other animals.

However, in the last quarter-century, the emergence of cognitive psychology as a distinct discipline has led to a new approach to many questions in animal behaviour, and the idea of studying "animal cognition" (rather than, say, "learning") is now firmly established. There remains much controversy on whether the study of animal cognition leads to an acceptance of what Griffin (1978) called "cognitive ethology". Nonetheless, given a thriving animal cognitive psychology, it makes sense to look again at the disjunction between lay and psychological approaches to animal thinking, and ask again, "Can animals think?" We are not, of course, claiming to be the first to have raised the question of animal thought in recent times. Important sources for our argument include ethologists (e.g. Cheney & Seyfarth, 1990; Griffin, 1978, 1984), psychologists (e.g. Pearce, 1987; Walker, 1983) and philosophers (e.g.

Dennett, 1988, 1991; Radner & Radner, 1989). A useful recent and thorough survey is the book edited by Ristau (1991). The aim of this chapter is to review the different ideas that have been brought forward, and to argue that a consensus has now been found.

When we talk about "animals" in this chapter we really mean warm-blooded vertebrates (other than humans, to avoid endless circumlocution). That is not to rule out the possibility that reptiles, or even some invertebrates such as certain molluscs, might be able to think. But as it is in question whether *any* animals other than humans can think, it makes sense to start consideration with the animals that are most like humans and therefore (in general) easiest to investigate. As almost all investigations in practice have used either mammals or birds, and many of the most important investigations have used primates, this sensible restriction is also a highly convenient one.

A PRIORI ISSUES: DARWINIAN CONTINUITY AND LINGUISTIC DISCONTINUITY

Both behaviourism and cognitive psychology have largely rejected the idea of animal thought. They have done so on the basis of a mixture of empirical and a priori arguments. The present chapter is mainly empirical in its thrust, but before we marshal evidence, we need to look at the reasons why such evidence might be beside the point.

Continuity and behaviourism
The starting point of behaviourism, both historically and logically, is the assumption of Darwinian continuity (Boakes, 1984). Humans are animals, and have evolved from non-human animals; in the absence of evidence to the contrary, we can assume that any process in humans will be the same as the corresponding process in the generality of animals, particularly animals that are phylogenetically close to humans. The behaviourists' studies of animal learning were designed to find out about learning in general, with the aim of applying the results to human learning; they were not motivated by any interest in the particular learning processes of particular species or individuals. This programme favours a rejection of animal thought in favour of behaviour. Thought is relatively difficult to observe, and may be very different in animals and humans, whereas behaviour is readily observed, and describable in a common language regardless of species.

From the point of view we are taking in this chapter, the behaviourists' programme was fundamentally misguided. Nonetheless it has produced evidence that is helpful to our argument. As a result of behavioural experiments, in psychology and ethology, we can take it for granted that all animals, or at least all the animals we shall discuss, are capable of learning. For any species we care to choose, this can be demonstrated by the techniques of habituation, and classical and operant conditioning. These we take as techniques for demonstrating an ability to learn, not necessarily as fundamental processes which in any sense account for learning. The capacity to learn effective behaviour in more complex situations, such as those calling for imitation or various kinds of problem-solving, also seems to be widespread if not universal, and we keep an open mind as to whether these situations demonstrate more advanced learning capacities or the same capacities being put to fuller use. Many kinds of animal specialise in particular types of learning that fit them to their ecological niche or socal structure, for example the learning of topographical maps of their home areas by sheep or the learning of the sites of stored food by some birds and squirrels (Macdonald, 1995; Vander Wall, 1990). Often these species-specific learning abilities are also "phase sensitive" (restricted to a particular period of life); examples include filial imprinting in ground-nesting birds, the learning of landmarks and celestial signs by migratory birds, and the immediate post-parturient learning to identify young by hoofed animals (e.g. Klopfer, Adams, & Klopfer, 1964).

We can also take it for granted that animals have emotional lives as well as cognitive ones. Animals respond to noxious or agreeable stimuli or situations in ways that suggest pain or pleasure to the human observer. We assume that they have corresponding feelings, at least at the "basic emotional" level (cf Smith & Kemp-Wheeler, this volume). Possibly, though, as we look more carefully at the issues of animal cognition and animal consciousness, we may want to attribute more complex emotions to them. Certainly animal, as well as human emotions extend and change in time (Smith & Kemp-Wheeler, this volume): an alsatian dog may begin by growling and snarling at a pekinese, and then after a while take to galloping around with him smelling common areas and wagging his tail. Thus there is no doubt that animals experience a range of emotions, but as yet we cannot ask them how they feel, only observe the correlated behaviour. Nor, of course, can we assume that animals' feelings are the same as ours; they could be just as complex but quite different (Toates, 1992)

Continuity and anthropomorphism
The assumption of continuity led the radical behaviourists to a rejection of human cognition. But continuity can as easily imply the acceptance of cognition in animals as its rejection in humans. Darwin himself believed that animals have rational and moral capacities similar to our

own (Rachels, 1991). Lorenz (1952, p.152), answered the charge that he anthropomorphised animal behaviour thus: "You think I humanize the animals? ... Believe me, I am not mistakenly assigning human properties to animals; on the contrary, I am showing you what an enormous animal inheritance remains in man".

What grounds could there be for assuming that Darwinian continuity ceases at the cognitive level? It is clear enough that there are qualitative and quantitative cognitive differences between humans and other animals, but in evolutionary theory, the uniqueness of each species goes hand in hand with the continuity of all species (Lea, 1984b). The fact that animals do not speak English, or send their conspecifics to the moon, does not mean that they have no mental life and no cognitive processes. Rollin (1989) elegantly points out that to assume animal cognitive vacuity on the basis of animal–human cognitive difference is not only irrational, but goes against the grain of what science is considered to be.

Continuity and pragmatism

We can give the argument for cognitive continuity an extra twist by considering the pragmatics of working with other humans and with animals. We take it for granted that other humans think, and we use this assumption, successfully, to predict their behaviour and plan our interactions with them. Similarly, people who work with other animals frequently assume that they can think, and plan accordingly (e.g. Johnson, 1995). If this assumption forms the basis of successful human–animal interaction, as in Johnson's training schemes for guide dogs, our evidence for animal thought seems as good as our evidence for human thought (Hearne, 1987).

Solipsism

The presumption that animals have no mental lives seems to have three roots. The first is an over-interpretation of Descartes' famous *cogito ergo sum*. "I think, therefore I am" means simply that I am aware of my own mental life, therefore I know that I must exist; I do not have the same evidence about anyone or anything else's existence. In theory that could drive us to doubt the existence of everything else, until it can be proved (a philosophical position known as solipsism). But for practical scientific purposes, we happily take for granted the existence of other people, and of their minds—even when, like babies or seriously intellectually handicapped people, their minds clearly do not work like ours. In this chapter, too, we shall assume without comment that other people can think. It is logically inconsistent if we then suddenly become solipsistic about other species' minds, and demand proof that they exist. Rollin's

(1989) argument is thus that it is consistent cognitive science, not animal-loving anthropomorphism, to accept and apply to animal cognition some common-sense psychology (what others have called folk psychology: Churchland, 1988; Radner & Radner, 1989).

Because any sensible person accepts that most other humans can indeed think, in spite of imperfect evidence, it would be legitimate to decide that animals can think even if the evidence for that also ends up as imperfect: we need to ask whether the two kinds of imperfection are actually different. There are special difficulties in deciding on the presence of thought in humans who are very young or very damaged (indeed, one of the reasons for being interested in the possibility of animal thought is that it may throw light on such cases). But all the healthy adult humans we know claim to engage in thinking. All solipsism can do is to cause us rephrase our question, pedantically, to become, "Can animals do anything like what we do when we say we are thinking?".

Culture

A second reason for the common presumption of animal cognitive vacuity probably lies in the cultural background of Western science. The Judaeo-Christian tradition makes very rigid distinctions between humans and other animals; from its beginnings, only humans were seen as made in the image of God and able to enter into a covenant with him, and, in the later development of the tradition, only humans were attributed an immortal soul. Our modern concept of mind is in part descended from that concept of the soul. Scientists are human, and so our approach is inevitably coloured by our culture. But we ought to make the effort to see past such influences.

Language

An undoubted cognitive difference between humans and animals is human language. We accept Rollins' argument that we cannot just assume from that fact that animals do not talk that they have no cognitive processes at all; but could a more extended argument lead us to the same point? Many authors assume it could. For example, Frey (1980) and Kennedy (1992) both argue for a distinction of treatment between humans and other animals, one on moral and the other on biological grounds, and for both the rationale is the fact that animals do not have language.

Such an argument begs two questions. First, do animals have communications systems that, although different from human language, could in some useful sense be called called languages (see Premack, 1976)? Second, to what extent does cognition depend on language?

Some would argue that to use the word "communication" implies intention and other cognitive processes. This is more than we want to assume at this stage of the chapter. But we know that animals can learn about the world, and respond emotionally to it, and it follows almost inevitably that they can pass on both feelings and facts to one another. If the human observer can discriminate the feelings of an animal, another animal of the same species can presumably also do so, and probably much more accurately. Furthermore, from the assembly calls of flock-feeding birds (e.g. Marler, Dufty, & Pickert, 1986) to the more elaborate gestures of chimpanzees (Menzel, 1971), animals behave in ways that give other animals practical information, and that information is then used. There may be an emotional overtone to such messages, but in at least some cases what is received is primarily information about the outside world. Krebs and Dawkins (1984) seek to reserve the word "communication" for cases where the animals sending and receiving the information both benefit. We do not need to enter into that debate. The point is that animals have ways of passing on knowledge about the world and reactions to it which serve some of the same purposes as human language. We cannot assume without discussion that they do not imply some of the same cognitive processes.

The surest way to demonstrate that animal communication works like human language would be to find a way in which both animals and humans could translate between the two. It would be easy, therefore, for this chapter to resolve into a discussion of whether animals can learn a language that is more obviously like the human version. As is well known, this question has been taken up in a series of experimental projects with chimpanzees, using human sign languages (initiated by Gardner & Gardner, 1971), or artificial languages constructed out of symbols, either plastic (as in the project initiated by Premack, 1976), or displayed by a specialised computer keyboard and display (an approach which began with Rumbaugh, 1977). These techniques, which have since been extended to other great apes, have opened up the question of animal language learning to experimental analysis. But in some ways they lead us away from the main question we are posing in this chapter. We are not asking whether animals can learn to think by means of learning a human language through human intervention. We are asking whether animals under normal conditions, without such a language, are able to think.

But even if we accepted that animal communication has nothing in common with human language, and that animals cannot learn any form of human language, would that imply that they have no mental processes at all? Does the absence of language imply the absence of either consciousness or thought? We accept of course that human thought and human consciousness are closely intertwined with human language. Already in this chapter we have argued that we know that humans can think because they claim to think—and the claim is made linguistically. But it does not follow that thought without language is impossible, either for humans who do have language, or for animals, who do not. Our argument is that this should be an empirical, not an a priori question, still less one to be settled by definitional fiat; and the question of animal thought is part of the evidence that should be brought to bear on it. Moreover, there are at least two a priori arguments against making language the criterion for the existence of cognition. First, if we take such a position, we have to argue that babies and seriously intellectually disabled people have no minds (just as Singer, 1976, argues that we would have to deny any moral responsibility to them), a position most people would reject as inhuman. Second, we have to invent a category of non-cognitive or mindless learning, because no-one could argue that animals do not learn. That is, of course, precisely what is connoted by the term "conditioning" as it has been used in psychology, particularly behavioural psychology; and it is significant that there is growing evidence that even the kinds of learning involved in conditioning experiments cannot be explained without reference to cognitive processes (see, for example, Dickinson, 1980).

WHAT IS THOUGHT?

If thought is not inextricably linked to language, what is it? Let us start with a rough characterisation. It is important not to have too restrictive a notion of thought at this stage of our chapter—part of the point of this entire inquiry is to expand our notion of what thought might be. In everyday terms, however, it is clear that thinking is associated with remembering, problem solving, planning, imagination, and goal-oriented behaviour. These are all what in psychology we call cognitive processes, and in everyday speech we call mental activities. Thought is something that goes on in the mind.

What, though, does that mean? Philosophers of mind have always divided as to whether or not the mind is a different entity from the central nervous system, dualists asserting that there are distinct mental and material substances, monists that there are not. Most modern psychologists are monists (and, more particularly, materialists), arguing that mental activity can in principle be accounted for in terms of material processes in the brain. In saying that thought is a mental activity, we are not taking a dualist position; we are saying that in the present state of our knowledge, it needs to be discussed at the level of the mind, not at the level either of nervous processes or of overt behaviour. More important to us than either monism or dualism would be the kind of pluralism that acknowledges many kinds of mind, whether or not they are identical with corresponding kinds of brain (Flew, 1979). There may be external signs of thought (knitted brows, perhaps), and there may be physical supports of thought (gestures, practical tests of possible problem solutions, speech, doodling, or writing may all aid thought in humans), but these are not what thought is. Thought goes on inside the thinker, and we refer to it as a mental rather than a brain activity, because that is the way humans experience it. Our question is whether animals can think in anything like the way we can.

Second, thought must involve more than mere reaction to stimuli, whether that is fixed or variable. The link from the signal Pavlov's dog heard to the saliva it released necessarily involved the central nervous system, because there is no other way sound waves arriving at the ears can trigger action at the salivary glands. But it need not follow that the dog thinks about the signal, or about its saliva, and the reason we use the word "conditioning" to describe the way Pavlov's dogs learned is that we are sceptical about the role of thought either in this kind of reaction or in the kind of learning that changes it. Thought, by contrast, must involve some kind of mental work on the stimulus input (or, indeed, on stimuli that were received in the past).

Because thought must involve mental work, there must be something for it to work on. Physical work manipulates objects in the physical world; mental work must manipulate objects in the mental world. But what is a mental object? The most obvious answer is that it is a mental representation of an object or event in the outside world. This leads to the conclusion that a prerequisite for thought is the ability to form mental representations of stimuli (present, and, preferably, past). This is a necessary condition for thought, but not a sufficient one—a representation that simply acted as an internal "repeater" of a current external stimulus would not really be said to be involved in thought. What we must look for is the capacity to do something with representations within the mind: to work mentally on mental representations. This is an ability we each know we possess ourselves, and we take it for granted that other people have it: we know that we think about people, objects, and events, and we take it for granted that other people can do so too. But can other animals do this?

It is clear enough why the ability to think, even in this limited sense, would be advantageous to an animal. Consider two examples. First, animals need to find their way about their environments, and to do this, a map is always useful. An elementary kind of mental representation is a "cognitive map" of the kind proposed by Tolman (1948) to explain rats' maze-learning behaviour and studied more recently in many other species, for example elephants (Moss, 1988) and horses (Kiley-Worthington, 1987). Second, most animals are faced with unfamiliar situations from time to time. The unknown is always potentially dangerous: it is safer to try out possible actions mentally than to try them out physically. If a mouse is waiting in its hole, and food is only to be found outside, how can it best assess whether it is safe to go out? The mouse that can try the action out in its mind, and meets a mental representation of a cat, is more likely to survive than the mouse that can only try it out with its body, and meets the cat itself.

To describe thought as involving mental representation immediately explains why language is so crucial to human thought. Language is precisely a system of representation, and the fact we can hear ourselves speak offers an obvious way in which thought as we know it might have evolved in prehominids who were beginning to be able to speak. Once an animal can talk to itself, and above all argue with itself, without physically uttering, it can certainly do everything we have described here as thinking. So language is a sufficient condition for thought, but it does not follow that it is the only possible vehicle for thought.

There is of course nothing new about this description of thought. Quite apart from what cognitive psychologists and mental philosophers have said, we can refer to Tolman (1932), the first systematic animal cognitive psychologist of the 20th century. Tolman (1932, p.446) defined "ideation" in rats as involving "the sampling of alternative or succedent means-ends possibilities by virtue of mere behavior-adjustments to runnings-back-and-forth", behaviour-adjustments in this context meaning internalised rather than overt activities. The focus on representation remains topical, and Gallistel (e.g. 1990) has put it at the centre of his discussion of animal cognition and discussed its history and epistemological status in some detail. Byrne (1995) similarly makes representation the hallmark of animal thought, although he draws its boundaries rather more closely than we are going to do. In terms of research strategy, animals' capacity to manipulate mental representations is a convenient focus. It does not constitute the whole of what we mean by thought in humans, still less the whole of what we might mean by thought in other animals. It is probably not a single coherent category of cognitive functioning. But it is something that we can look for in a variety of ways in a variety of species.

SOME UNANSWERED QUESTIONS

Our preliminary description of thought leaves many questions unanswered. Does thought require consciousness, for example, as Griffin (e.g. 1978) implies? And if "consciousness" is used to describe several different kinds or levels of phenomenon, as Young and Block (this volume) argue, which of them is necessary for thought, and which of them can be demonstrated in animals? We will take up these questions in more detail later. For the moment, though, let us simply note that at least some authors seem to allow thought to occur without consciousness. For example, Hofstadter (1979) argues that consciousness comes from reflexive thought—from having a mental representation of the self, whereas Mead (1934, p.18) sees it as emergent from social action. Both these make consciousness look like an additional process, or a specialised kind of thought. Because we would not want to rule these analyses of consciousness out at this stage, we will, for the time being at least, allow the possibility that thought can go on without consciousness. This position has, after all, a long pedigree in human psychology (e.g. Freud, 1922).

Another key question is the inevitability of thought. Given that an animal can think at all, does it follow that it will think about every situation? To put it another way, is thought a cognitive style, a way of using the brain that, once evolved, is involved in every response to stimuli, present or past; or is it an extra faculty, working in parallel to other, more primitive, cognitive functions, perhaps only to be engaged when simpler systems fail? Broad and undemanding as our description of thought is, there is reason to suppose that the activity it describes is difficult even for humans. The moment we start to do any serious thinking, we take steps to use external representations of key elements of the problem, using words, pictures, or objects. Mental arithmetic is much harder than arithmetic using pencil and paper. Although mental rotation is possible (Shepard & Metzler, 1971), when it is a matter of life or death, it is better to rotate a map in the real than in the mental world, as Army instructions to jeep navigators show. Problem-solving is often aided by physically showing the solver a partial solution (Maier, 1931).

In one form or another, human psychology has repeatedly argued that thoughtful and less thoughtful cognitive processes exist side-by-side—whether in terms of rule-governed behaviours alongside contingency-governed ones in human operant psychology (Lowe, Harzem, & Bagshaw, 1978); unconscious alongside conscious motives in psychoanalytic thinking (Freud, 1922, p.16ff.); automatic versus purposive processing in semantic memory (Posner & Snyder, 1975); the "grasp of consciousness" whereby children become able to describe actions they could perform at a much earlier developmental stage (Piaget, 1977); or the formation of motor programs to replace deliberate response sequences as skilled responding develops (Keele, 1973). We will follow this lead, and argue that animals, too, may think about some situations while reacting unthinkingly in others. There is some evidence for the replacement of deliberate choice by motor programmes, for example, both in rats learning mazes (Tolman, Ritchie, & Kalish, 1946) and in some of the training of guide dogs (Johnson, 1995). However, the boundary between behaviours that are and are not under the control of thought is not in general easy to draw, and may not lie in the most obvious place. Nor need it necessarily be drawn very conservatively, as would be implied by a strict usage of Lloyd Morgan's canon (we should not attribute to animals higher mental processes than are needed to explain their behaviour: Morgan, 1894, p.53): in human affairs, we tend to assume that behaviour is underlain by thought unless we have evidence to the contrary.

WHAT DO WE KNOW ABOUT ANIMAL THOUGHT?

In recent years, many psychologists of animal learning have adopted a (loosely) cognitive approach. It has become widely accepted that animals do form internal representations of external stimuli and responses, and that even the simplest forms of learning involve changes in the connections to these representations rather than to the direct stimulus inputs or response outputs themselves. Why has this approach become widespread? The question of representation has been argued at great length by psychologists working on classical and (to a lesser extent) operant conditioning, mainly in rats. It is summarised briefly by Pearce (1987 Ch 4) and in more detail by Dickinson (1980 Ch 3) and Holland (1990). We shall give just a few examples of the kinds of experiments involved.

Behaviourally silent learning

Even in the simplest conditioning experiments, there are a number of situations where learning takes place without any accompanying change in behaviour. Such learning can be described as "behaviourally silent" (Dickinson, 1980, pp.15 ff.). For example, Rescorla (1969) repeatedly exposed rats, who were receiving occasional mild electric shocks, to an audible tone. Events were programmed so that shock never occurred within a few seconds of the tone: in effect the tone was a signal that no shock was coming, though the rats did not respond to it in any obvious way. Some time afterwards, in a different environment in which the rats were pressing a lever for occasional food reward, Rescorla used the tone as a signal that a shock was coming. Normally, rats learn the significance of such signals very quickly, and stop food-oriented behaviour such as lever pressing when they hear them. But the rats for whom the tone had previously been a signal of no shock were unusually slow to learn. They had learned previously that the tone signalled no shock; but this learning was behaviourally silent, until the tone was put to a new use, when what they had already learned about it conflicted with what they now had to learn. They had to change their representation of the tone from a signal of safety to a signal of danger.

Devaluing food

Holland and Straub (1979) first conditioned rats to approach a food cup in response to a tone, then gave them experience in which eating the food concerned was followed by illness (induced in fact by an injection of lithium chloride); the rats stopped reacting to the tone, implying that it elicited not a direct tendency to approach the food tray but a representation of the food, and with it its newly acquired aversive properties. Holland and Ross (1981) paired lithium-induced illness with a tone that had previously been used as a signal for food; although no food was presented anywhere near the time of the injection, the rats subsequently avoided the food that the tone had signalled. This implies that, because of the previous conditioning, the tone elicited a representation of the food, which became associated with the illness induced by the injection when tone and illness occurred together.

Such experiments, by their nature, can only demonstrate very simple manipulation of mental representations, and a critic might legitimately say that it is not really what we mean by thought at all. The importance of this line of research is that it establishes on a firm basis a necessary condition for animal thinking—a result that is the more impressive because it comes from the most anti-mentalistic experimental tradition. But is this sufficient for us to say that animals can think?

Animals' concepts

The next step from demonstrating that animals have, and work on, representations of external stimuli is to show that they have representations of stimuli that have never actually occurred in the external world. This question has been addressed by the extensive literature on concept discrimination by animals. Herrnstein and Loveland (1964) showed that pigeons could discriminate accurately between sets of colour slides which were defined using a natural human concept: positive slides included a human being somewhere in the picture, negative slides did not. Discrimination of many other natural concepts, and some artificial ones, has been demonstrated since (Herrnstein, 1985; Watanabe, Lea, & Dittrich, 1993), and after training the birds can normally respond correctly to novel instances of the concepts. Examples include the discrimination of pigeons from other birds (Poole & Lander, 1971), and the discrimination of photographs of a university campus taken from one camera position from photographs taken from another position (Honig & Stewart, 1988).

At first, such experiments were referred to as involving "concept formation" by the pigeons, but as Lea (1984a) pointed out, this description goes well beyond the data. We know for certain only that the concept exists in the mind of the experimenter; the subjects in the experiment may or may not use the concept to make the discrimination, and if they do use it, it may be one that already exists rather than one that is formed in the experiment. Lea (1984a) proposed some tests that might give clearer evidence that subjects were using a concept, in the sense of an internal representation that incorporated the general properties of a set of positive (or negative) stimuli rather than any particular member of it. For example, Lea argued that if an internal concept was involved in concept discrimination, learning a new response to one or a few members of the set ought to lead to its generalising to all members. Several authors have tried to use this or related tests, with mixed results (Herrnstein, 1990; Watanabe et al., 1993).

Herrnstein (1979) showed that after repeated reversals of a discrimination of the concept "tree", pigeons showed reversal to all stimuli following exposure to just one or two at the beginning of each new reversal; Vaughan and Herrnstein (1987) got a similar result in an experiment in which the two stimulus categories signalled, not the presence or absence of food reward, but which of two intermittent schedules of reinforcement was in force; and Vaughan (1988) showed instance to category generalisation with successive reversal of a "pseudoconcept" discrimination, in which both stimulus categories consisted of an arbitrary mixture of tree and non-tree pictures. Single reversals, however, have not in general shown evidence that pigeons use concepts. Bhatt and Wasserman (1989, Experiment 2) found no evidence of instance to category generalisation after they had trained pigeons in a four-way categorisation task, and von Fersen and Lea (1980) found that following partial reversal of a concept discrimination, generalisation only occurred to stimuli that shared identifiable features with the instances used in reversal.

Watanabe et al. argue that the structure of von Fersen and Lea's stimulus sets was in fact unlike that of natural concepts, and would discourage concept formation. One could equally say, though, that the repeated reversal procedure makes it essential to use a concept, whereas with a single concept discrimination, alternative mechanisms are adequate; on this argument, the evidence suggests that animals do not spontaneously use or form concepts, whereas for humans they are a natural part of thinking. Perhaps pigeons are not the most promising candidates for this kind of mental activity. Although some concept discrimination experiments have been carried out with primates (e.g. D'Amato & Van Sant, 1988; Dittrich, 1988; Schrier, Angarella, & Povar, 1984; Yoshikubo, 1985), the more elaborate tests for concept use have not yet been performed. The experiments on language-learning in apes are of considerable help here, however. Chimpanzees who have been taught American Sign Language occasionally coin new gesture combinations to describe objects for which they have not yet been taught names: "smell-fruits" for citrus fruits, for example (Fouts, 1974). Such reports imply that the animal is locating a concept into a semantic network, which is what humans do when we "understand" something; Savage-Rumbaugh, Romski, Hopkins, and Sirak (1989) argue strongly that the bonobo (pygmy chimpanzee) Kanzi is able to understand spoken human language in just this sense. Because sea-lions are capable of responding to commands in new contexts (e.g. to do on land what they have previously only done in water) Schusterman and Krieger (1984) argued that they, too, comprehend semantically.

Problem solving

Concept formation, as Lea (1984a) defined it, involves the putting together at the mental level of diverse stimulus elements or features. Another mental operation that has been investigated extensively is putting together information that has been received at different times. Early learning theorists (e.g. Maier, 1929) used this as the definition of "reasoning"; Deutsch (1960, pp.101–102) argued that it is the essence of what Köhler (1927) called "insight", and what we would nowadays call problem solving.

At its simplest, indeed, Tolman's "internalised running back and forth" is precisely a way of putting together information gathered at different times. Tolman (1932, Ch 13) noted that rats at choice points in mazes or discrimination chambers repeatedly moved a small way into each alley. He argued that they were re-experiencing, in memory, the consequences of their last entries into the alleys, so as to compare them (hence Muenzinger, 1938, called this behaviour vicarious trial and error, or VTE). At a later stage in learning, Tolman supposed that the entire process took place internally, so that the rat did not have to overtly move towards each alley in order to be reminded of its consequences. More recent research, reviewed by Miller, Kasprow, and Schachtman (1986), has demonstrated the great importance of "reminder" stimuli in enabling animals to respond appropriately on the basis of past experience, and this strongly supports Tolman's account of VTE. The significance of VTE is that on any one trial, the rat can only fully enter one alley; so past entries to the two alleys must have occurred at different times, and VTE therefore involves working on mental representations of events that occurred at different past times.

The classic definition of "reasoning", as used by Maier (1929), demands the integration of information derived at distinct times. Morgan (1894) had drawn the distinction between reason in this sense and "intelligence", the simple ability to learn by trial and error. Although Maier claimed to show evidence of reasoning in rats, the classic insight experiments of Köhler (1927), despite lacking the formality of Maier's work, were in many ways more immediate and compelling. They remain relevant to the issue of how animals solve problems. As is well known, Köhler set chimpanzees novel tasks such as using a branch to rake in food that was out of reach through the bars of a cage, or piling boxes one on top of another to reach food that was otherwise too high to reach. He claimed that the apes solved these tasks without the process of trial and error that is required by early behaviourist theories of learning such as that of Morgan (1894) and Thorndike (1911). Köhler's way of putting it was to describe a "perceptual reorganisation" in which what had been seen as a branch came to be seen as an extension of the arm, and it is hard to avoid the description that the apes had to "think about" the problem. Although the elements of the solution were always present, the ape did not solve the problem by working with them physically until a solution appeared by chance, but rather by retiring from the task, and then coming back with it apparently solved.

However, this sudden "insight" is not an uncontrollable phenomenon. Birch (1945) showed that it was more likely to occur in apes that had had experience of the possible tools and the things that could be done with them. Parker and Poti' (1990) have carried out a thorough analysis of the genesis of insightful tool-using, showing that in cebus monkeys only young animals, whose play ensured that they used the necessary component behaviours, learned to use sticks as tools. A more challenging recent report is Epstein and Medalie's (1983) demonstration that the achievements of Köhler's apes could be replicated in pigeons by ensuring that the component responses were already present in the animal's repertoire. Pigeons that were trained to obtain food either by pushing a platform across the floor of a test chamber, or by pecking a disc on the chamber wall, spontaneously pushed the platform to the wall and jumped on it when the disc was moved too high up the wall for them to reach. Similarly, Nakajima and Sato (1993) showed that if (and only if) pigeons were first trained to peck a key and to move a block around a test chamber, they could, without further training, solve the problem of finding that access to the key was now obstructed by the block. One of their birds showed the abrupt emergence of a solution, usually taken as evidence of insight. Were the pigeons in these experiments "thinking about" the relation between the platform and the key? And if we are unwilling to say that they were, why do we say that Köhler's apes thought about the relation between a packing case and a bunch of bananas?

Remembering

Another way of demonstrating that animals work with mental representations is to consider what happens to the representations of objects that are not currently present; that is, to memories. There has been a spate of work on animal memory since the concept came back into fashion with the early studies summarised by Honig and James (1971) and Medin, Roberts, and Davis (1976). It is now clear that animals have remarkable long-term memories. Vaughan and Greene (1984), for example, trained pigeons in a discrimination in which there were 320 different colour slide stimuli. In the presence of half of the slides, food was available if the pigeon pecked a switch; in the presence of the other slides, no food was given. The positive and negative slides were chosen at random before the experiment. Not only did the pigeons learn this discrimination, they were still able to perform correctly after a two-year break. Under natural conditions, even more formidable memory capacities have been seen. After a 20-day interval, grey squirrels return to within 2cm of the position of a buried nut on over 75% of trials (Macdonald, 1995). A single Clark's nutcracker (nutcrackers are birds of the crow family) may bury as many as 100,000 seeds, in tens of thousands of separate caches, each autumn; in the course of the winter months, it returns to almost all its caches to collect the seeds, even though the ground may now be covered in snow (see Vander Wall, 1990).

Such results show that animals can store large amounts of information, and act on it after a long delay. By themselves, however, they say nothing about the mental events involved. A much older study, of short-term rather than long-term memory, does shed some light on this question. Tolman (1948) reports a study by Hudson in which rats were given electric shocks shortly after eating from a food cup surrounded by a distinctive striped stimulus. Subsequently, they avoided both the food cup and the striped wall. However, for some rats, the chamber lights were turned off immediately after the shock, and the food cup and stripes were removed under cover of darkness. These rats showed no avoidance of the stripes. Tolman's suggestion is that after the shock, the rats look at their environments to see what has recently changed, and attribute the painful stimulus to that. This implies that they are working on the memory of the shock to link it to the stimulus.

The training of domestic animals such as sheep dogs, guide dogs, and circus animals (see Kiley-Worthington, 1990) often implicitly relies on this ability to link current consequences to remembered stimuli. For example, a sheep dog needs to remember where the sheep are in order to find them and select the best strategy for moving the flock, or an individual sheep, in the required direction. A similar ability is apparently seen in untrained behaviour when dolphins find their way out of nets by gaps that they have previously passed (Pryor & Schallenberger, 1991).

Arguably, fluent navigation in an unfamiliar environment necessarily depends on the same cognitive skill. Consider the following incident, seen last year. A loose horse was following a group of horses being ridden across Dartmoor, but fell behind. The group came to a wide, deep leat, and crossed on a small bridge. The loose horse, arriving later, galloped straight past the bridge towards the other horses, but then found his way blocked by the leat. He paused for about half a minute, then turned and galloped back to the bridge and crossed by it. So he had seen and remembered the bridge when he passed it, and when posed the problem of crossing the leat was able to use the information from memory. This is of course an anecdotal account, and although it was seen by a trained observer, needs supporting either by experiment or by the systematic collection and examination of related anecdotes (e.g. Byrne & Whiten, 1988). But the incident illustrates the need to be able to manipulate memories if one error in a strange environment is not to lead to hopeless floundering.

A common technique when studying short-term memory is to use a delayed-response task, where stimuli are presented, removed for a retention interval, and only after that interval is there an opportunity to respond to the stimuli. Roitblat (1980) used a version of this design, the "delayed symbolic matching to sample" task, to show in a striking way what pigeons were apparently thinking about during the delay interval. Pigeons were presented with one of three sample stimuli (A, B, and C, say) before the delay interval, then after it three test stimuli (X, Y, and Z) were presented. The pigeon's task was to respond to X if A was presented earlier, to Y if B was presented earlier, and to Z if C was presented earlier. The twist in Roitblat's experiment was that stimulus A was made highly confusible with B, and stimulus Y was made highly confusible with Z. When there was no delay between the sample and test stimuli, the pigeons could perform this task reasonably accurately.

As the delay was increased, performance got worse. But it got worse in a particular way: the pigeons tended to make errors between test stimuli Y and Z, not between stimuli X and Y. Roitblat argued that this showed that the pigeons had "recoded" the sample stimulus into something resembling the corresponding test stimulus. During the delay interval, they were not remembering (we might say, thinking about), the stimulus they had just seen, but the stimulus they would have to respond to at the end of the delay.

Deception

A further line of evidence for animals working on representations of things that are not present is their use of bluff and deception. This has been a matter of intense interest in the recent literature. There are species that practise forms of deception as a matter of course; the Green Plover gets its alternative name of Lapwing from the way it leads potential predators away from its nest by appearing to be injured. Despite the detailed case made out by Ristau (1991, Ch 5), on the basis of the behaviour of other plovers, most people would tend to see this sort of "instinctive" deception as very different from deception as practised by humans. The hallmark of human deception is, indeed, its unsystematic, opportunistic nature, for the good reason that predictable attempts at deception are likely to fail. This makes it a tricky phenomenon to investigate, because reports are almost bound to be anecdotal. If enough anecdotes can be collected, however, they can be studied systematically, and Byrne and Whiten (1988) have attempted to do this for primates in general; Jolly (1991) has provided a collection of accounts of deception in chimpanzees and bonobos, de Waal (1982) for chimpanzees, Miles (1990) for apes in general, and Cheney & Seyfarth (1990) for vervet monkeys. Unlike the anecdotes collected by early anthropomorphisers like Romanes (1886), these accounts of behaviour come from primatologists with detailed knowledge of the species concerned, engaged in the scientific study of behaviour. They leave little room for doubt that apes, and probably most monkeys, can and routinely do engage in deceptive acts, which require them to respond to objects or (most commonly) individuals not currently present, or to circumstances that have not yet, and may never, come to pass. In a famous early report, Menzel (1971, 1974) showed that chimpanzees in a group would report to each other the location of food—but also that a subdominant female repeatedly gave false information to a dominant male. More recently Savage-Rumbaugh and McDonald (1988) report that the sign-language trained bonobo Kanzi, denied access to the chimpanzees Sherman and Austin, achieved it by requesting access to food located beyond their quarters, then diverting to join them on his way to it.

WHAT DON'T WE KNOW?

The evidence of the previous section seems clear to us: animals do form internal representations of their external worlds, and they do work with them in the absence of the relevant external stimuli to produce new rules for behaviour. Unless it is seen in a proper context, some of the work we have cited will nonetheless seem unsatisfactory as evidence for thought in animals. Without even using computers, it is not hard to invent automata that will perform in the same way as rats in maze experiments, including those that are supposed to demonstrate insight or reasoning (Deutsch, 1960), if that is all they have to do; what is difficult is to build a robot that will behave "intelligently" in the sense of coping with a wide variety of different learning situations. Something more than mental representation is needed for us to be comfortable talking about thought: something closer, perhaps, to the issues of consciousness and self-awareness that we were cautious, earlier, in adopting as necessary conditions for thought. When we, as humans, manipulate our mental representations of the world (that is, when we think), we know that we are thinking. We know what it is to "think" and we know who "we" are (the self-reflective criterion of Hofstadter, 1979). As a result, we assume that others think and know who they are. Do these processes have any parallels in animal cognition? Are animals aware of their own minds, and of the minds of others?

This brings us back to the question of consciousness. We have argued that animals can, indeed, think. Does that imply that they are conscious, and if so, in what sense? There remains considerable dispute about what consciousness is, and how it should be assessed (see Young & Block, this volume; Davies & Humphrey 1993). To avoid the vagueness and open-endedness that seem endemic in debates about these topics, Griffin (1984) continually refers to "conscious thinking". We shall make use instead of the distinctions drawn by Young and Block, between "phenomenal consciousness", "access consciousness", and "self consciousness". We shall argue that it goes without saying that warm-blooded vertebrates are "phenomenally conscious", that evidence is accumulating that at least some of them have "access consciousness", and that some animals at least may have "self-consciousness". That will still leave us with the difficulty of what any of these imply about thought.

As Young and Block explain, we use the word "consciousness" in several quite different ways. First, we use it to distinguish between different "states of consciousness"—waking, deep sleep, dreaming, hypnotic trance, coma, drugged states. The evidence is strong that most mammals, at least, pass through all these states in the same way, and with the same neurophysiological and neuropharmacological basis, as humans do (Horne, 1988, Ch 7). This is not a trivial point; if animals can be unconscious because of sleep or anaesthetics, there is an important sense in which, at other times, it is proper to say that they are conscious. This is the "phenomenal consciousness" of Young and Block.

Phenomenal consciousness immediately raises further questions. How do we know when a human is conscious, rather than in a trance, for example? The ability to react to external stimuli is certainly part of it, but not the whole story. To count as conscious in everyday terms, I must also have some idea about where I am (or know that I have no idea). This criterion, for example, seems to imply that a thoroughly deluded schizophrenic should not be classified as fully conscious, which is contrary to common sense, although it may make sense to describe schizophrenia as a state of disordered consciousness. On the most conservative reckoning, there is at least some sense in which an animal like a dog, cat, or horse waking up "knows where it is". If (as is normal) it is in a familiar place, it is greeted by a range of known stimuli, with known meanings; it has a battery of practised responses to likely situations. Earlier in this chapter, we have argued that the animal also has internal representations of those stimuli, which give them meaning, and enable it to think about them (though not talk about them) and use them as a guide to action. Except for the lack of language, this capacity to reflect on the perceived world corresponds closely to Young and Block's "access consciousness", and so we reach the point of attributing access consciousness to animals.

But does the waking animal also have that sense of self, and place, and time that is a critical part of what we mean by "being conscious" in humans—the "self consciousness" of Young and Block? We describe a human waking as "coming to himself" (or herself). In humans, the different senses of consciousness coalesce. Phenomenal consciousness and access consciousness between them cover the sense of being capable of thought, intention, and belief (Dennett, 1991; Radner & Radner, 1989). On the other hand, self consciousness covers the idea of an awareness of self, the self-reflective process emphasised by Hofstadter (1979). In humans these go hand in hand; we cannot imagine being awake but unaware of ourselves. But do other animals also have selves to come to?

Jolly (1991) and Cheney and Seyfarth (1990) argue that the research on deception enables us to approach this question. They use Dennett's (1983) ranking of orders of complexity of social awareness, from "I know" up to "I know that he knows that I know" and beyond. Effective deception requires the deceiver to conceive of how his or her actions will appear to the intended victim. This means that the deceiver must be aware of the victim's mind. How could the deceiver be aware of the victim's mind without being aware of his or her own mind?

An alternative test for the presence of a self-concept was proposed by Gallup (1970). While an animal was under an anaesthetic, he applied a coloured patch to its face. When the animal woke, he allowed it to see itself in a mirror. A chimpanzee given this test immediately scratched the patch on its own face. Later research has shown that orang utans react in the same way as chimpanzees, but other primates (including gorillas) did not (Gallup, 1983). Gallup argued that only the chimpanzee had a concept of itself. Not everyone believes that Gallup's results have anything to do with self-concepts; for a detailed critque see Heyes (1994). Even if we take them at closer to face value than Heyes does, there are other possible interpretations—perhaps gorillas have self-concepts but do not recognise mirror images as being themselves. But it does seem clear that the chimpanzee and the orang utan reacted to images of themselves in a way that would be natural for a self-aware human, so it is natural to attribute self-awareness to them, whereas with the other primates Gallup tested, we cannot be so confident.

What do these different definitions of consciousness imply for thought? For humans, phenomenal consciousness is a necessary but not sufficient condition for thinking. Access consciousness comes close to the way we have described thought, as the ability to manipulate mental representations. Self consciousness seems to go a step further, and, we would argue, a step further than we need to go. The knowledge that one is thinking (and therefore that one has, or is, a self that can think) may be too stringent a criterion for thought. There are other ways in which we operate on our mental representations which are perhaps less advanced than self-consciousness, but also look less like the processes of an automaton than the manipulations required to solve mazes or discriminate concepts. For example, does it make sense to talk about animals as holding beliefs, forming intentions, or laying plans? In human terms, all these are things that we do with our mental representations of objects, actions, or events we have experienced in the past or hope to experience in the future.

What does it mean to hold a belief or expectation about the world rather than simply to react to the stimuli it produces? In everyday terms, what is distinctive about beliefs is that they give rise to considered reactions; when our behaviour is based on a belief, we can give an account of what we are doing which is fuller than that an outside observer could give (Harré & Secord, 1972, Ch 6). Hand in hand with that goes the implicit or explicit acceptance that what we believe may be untrue: we are able to conceive of the possibility that the world is not the way we believe it to be. Not all our responses are considered in this way, even when they are based on experience—for example, a sudden illness can produce a taste aversion even when one knows that the flavour concerned was quite unconnected with the illness (Logue, Ophir, & Strauss, 1981, Table 5), and social psychologists recognise a class of "mindless" reactions (Langer, 1989). But the very fact that some responses are demonstrably mindless shows that others are rightly called "mindful". Are animals mindful of their behaviour in this way?

Beliefs, intentions, and plans are closely linked, as may be seen from an old experiment of Tinklepaugh (1928), which is often cited as evidence that monkeys, at least, have expectations. Tinkelpaugh tested four macaque monkeys (three rhesus and one cynomologus) in a delayed reaction task, in which an item of food was put into one of two cups, a screen was raised to hide the cups, and subsequently the monkey was allowed to go behind the board and retrieve the food (the delayed symbolic matching to sample task used by Roitblat in the experiments described earlier in the chapter is just a modern, automated, version of this situation). Monkeys can remember the location of hidden food easily, and Tinklepaugh's subjects performed correctly even with overnight delays. The test worked with a variety of kinds of food, for example pieces of banana or a lettuce leaf. In a variant of the task, Tinkelpaugh substituted lettuce for banana during the delay period. On finding the lettuce leaf where the banana should have been, the monkeys showed repeated searching behaviour followed by aggressive responses, and did not eat the lettuce. It is hard to avoid the conclusion that they believed they were going to find the preferred banana, and indeed intended to obtain banana and had planned how to obtain banana. Or consider a guide dog whose handler asks him to cross a road (cf Johnson, 1995). The handler's signal only communicates the goal. It is the dog who must judge whether or when it is safe to cross, assessing the speed, direction, and nature of traffic, and predicting its likely future actions; and plan a course from one side of the road to the other that will avoid obstacles and other pedestrians. At a more global level, the dog must also learn from any mistakes how to make better plans in future— although, as we have already discussed, trial and error is an unsatisfactory way of learning when the consequences of error can be fatal.

WHAT DO ANIMALS THINK ABOUT?

The problem with the research we have been describing is that it involves experimenter-imposed tasks. In trying to see whether animals can think, we try to get them to think about things we specify for them. Whenever we try to do this to other humans, we run into trouble: consider the teacher who wants a class of 12-year-olds to think about algebra, the magistrate who wants a petty thief to think about the distress his activities cause his victims, or the forlorn youth who wants his beloved to think about him. Why should it be any easier for the psychologist who wants a chimpanzee to think about the best way of piling boxes? By using strong biological incentives, we hope to persuade animals to think about the tasks we pose them; but it may be that all they do is think about the (potential) rewards.

What would animals think about, left to themselves? Very probably they would indeed spend much time thinking about strong biological incentives. Jane Goodall (van Lawick-Goodall, 1971, p.180) describes a chimpanzee who had been keeping company with a young female one evening; they went to their separate nests, but when the male woke, "he suddenly swung from his nest and, moving rapidly through the tree, leapt straight into the female's bed ... it certainly showed that the female was very much in old McGregor's mind when he woke that morning".

Jane Goodall's anecdote is entertaining because the chimpanzee's behaviour, and his presumed thoughts, are recognisably human. But biological drives do not dominate all human thought, and it is unlikely that they dominate all animal thought either. It is also unlikely that the thoughts of all animal species are the same, and here we encounter the limits of our own imaginations. If we could guess what the thoughts of a chimpanzee, or a bat, or a lion, might be like, we might be able to find evidence of them or create tests to demonstrate them; but it is precisely this guessing that is most difficult. Wittgenstein (1968) famously argued that if a lion could talk we would not understand him; and Nagel (1979, Ch 12) argued that a bat's world is so very different from ours that there is no way we can relate to him and understand it, so there is no point in trying. As cognitive psychologists or ethologists, we need not be so pessimistic. Although the task is not easy, there are many ways in which we can try to understand the mental worlds of other species. An important technique is to bring together the sceptical scientist and the anthropomorphic lay person: to think critically and constructively about the folk psychology of animal behaviour and its use in living and working with animals, both in training them and in interacting emotionally with them. We do recognise similarities between humans and some other animals, and we need to make use of them. We need not start the analysis of animal cognition from a position of complete ignorance. It is this kind of "conditional anthropomorphism" that seems to us to underly some of the most interesting recent advances in the study of animal cognition, such as Cheney and Seyfarth's (e.g. 1990) work with vervets, Pepperberg's (e.g. 1981, 1983, 1987) with the African Grey parrot Alex, Johnson's (1995) with guide dogs, Herman's (e.g. 1986) with dolphins, and Savage-Rumbaugh's (1994) with the bonobo Kanzi.

To say that the thoughts of different species are likely to be different is to admit what is anyway obvious, that no animal arrives in the world as a cognitive "*tabula rasa*", and that no animal's thinking is unmodified by its environment. To take a simple example, consider the domestic chick that, soon after it hatches, instinctively follows the first conspicuous moving object it sees, learns the characteristics of that object, and in general treats it as its mother. We can say of the chick that its genetics give it a concept of mother: it is hatched knowing, in some sense, that it will have a mother, and equipped with a mechanism for learning what she will look like. It is biologically prepared to think about a mother (just as humans are—this is the point that lies behind Jung's idea of a mother archetype in the human collective unconscious). But its concept of what a mother is and does is elaborated by experience, especially but not exclusively during the sensitive period for imprinting. Where domestic animals are concerned, interaction with humans, and tasks and rules set by humans, form an important part of their experience. It is not anthropocentrism, but common sense, to suppose that horses think about their riders and cats about their owners, that sheepdogs think about sheep and guide-dogs about traffic.

So, from what we know about their societies, we can guess that the thoughts of social primates are likely to centre around social status, manipulation, who is where, who is holding what infant, who is mating with whom, how can objects be pulled and pushed to attract social attention or secure a social advantage; whereas the thoughts of the equally social equines are more likely to centre around keeping together, keeping watch, avoiding conflicts, moving fast, maintaining lifelong social relationships, and keeping track of where they are, where others are, and what food resources are around them. Both groups' thoughts are likely to reflect their needs for social knowledge and ecological knowledge, but their different societies and different ecologies will surely be reflected in different mental lives.

There are other lines of difference that we can identify. The thoughts of language-taught primates, such as Washoe or Kanzi, are likely to be different from those of wild apes; the thoughts of a highly trained guide dog are likely to be different from those of a pet whose owners demand nothing but social response, let alone those of a wild wolf. Such specialised training may well give an animal skills and problem-solving strategies that are not typical for its species. So as well as the kinds of learning that are a part of the normal development of members of a species, there are specialised "cultures" which may channel the possibilities of thought, just as ethnological or occupational cultures may channel human thought (cf. Benedict, 1935; Midgley, 1992).

SOME LINES FOR FUTURE RESEARCH

First, we make three obvious methodological points. It would be natural to look to the things we don't yet know about animal thinking when we ask what the next research questions should be. But some of those questions may be unanswered because they are unanswerable, at least as we have posed them: we don't know how to translate the words of the question into empirical observations that we could make. One essential line of continuing enquiry, therefore, is the business of clarifying terms and operations, so that we know more clearly what we mean when we ask about animal thinking.

Armchair analysis, however, can never be the end of the matter. The second essential is to know animals better—to know what they normally do, and what they can be taught to do. Both observation and experiment have their place in this, but both need to be pursued with an open mind. Preconceived questions can prevent us seeing animals' most exciting cognitive achievements. This is particularly important from the point of view of animal thought, because, as remarked earlier, if animals are at all like humans, they will not think much or willingly about tasks that are imposed on them by others. This suggests looking closely at situations where animals seem to be trained naturally and easily to do certain things, and especially at tasks they appear to enjoy.

Third, we are unlikely to find evidence of animal thought unless we approach animals with a presumption that they might think. This implies a kind of qualified anthropomorphism: not the naive anthropomorphism of Romanes or the pet-owner, but a recognition that human thought is the only kind of animal thought we know much about, and we should be looking for something a little like it in other species. At the same time we need to be aware of the different ways in which different species differ from humans. In terms of perceptual capacities, humans (and also cats and owls) have forward-looking, binocular vision, and have to look at one thing at a time; pigeons, rabbits, and many other animals have nearly 360° vision, and can see in detail over most of it; would we expect an animal with that kind of visual experience to show the focal attention (Neisser, 1967), the single channel of thought (cf Welford, 1968), that is so characteristic of human consciousness? In terms of ecological niche, humans are omnivores: how does that make our thought unlike that of an exclusively prey species like a cow or sheep, or an exclusive predator like a lion? In terms of social structure, is the thought of the solitary orang utan like that of the gregarious chimpanzee?

What substantive questions most need investigation? Given the emphasis we have put on mental representation as the precondition of thought, it will be no surprise that we see the process of abstraction as a key field of study. Human thought is all-pervasive because of the symbol system of language. Do animals have natural symbol systems that we have not yet discovered? As more is learned about the power of animal communication (e.g. Cheney & Seyfarth, 1988; Griffin 1992, Ch 9; Seyfarth, Cheyney & Marler, 1980), we discover the elements on which mental symbols might be based. But there are many plausibly thoughtful animals whose communications systems are not known in anything like sufficient detail. The East African vervets' auditory communication has been studied in detail, but even their visual communication is relatively unexplored. We know much less about communication in equines, or parrots, or dolphins, especially under natural or near-natural conditions (for some data on each, see Silber, 1986; Busnel & Mebes, 1975; Rubenstein & Hack, 1992 respectively). The experiments of Kiley-Worthington (1985, 1987), Pepperberg (e.g. 1981, 1983, 1987) and Herman (e.g. Herman, Richards, & Wolz, 1984), respectively, suggest that all three groups are good candidates for symbolic thought. Animals of all these groups have been shown to respond to arbitrary, learned, gestures or sounds "as if" they were the actions they stand for.

As we noted earlier, much recent research on animal cognition has focused on the question of bluff and deception. This is partly because of sound technical reasons—if an animal is deceiving another, that may involve thinking about states of the world that do not currently subsist, and so it implies a particular kind of mental manipulation. It is also the product of an era when selfishness and conflict have seemed to be the keys to understanding animal social behaviour (Dawkins, 1976). But the reason the "selfish gene" is an interesting idea is that it is able to explain co-operative behaviour; far from denying that co-operation exists, sociobiology predicts that most social animals will show at least some altruism and co-operation under at least some circumstances. It is genes, not animals, that are "selfish", and we need to consider how animals think about sharing and co-operating with each other, as well as how they think about competing and deceiving.

Our interest in animal cognition should not be at the cost of ignoring animal emotion. Behaviourism at its most severe could not expunge the word "fear" from its vocabulary (Mowrer, 1960, Ch 2), and post-behaviourist animal psychology certainly should not do so. And if a rat can experience fear, can we really deny that a dog or a horse can experience joy, for example in swift and skilful movement, or successful co-operation with a handler? In practical interaction with animals, it is as important to attribute emotions to them as it is to attribute thoughts. Physiological psychology routinely discusses at least a set of basic emotions in animals (e.g. Gray, 1971). If we allow animals to have thoughts, we can see how those basic emotions can be differentiated into a range of more subtle feelings such as humans experience: for example, humour, imagination, creativity, and aesthetic appreciation. "Do dogs laugh?" asked the social anthropologist, Mary Douglas (1971); but she had to reject the question as too complex. A further task for research, therefore, is to find less crude ways of recognising emotions in animals than the physiologists use. In humans a smile is first and foremost a way of communicating that we are enjoying a present experience; secondarily, it can show that we are enjoying a remembered or a planned experience. Ethological research can tell us fairly easily what responses in other species are analogical to our smile. Because we believe that animals, like us, both remember and plan, we would expect them to be able to enjoy both reminiscence and anticipation, and we should be able to observe them doing both. Most dog owners would believe they can recognise their pets enjoying the anticipation of a walk when they see coats and shoes being put on at the right time of day. Can that commonplace observation be put on a more rigorous basis?

All these questions for future research, however, fade into insignificance compared with one central problem. It is one thing to agree that animals can, after all, think. It is another to know what they think about. We accept without question that other people think, but we do not, in general, believe that we can know what they think, without a long process of finding evidence. Many of the problems of life result from being mistaken, unimaginative, or deceived about what other people are thinking. We should not expect to do any better at guessing what animals are thinking; in fact, there is good reason to suppose we will usually do worse. Many of the errors of early, anthropormorphic animal psychology can be seen as resulting, not from the assumption that animals can think, but from over-simplified assumptions about what they are thinking. Accepting the principle of animal thought should not be used as an excuse for another round of unbridled speculation about the contents of animal thought; if it does, it is likely to lead to nothing but a retreat of serious scientists into a new behaviourism. The central challenge to animal cognitive psychology, therefore, is to find disciplined ways of exploring what animals think.

AN UNSOLVED MYSTERY?

So, is it a mystery whether animals can think? We argue that it is not. There are ways of defining terms so as to make it not just unsolved but unsolvable, but we think that they lead to an arid and unprofitable view of all kinds of thought, animal or human (or, indeed, machine). With a concept of thought that comes closer to our own experience of thinking, we argue that there is good evidence that animals can think at some levels at least, but little evidence of where the limits might lie. The unsolved mystery is no longer whether animals can think, it is what they think about. We do not believe that this is an unsolvable mystery. In the past 25 years, taking the idea of animal cognition seriously has led to a radical expansion of our ideas of what animals can learn. Taking the possibility of animal thought seriously may lead to an equally radical expansion of our ideas of what they can think. Such an expansion would have profound practical consequences for the kinds of interaction between humans and animals that would be practically possible and ethically acceptable. Not all the changes would be convenient. But they would enrich the lives both of humans and of the other animals with whom we interact.

REFERENCES

Bartlett, F.C. (1932). *Remembering: A study in experimental and social psychology*. Cambridge: Cambridge University Press.

Benedict, R. (1935). *Patterns of culture*. London: Routledge & Kegan Paul.

Bhatt, R.S., & Wasserman, E.A. (1989). Secondary generalization and categorization in pigeons. *Journal of the Experimental Analysis of Behavior, 52*, 213–224.

Birch, H.G. (1945). The relation of previous experience to insightful problem solving. *Journal of Comparative Psychology, 38*, 367–383.

Boakes, R. (1984). *From Darwin to behaviourism*. Cambridge: Cambridge University Press.

Bruner, J.S. (1990). *Acts of memory*. Cambridge, MA: Harvard University Press.

Busnel, R.G., & Mebes, H.D. (1975). Hearing and communication in birds: The cocktail party effect in intra-specific communication of *Agapornis roseicollis*. *Life Science, 17*, 1567–1570.

Byrne, R. (1995). *The thinking primate*. Oxford: Oxford University Press.

Byrne, R.W., & Whiten, A. (Eds.) (1988). *Machiavellian intelligence*. Oxford: Oxford University Press.

Cheney, D.L., & Seyfarth, R.M. (1988). Assessment of meaning and the detection of unreliable signals by vervet monkeys. *Animal Behaviour, 36*, 477–486.

Cheney, D.L., & Seyfarth, R.M. (1990). *How monkeys see the world: inside the mind of another species*. Chicago: Chicago University Press.

Churchland, P.M. (1988). *Matter and consciousness*. Cambridge, MA: MIT Press.

D'Amato, M.R., & Van Sant, P. (1988). The person concept in monkeys (*Cebus apella*). *Journal of Experimental Psychology: Animal Behavior Processes, 14*, 43–55.

Davies, M. & Humphreys, G.W. (1993). Introduction. In M. Davies & G.W. Humphreys (Eds.), *Consciousness* (pp.1–39). Oxford: Blackwell.

Dawkins, R. (1976). *The selfish gene*. Oxford: Oxford University Press.

Dennett, D.C. (1983). Intentional systems in cognitive ethology: the Panglossian Paradigm defended. *The Behavioral and Brain Sciences, 6*, 343–391.

Dennett, D.C. (1988). Précis: The intentional stance. *Behavioral and Brain Sciences, 11,* 496–511.

Dennett, D.C. (1991). *Consciousness explained.* Boston: Little Brown

Deutsch, J.A. (1960). *The structural basis of behavior.* Cambridge: Cambridge University Press.

de Waal, F. (1982). *Chimpanzee politics.* New York: Harper & Row.

Dickinson, A. (1980). *Contemporary animal learning theory.* Cambridge: Cambridge University Press.

Dittrich, W.H. (1988). Wie klassifizieren Javaneraffen (*Macaca fascicularis*) natürliche Muster? *Ethology, 77,* 187–208.

Douglas, M. (1971). Do dogs laugh? *Journal of Psychosomatic Research, 15,* 387–390.

Epstein, R., & Medalie, S.D. (1983). The spontaneous use of a tool by a pigeon. *Behavior Analysis Letters, 3,* 241–247.

Flew, A. (Ed.) (1979). *Dictionary of philosophy.* London: Pan.

Fouts, R.S. (1974). Language: origins, definitions and chimpanzees. *Journal of Human Evolution, 3,* 475–482.

Freud, S. (1922). *Introductory lectures on psycho-analysis* [Trans. J. Riviere]. London: Allen & Unwin.

Frey, R.G. (1980). *Interests and rights: The case against animals.* Oxford: Clarendon Press.

Gallistel, C.R. (1990). Representations in animal cognition: An introduction. *Cognition, 37,* 1–22.

Gallup, G.G. (1970). Chimpanzees: Self-recognition. *Science, 167,* 86–87.

Gallup, G.G. (1983). Towards a comparative psychology of mind. In R.L. Mellgren (Ed.), *Animal cognition and behavior* (pp.473–510). Amsterdam: North Holland.

Gardner, B.T., & Gardner, A. (1971). Two-way communication with an infant chimpanzee. In A.M. Schrier & F. Stollnitz (Eds.), *Behavior of non-human primates* (Vol 4, pp.117–185). New York: Academic Press.

Gray, J.A. (1971). *The psychology of fear and stress.* London: Weidenfeld & Nicolson.

Griffin, D.R. (1978). Prospects for a cognitive ethology. *Behavioral and Brain Sciences, 1,* 527–538.

Griffin, D.R. (1984). *Animal thinking.* Cambridge, MA: Harvard University Press.

Griffin, D.R. (1992). *Animal minds.* Chicago: University of Chicago Press.

Harré, R., & Secord, P.F. (1972). *The explanation of social behaviour.* Oxford: Blackwell.

Hearne, V. (1987). *Adam's task: Calling animals by name.* New York: Heinemann.

Herman, L.M. (1986). Cognition and language competencies of bottlenosed dolphins. In R.J. Schusterman, A.J. Thomas, & F.G. Wood (Eds.), *Dolphin cognition and behavior* (pp.221–252). Hillsdale, NJ: Lawrence Erlbaum Associates Inc.

Herman, L.M., Richards, D., & Wolz, J. (1984). Comprehension of senstences by bottlenosed dolphins. *Cognition, 16,* 129–219.

Herrnstein, R.J. (1979). Acquisition, generalization, and discrimination reversal of a natural concept. *Journal of Experimental Psychology: Animal Behavior Processes, 5,* 118–129.

Herrnstein, R.J. (1985). Riddles of natural categorization. In L. Weiskrantz (Ed.), *Animal intelligence* (pp.129–143). Oxford: Clarendon.

Herrnstein, R.J. (1990). Levels of stimulus control: A functional approach. *Cognition, 37,* 133–146.

Herrnstein, R.J., & Loveland, D.H. (1964). Complex visual concept in the pigeon. *Science, 146,* 549–551.

Heyes, C.M. (1994). Reflections on self-recognition in primates. *Animal Behaviour, 47,* 909–919.

Hofstadter, D.R. (1979). *Gödel, Escher, Bach : An eternal golden braid.* Brighton, UK: Harvester.

Holland, P.C. (1990). Event representation in Pavlovian conditioning: Image and action. *Cognition, 37,* 105–131.

Holland, P.C., & Ross, R.T. (1981). Associations in serial compound conditioning. *Journal of Experimental Psychology: Animal Behavior Processes, 7,* 228–241.

Holland, P.C., & Straub, J.J. (1979). Differential effects of devaluing the unconditioned stimulus after Pavlovian appetitive conditioning. *Journal of Experimental Psychology: Animal Behavior Processes, 5,* 65–78.

Honig, W.K., & James, P.H.R. (Eds.) (1971). *Animal memory.* New York: Academic Press.

Honig, W.K., & Stewart, K.E. (1988). Pigeons can discriminate locations presented in pictures. *Journal of the Experimental Analysis of Behavior, 50,* 541–551.

Horne, J. (1988). *Why we sleep.* Oxford: Oxford University Press.

Johnson, B. (1995). *Harnessing thought: The guide dog, a thinking animal with a skilful mind.* Harpenden, UK: Lennard.

Jolly, A. (1991). Conscious chimpanzees: A review of recent evidence. In C.A. Ristau (Ed.), *Cognitive ethology* (pp.231–252). Hillsdale NJ: Lawrence Erlbaum Associates Inc.

Keele, S.W. (1973). *Attention and human performance.* Pacific Palisades, CA: Goodyear.

Kemp, S., & Strongman, K.T. (1994). Consciousness—a folk theoretical view. *New Zealand Journal of Psychology,* in press.

Kennedy, J.S. (1992). *The new anthropomorphism.* Cambridge: Cambridge University Press.

Kiley-Worthington, M. (1985). Horse communication: Do they have language. *Proceedings of the International Ethological Conference.* Toulouse, France: I.E.C.

Kiley-Worthington, M. (1987). *The behaviour of horses in relation to management and training.* London: Allen.

Kiley-Worthington, M. (1990). *Animals in circuses and zoos: Chiron's world?* Basildon, UK: Little Eco-Farms.

Klopfer, P.H., Adams, D.K., & Klopfer, M.S. (1964). Maternal "imprinting" in goats. *Proceedings of the National Academy of Sciences, 52,* 911–924.

Köhler, W. (1927). *The mentality of apes* (2nd edn.). London: Routledge & Kegan Paul.

Krebs, J.R., & Dawkins, R. (1984). Animal signals: Mind-reading and manipulation. In J.R. Krebs & N.B. Davies (Eds.), *Behavioural ecology* (2nd edn, pp.380–402). Oxford: Blackwell.

Langer, E.J. (1989). *Mindfulness.* Reading, MA: Addison-Wesley.

Lea, S.E.G. (1984a). In what sense do pigeons learn concepts? In H.L. Roitblat, T.G. Bever and H.S. Terrace (Eds.), *Animal cognition* (pp.263–276). Hillsdale, NJ: Lawrence Erlbaum Associates Inc.

Lea, S.E.G. (1984b). *Instinct, environment and behaviour.* London: Methuen.

Logue, A.W., Ophir, I., & Strauss, K.E. (1981). The acquisition of taste aversion in humans. *Behaviour Research and Therapy, 19*, 319–333.

Lorenz, K.Z. (1952). *King Solomon's ring* [Trans. M.K. Wilson]. London: Methuen.

Lowe, C.F., Harzem, P., & Bagshaw, M. (1978). Species differences in temporal control of behavior II: Human performance. *Journal of the Experimental Analysis of Behavior, 29*, 351–361.

Macdonald, I.M.V. (1995). *Mechanisms of cache recovery in the grey squirrel.* Unpublished dissertation, University of Exeter.

Maier, N.R.F. (1929). Reasoning in white rats. *Comparative Psychology Monographs, 6*, Whole no. 29.

Maier, N.R.F. (1931). Reasoning in humans II. The solution of a problem and its appearance in consciousness. *Journal of Comparative Psychology, 12*, 181–194.

Marler, P., Dufty, A., & Pickert, R. (1986). Vocal communication in the domestic chicken: I. Does a sender communicate information about the quality of a food referent to a receiver? *Animal Behaviour, 34*, 188–193.

Mead, G.H. (1934). *Mind, self and society from the standpoint of a social behaviorist.* Chicago: University of Chicago Press.

Medin, D.L., Roberts, W.A., & Davis, R.T. (Eds.) (1976). *Processes of animal memory.* Hillsdale, NJ: Lawrence Erlbaum Associates Inc.

Menzel, E.W. (1971). Communication about their environment in a group of young chimpanzees. *Folia Primatologica, 15*, 220–232.

Menzel, E.W. (1974). A group of young chimpanzees in a one-acre field. In M. Schrier & F. Stolnitz (Eds.), *Behavior of non-human primates, Vol. 5.* New York: Academic Press.

Midgley, M. (1992). *Science as salvation.* London: Routledge.

Miles, H.L.W. (1990). The cognitive foundations for reference in a signing orang utan. In S.T. Parker & K.R. Gibson (Eds.), *"Language" and intelligence in monkeys and apes* (pp.511–539). Cambridge: Cambridge University Press.

Miller, R.R., Kasprow, W.J., & Schachtman, T.R. (1986). Retrieval variability: Sources and consequences. *American Journal of Psychology, 99*, 145–218.

Morgan, C.L. (1894). *An introduction to comparative psychology.* London: Walter Scott.

Moss, C. (1988). *Elephant memories.* Columbine, NY: Fawcett.

Mowrer, O.H. (1960). *Learning theory and behavior.* New York: Wiley.

Muenzinger, K.F. (1938). Vicarious trial and error at a point of choice: I. A general survey of its relation to learning efficiency. *Journal of Genetic Psychology, 53*, 75–86.

Nagel, T. (1979). *Mortal questions.* Cambridge: Cambridge University Press.

Nakajima, S., & Sato, M. (1993). Removal of an obstacle: Problem-solving behavior in pigeons. *Journal of the Experimental Analysis of Behavior, 59*, 131–145.

Neisser, U. (1967). *Cognitive psychology.* New York, Appleton-Century-Crofts.

Parker, S.T., & Poti', P. (1990). The role of innate motor patterns in ontogenetic and experiential development of intelligent use of sticks in cebus monkeys. In S.T. Parker & K.R. Gibson (Eds.), *"Language" and intelligence in monkeys and apes: Comparative developmental perspectives* (pp.219–243). New York: Cambridge University Press.

Pearce, J.M. (1987). *Introduction to animal cognition.* Hove, UK: Lawrence Erlbaum Associates Ltd.

Pepperberg, I.M. (1981). Functional vocalizations by an African Grey parrot (*Psittacus erithacus*). *Zeitschrift für Tierpsychologie, 55*, 139–160.

Pepperberg, I.M. (1983). Cognition in the African Grey parrot: Preliminary evidence for auditory/vocal comprehension of the class concept. *Animal Learning and Behavior, 11*, 179–185.

Pepperberg, I.M. (1987). Acquisition of the same/different concept by an African Grey parrot (*Psittacus erithacus*): Learning with respect to categories of color, shape, and material. *Animal Learning and Behavior, 15*, 423–432.

Piaget, J. (1977). *The grasp of consciousness* [Trans. S. Wedgwood]. London: Routledge & Kegan Paul.

Poole, J., & Lander, D.G. (1971). The pigeon's concept of pigeon. *Psychonomic Science, 25*, 157–158.

Posner, M.I., & Snyder, C.R.R. (1975). Facilitation and inhibition in the processing of signs. In P.M.A. Rabbitt & S. Dornic (Eds.), *Attention and performance V.* London: Academic Press.

Premack, D. (1976). *Intelligence in ape and man.* Hillsdale, NJ: Lawrence Erlbaum Associates Inc.

Pryor, R. & Schallenberger, I.R. (1991). Social structure in spotted dolphins (*Stenella attenuata*) in the tuna purse seine fishery in the eastern tropical Pacific. In K. Pryor & K.S. Norris (Eds.), *Dolphin societies: discoveries and puzzles.* Berkeley, CA: University of California Press.

Rachels, J. (1991). *Created from animals.* Oxford: Oxford University Press.

Radner, D., & Radner, M. (1989). *Animal consciousness.* Buffalo, NY: Prometheus.

Rescorla, R.A. (1969). Conditioned inhibition of fear resulting from negative CS-US contingencies. *Journal of Comparative and Physiological Psychology, 67*, 260–263.

Ristau, C.A. (Ed.) (1991). *Cognitive ethology.* Hillsdale, NJ: Lawrence Erlbaum Associates Inc.

Roitblat, H.L. (1980). Codes and coding processes in pigeon short-term memory. *Animal Learning and Behavior, 8*, 341–351.

Rollin, B.E. (1989). *The unheeded cry.* Oxford: Oxford University Press.

Romanes, G.J. (1886). *Animal intelligence* (4th edn). London: Kegan Paul, Trench.

Rubenstein, D.I., & Hack, M.A. (1992). Horse signals: the sounds and scents of fury. *Evolutionary Ecology, 6*, 254–260.

Rumbaugh, D.M. (1977). *Language learning by a chimpanzee.* New York: Academic Press.

Savage-Rumbaugh, E.S. (1994). *Kanzi: The ape at the brink of the human mind.* New York: Wiley.

Savage-Rumbaugh, E.S., & McDonald, K. (1988). Deception and social manipulation in symbol-using apes. In R.W. Byrne & A. Whiten (Eds.), *Machiavellian intelligence,* pp. 224–237. Oxford: Oxford University Press.

Savage-Rumbaugh, E.S., Romski, M.A., Hopkins, W.D., & Sirak, R.A. (1989). Symbol acquisition and use by *Pan troglodytes, Pan paniscus,* and *Homo sapiens.* In P.G. Heltne & L.A. Marquardt (Eds.), *Understanding chimpanzees.* Cambridge, MA: Harvard University Press.

Schrier, A.M., Angarella, R., & Povar, M.L. (1984). Studies of concept formation by stumptailed monkeys: Concepts humans, monkeys, and letter A. *Journal of Experimental Psychology: Animal Behavior Processes, 10*, 564–584.

Schusterman, R.J., & Krieger, K. (1984). California sea lions are capable of semantic comprehension. *Psychological Record, 34*, 3–23.

Seyfarth R.M., Cheney, D.L., & Marler, R.M. (1980). Vervet monkey alarm calls: Semantic communication in a free-ranging primate. *Animal Behaviour, 28*, 1070–1094.

Shepard, R.N., & Metzler, J. (1971). Mental rotation of three-dimensional objects. *Science, 171*, 701–703.

Silber, C.K. (1986). The relationship of social vocalizations to surface behavior in the Hawaiian humpback whale (*Megaptera novaeangliae*). *Canadian Journal of Zoology, 64*, 2075–2080.

Singer, P. (1976). *Animal liberation*. London: Cape.

Skinner, B.F. (1950). Are theories of learning necessary? *Psychological Review, 57*, 193–216.

Skinner, B.F. (1969). *Contingencies of reinforcement*. New York: Appleton-Century-Crofts.

Thorndike, E.L. (1911). *Animal intelligence: Experimental studies*. New York: Macmillan.

Tinklepaugh, O.L. (1928). An experimental study of representative factors in monkeys. *Journal of Comparative Psychology, 8*, 197–236.

Toates, F.M. (1992). *Animal motivation and cognition*. Paper read at the conference on Animal Cognition and Society, Aix-en-Provence, France, August.

Tolman, E.C. (1932). *Purposive behavior in animals and men*. New York: Century.

Tolman, E.C. (1948). Cognitive maps in rats and men. *Psychological Review, 55*, 189–208.

Tolman, E.C., Ritchie, B.F., & Kalish, D. (1946). Studies in spatial learning. II: Place learning versus response learning. *Journal of Experimental Psychology, 36*, 221–229.

Vander Wall, S.B. (1990). *Food hoarding in animals*. Chicago: University of Chicago Press.

van Lawick-Goodall, J. (1971). *In the shadow of man*. London: Collins.

Vaughan, W. (1988). Formation of equivalence sets in pigeons. *Journal of Experimental Psychology: Animal Behavior Processes, 14*, 36–42.

Vaughan, W., & Greene, S.L. (1984). Pigeon visual memory capacity. *Journal of Experimental Psychology: Animal Behavior Processes, 10*, 256–271.

Vaughan, W., & Herrnstein, R.J. (1987). Choosing among natural stimuli. *Journal of the Experimental Analysis of Behavior, 47*, 5–16.

von Fersen, L. & Lea, S.E.G. (1990). Category discrimination with polymorphous features. *Journal of the Experimental Analysis of Behavior, 54*, 69–84.

Walker, S.F. (1983). *Animal thought*. London: Routledge.

Watanabe, S., Lea, S.E.G., & Dittrich, W.H. (1993). What can we learn from experiments on pigeon concept discrimination? In H.P. Zeigler & H.-J. Bischof (Eds.), *Bird vision and cognition* (pp.351–376). Cambridge, MA: MIT Press.

Watson, J.B. (1913). Psychology as the behaviorist views it. *Psychological Review, 20*, 158–177.

Welford, A.T. (1968). *Fundamentals of skill*. London: Methuen.

Wittgenstein, L. (1968). *Philosophical investigations* (3rd edn; Trans. G.E.M. Anscombe). Oxford: Blackwell.

Yoshikubo, S.I. (1985). Species discrimination and concept formation by rhesus monkeys. *Primates, 26*, 285–299.

Author index

Subject Index